George Barrington's Voyage to Botany Bay

THE LITERATURE OF TRAVEL, EXPLORATION AND EMPIRE

Series Editors: Iain McCalman and Nicholas Thomas

There is now an unprecedented level of interest in travel, cross-cultural relations and colonial histories. Scholars in cultural history, literary studies, art history, anthropology and related fields have become increasingly interested in the history of encounters between Europeans and other peoples, in the intellectual and scientific dimensions of exploration and travel, and in the development of travel-writing genres.

Despite this burgeoning scholarly interest, many important texts are unavailable, or available only in expensive facsimiles that lack up-to-date commentary. This new series makes key texts more widely available, including not only remarkable but previously unpublished or poorly known texts, but also new editions of well-known works. Accessible introductions situate the works in the light of recent historical and anthropological research, and theoretical developments in the understanding of travel and colonial representation, while annotations provide relevant contextual information and emphasize questions of interpretation.

Published titles:

Maiden Voyages and Infant Colonies: Two Women's Travel Narratives of the 1790s, edited by Deirdre Coleman

George Keate, *An Account of the Pelew Islands* (1788), edited by Nicholas Thomas and Karen Nero

Ada Pryer, *A Decade in Borneo* (1894), edited by Susan Morgan

Forthcoming titles include:

F. E. Manning, *Old New Zealand and Other Writings* (1863), edited by Alex Calder

Hester Lynch Piozzi, *Observations and Reflections Made in the Course of a Journey Through France, Germany and Italy* (1789), edited by Chloe Chard

David Samwell, *The Death of Captain Cook and Other Writings* (1786), edited by Iain McCalman, Martin Fitzpatrick and Nicholas Thomas

C. F. Volney, *Ruins, or a Survey of the Revolutions of Empire* (c. 1791), edited by Iain McCalman

For further information, see
www.anu.edu.au/culture/projects/cultural_history.html

GEORGE BARRINGTON'S VOYAGE TO BOTANY BAY

Retelling a Convict's Travel Narrative of the 1790s

Edited by Suzanne Rickard

Leicester University Press
London and New York

Leicester University Press
A Continuum imprint
The Tower Building, 11 York Road, London SE1 7NX
370 Lexington Avenue, New York NY 10017–6503

First published 2001
Introduction and editorial apparatus © Suzanne Rickard 2001

British Library Cataloguing-in-Publication Data
A catalogue record for this book is available from the British Library.

ISBN   0-7185-0185-3 (hardback)
        0-7185-0186-1 (paperback)

Library of Congress Cataloging-in-Publication Data
Barrington, George, 1755–1804.
    [Voyage to Botany Bay]
    George Barrington's Voyage to Botany Bay : retelling a convict's travel
    narrative of the 1790s / edited by Suzanne Rickard.
        p. cm. — (Literature of travel, exploration and empire)
    Barrington's work has become known as Voyage to Botany Bay.
    The version of Barrington's Voyage used in this work is entitled: An impartial
    and circumstantial narrative of the present state of Botany Bay, in New South
    Wales ... by George Barrington, now superintendant of the convicts at Paramata,
    published circa 1793 by S. & J. Bailey, London.
    Includes bibliographical references and index.
    ISBN 0-7185-0185-3 — ISBN 0-7185-0186-1 (pbk.)
    1. Botany Bay (N.S.W.)—Description and travel—Early works to 1800. 2. New South
    Wales—Description and travel—Early works to 1800. 3. Penal colonies—Australia—
    New South Wales—Early works to 1800. 4. Australia—Description and travel— Early
    works to 1800. 5. Barrington, George, 1755–1804—Journeys—Australia—Botany Bay
    (N.S.W.) 6. Prisoners—Australia—New South Wales—Social life and customs. 7. Travel
    writing. I. Title: Title used in introduction Impartial and circumstantial narrative of the
    present state of Botany Bay, in New South Wales—by George Barrington, now
    superintendant of the convicts at Paramata. II. Rickard, Suzanne, 1948– III. Series.
    DU180.B6 B37 2001
    994.4′102′092—dc21
    [B]   00-055655

Editorial work towards this publication has been supported by

the centre for cross-cultural research
AN AUSTRALIAN RESEARCH COUNCIL SPECIAL RESEARCH CENTRE
THE AUSTRALIAN NATIONAL UNIVERSITY, CANBERRA, ACT 0200
www.anu.edu.au/culture

Typeset by BookEns Ltd, Royston, Herts
Printed and bound in Great Britain by Biddles Ltd, Guildford and King's Lynn

CONTENTS

ILLUSTRATIONS

Illustrations

Illustrations

Acknowledgements

I am grateful to the Series Editors, Iain McCalman and Nicholas Thomas, for their invitation to contribute a volume to *The Literature of Travel, Exploration and Empire*. Christine Winter and Jenny Newell, research and editing assistants to the series at the Centre for Cross-Cultural Research, Canberra, are also to be thanked for their efficient back-up and enthusiasm on all fronts.

This edition has been supported by the Centre for Cross-Cultural Research, and during my postdoctoral fellowship at the History Program, Research School of Social Sciences, Australian National University, I was fortunate to be able to divert part of my time to researching and writing this annotated edition. I am grateful to all those who asked searching questions at academic seminars about George Barrington and about the times and context in which he lived. My thanks also to Professor Joan Kerr for her pictorial knowledge of the period and her willingness to share her insights and sources with me.

Beyond the Australian National University, I have received generous research assistance and inspiration from Richard Neville, Picture Curator at the State Library of New South Wales, and Simon Burroughs of the University of Leeds. Librarians at the Mitchell and Dixson Libraries, State Library of New South Wales, the Menzies Library, Australian National University, the National Gallery of Australia, and the National Library of Australia, as well as the John Rylands Library, University of Manchester, and the British Library, London, have been helpful and efficient in providing me with access to and knowledge of 'Barringtonia' in all its editions, forms and variations.

George Barrington entered my life when I wrote an honours thesis on his celebrity and impact on eighteenth- and nineteenth-century history and fiction; my focus then was upon his presence in the world of British publishing and writing. At that point, Barrington's actual existence in New South Wales, while of interest, did not command my full attention. In that study, as in this, my work would have been almost impossible without the bibliographical expertise and rare books collection of the late J. A. Ferguson (1881–1969). Ferguson's *Bibliography of Australia* (Volume

Acknowledgements

1, 1784–1830), published by the National Library of Australia, provides an essential guide to the countless variations of Barrington's histories. I salute Ferguson for his persistence in tracking down all known publishing references to the 'Prince of Pickpockets'. In this regard, I also acknowledge the 'Barringtonia' acquired by the late collectors, E. A. Petherick and Rex Nan Kivell, whose mighty collections of books, pictures, artefacts and ephemera now reside in the National Library of Australia.

In this edition, the sights and experiences that Barrington undoubtedly saw or experienced in the penal colony have become of abiding interest to me, and I am grateful that my enthusiasm has been shared by friends and colleagues, particularly Julia Clark, Margaret Steven, Paul Hetherington, Peter Cochrane, Penny Smith and John Iremonger. All have, in their own way, contributed valuable insights and information.

On the home front, I wish to thank Colin for his forbearance and willingness to let George Barrington into our home again, as well as Louise and David, who almost grew up with him. Finally, I owe a debt to Deirdre Coleman, who was the pathfinder for this series and who provided advice and encouragement.

Suzanne Rickard
Canberra, December 2000

CHRONOLOGY

Date	Events in Barrington's life	Publications	Historical events
1788	Barrington arrested for robbery and outlawry, July 1788.	*The Famous Speech of George Barrington Esq., before the Judge and Jury at the Old Bailey, London, together with the learned Recorder's Answer*, dated 18 September 1788, published, London.	Arrival of First Fleet at Port Jackson, New South Wales. Convict transports, *Alexander, Charlotte, Friendship, Lady Penhryn, Prince of Wales*; stores ships, *Borrowdale, Fishburn, Golden Grove*; warships, HM *Sirius* and *Supply*.
			Governor Arthur Phillip formally establishes the settlement of Sydney on 26 January 1788, with a civil administration.
			French navigators, La Pérouse and De Langle visit Botany Bay in the *Boussoule* and *Astrolabe*.
			Lt. Philip Gidley King sails to settle Norfolk Island as Superintendent and Commandant.
1789	Barrington confined in Newgate Gaol for almost twelve months.	*The Voyage of Governor Phillip to Botany Bay; with an Account of the*	The *Guardian*, bringing fresh supplies to the colony, is wrecked

Date	Events in Barrington's life	Publications	Historical events
1789 (cont'd)	The trial takes place at the Old Bailey, but the Jury finds Barrington 'Not Guilty', and he is released.	*Establishment of the Colonies of Port Jackson & Norfolk Island; compiled from Authentic Papers, which have been obtained from several Departments. To which are added, the Journals of Lieuts Shortland, Watts, Ball, & Capt. Marshall, with an Account of their New Discoveries embellished with fifty-five Copper Plates, the Maps and Charts taken from Actual Surveys, & the Plans & Views drawn on the Spot, by Capt. Hunter, Lieuts Shortland, Watts, Dawes, Bradley, Capt. Marshall, &c.* Printed for John Stockdale, Piccadilly.	off the Cape of Good Hope in December 1789. Colony imperilled by threat of starvation.

Smallpox epidemic at Port Jackson decimates the Aboriginal inhabitants around Port Jackson.

The Second Fleet sets sail for Port Jackson. The Convict transport, *Lady Juliana*, leaves Plymouth July 1789, with 226 female convicts on board and is followed by the *Surprize*, *Neptune* and *Scarborough*.

The French Revolution begins, May 1789. |
| | | *A Narrative of the Expedition to Botany Bay with an Account of New South Wales ... by Captain Watkin Tench of the Marines,* Printed for J. Debrett, Piccadilly. | James Ruse, the first emancipist granted land at Parramatta, New South Wales, becomes self-sufficient in food. |
| | | *An Authentic and Interesting Narrative of the late Expedition to Botany Bay, As performed by Commodore Phillips, and The Fleet of the* | Fletcher Christian leads a mutiny on HMS *Bounty*.

Captain William Bligh is set adrift near Tahiti with eighteen men in an eight-metre |

Date	Events in Barrington's life	Publications	Historical events
1789 (cont'd)		*Seven Transport Ships under his command: Containing a circumstantial Account of their perilous voyage ... by an Officer,* Printed for W. Clements, and J. Sadler, in the year 1789, London	open long boat. In six weeks, he sails 6000 kilometres to land in Timor.
1790	Barrington arrested for stealing the gold watch of Mr Henry Hare Townsend, September 1790. Barrington's trial at the Old Bailey widely reported. Jury find Barrington 'guilty' and Judge Baron Eyre sentences Barrington to transportation, 'for a term of seven years to parts beyond the seas'. 'An Heroic Epistle from George Barrington to Major Semple, on his transportation to the Coast of New South Wales', published in the *Attic Miscellany*, London.	Reprint of *The Voyage of Governor Phillip to Botany Bay.* *A Narrative of the Mutiny, on board His Majesty's Ship Bounty ... Written by Lieutenant William Bligh,* Printed for George Nicol, Pall Mall. *Journal of a Voyage to New South Wales with sixty-five plates of Non-descript Animals, Birds, Lizards, Serpents, curious Cones of Trees and other Natural Productions By John White Esqr. Surgeon-General to the Settlement at Port Jackson,* J. Debrett, Piccadilly. *Memoirs of George Barrington; A New Flash Song, made on*	The Marine Corps is replaced by the New South Wales Corps under the command of Capt. Nepean. The NSW Corps to perform police operations. Inexperienced men and conscripts serving out punishments for misconduct in the English service are recruited for the NSW Corps. Bligh arrives in England, returning from Batavia, to face a court martial. He is exonerated and returns to sea.

Date	Events in Barrington's life	Publications	Historical events
1790 (cont'd)		*the noted George Barrington; The Genuine Life and Trials of George Barrington; The Life, Amours, and Wonderful Adventures of that most Notorious Pickpocket, George Barrington; The Trial at Large of George Barrington, before Lord Chief Baron Eyre ...; Arraignment of George Barrington – The Whole Proceedings on the King's Commission ... and Gaol Delivery for the City of London; and also the Gaol Delivery for the County of Middx.* Edmund Burke publishes *Reflections on the Revolution in France*, November 1790.	
1791	March. Barrington is finally embarked on the convict transport ship, *Active*, for Port Jackson. Official reports of the voyage to New South Wales state that Barrington underwent a religious conversion at sea, and gave a sermon twice on Sundays on board the *Active*.	Jeremy Bentham publishes *Panopticon; or, The Inspection House*, a pamphlet attacking the transportation and colonization scheme to New South Wales. Thomas Paine's *Rights of Man* published.	Third Fleet departs England. Sailing in two divisions, from Portsmouth and Plymouth: the *Matilda, Atlantic, Salamander, William and Ann, Active*, the *Queen* (originating from Cork), the *Albemarle, Britannia, Admiral Barrington, Mary Ann*.

Date	Events in Barrington's life	Publications	Historical events
1791 (cont'd)	Barrington arrives in Port Jackson on 26 September 1791. Sent to work at the Government Farm at Toongabbie. Barrington's exemplary conduct is noted by the authorities.		Rationing is introduced in the Colony of New South Wales. 1696 convicted men and 169 convicted women arrive at Port Jackson. More than 200 deaths occurred at sea. Overcrowding, malnutrition and sickness account for death toll.
1792	Barrington receives conditional pardon and is appointed Superintendent of Convicts at Parramatta. Barrington granted sixty acres of land at Parramatta by Governor Phillip, and purchases a further fifty acres on the Hawkesbury River.	Publication in London of *The Life of George Barrington, containing every Remarkable Circumstance, from his Birth to the Present Time*; the book appears in London and the provinces. *Extracts of letters &c, from Governor Phillip, relating to New South Wales, ...* Printed for J. Debrett, Piccadilly. William Bligh publishes in London *Voyage to the South Sea, undertaken by command of His Majesty, for the purpose of conveying the Bread-fruit Tree to the West Indies ...*	Governor Arthur Phillip returns to England, compelled by ill health. Captain John Hunter, who held the dormant commission as Governor, returns to England. Major Francis Grose, Lieutenant-Governor and commander of the New South Wales Corps, conducts the colony in Hunter's absence as administrator and establishes military rule. Captain Watkin Tench returns to England.

Date	Events in Barrington's life	Publications	Historical events
1792 (cont'd)			Bennelong and Yemmerrawannie, two Aboriginal men captured in 1790, travel with Phillip to England. Yemmerrawannie dies in Kent. France declared a republic.
1793		*An Historical Journal of the Transactions at Port Jackson and Norfolk Island, with the Discoveries which have been made in New South Wales and in the Southern Ocean ... By John Hunter, Esqr. Post Captain in His Majesty's Navy*, printed by John Stockdale, Piccadilly, London, 1793. *An Impartial and Circumstantial Narrative of the present state of Botany Bay, in New South Wales ... by George Barrington, now Superintendant of the Convicts at Paramata*, published in London. *A Complete Account of the Settlement at Port Jackson, including an accurate*	Outbreak of war with France. Watkin Tench taken prisoner by the French from his ship, the *Alexander*. Revd Richard Johnson, the first chaplain to New South Wales, builds the colony's first church at his own expense.

Date	Events in Barrington's life	Publications	Historical events
1793 (cont'd)		*description of the Situation of the Colony; of the Natives; and of its natural productions. By Captain Watkin Tench, of the Marines*, Sold by G. Nicol, Pall Mall, London, 1793	
1794	*The Revenge* performed at the York Theatre, Sydney Town, featuring the 'Prologue', which is incorrectly attributed to Barrington. *Lt. Gov. Francis Grose grants George Barrington thirty acres of land at North Brush, in the Field of Mars, near Parramatta.* As Chief Constable of the Watch Barrington hunts for the murderer of John Lewis, a stock-keeper at Parramatta.	Revd Richard Johnson's *An Address to the Inhabitants of the Colonies, established in New South Wales and Norfolk Island* (written in 1792) published in London. Letters from an exile *at Botany Bay, to his* Aunt in Dumfries; *giving a particular account of the Settlement of New South Wales, with the Customs and manners of the Inhabitants*, by Thomas Watling, (forger and painter, assigned to Surgeon White), published in Dumfries, for distribution in Great Britain.	*Habeas Corpus* suspended in England. Grose returns to England and is replaced by Captain William Paterson of the NSW Corps, who continues military rule.

Date	Events in Barrington's life	Publications	Historical events
1795		*A Voyage to New South Wales; With a Description of the Country; The Manners, Customs and Religion, &c, of the Natives, In the Vicinity of Botany Bay. By George Barrington, now Superintendant of the Convicts at Paramatta*, published in London.	Bennelong returns to Port Jackson.
			John Hunter, second in command to Governor Phillip in the colony of New South Wales from 1788 to 1790, returns and is appointed Governor.
		A Voyage round the World, in the Gorgon Man of War: Captain John Parker. Performed and written by his widow ... Mary Ann Parker, sold by Mr Debrett, Piccadilly.	Hunter re-establishes civil administration in the Colony. British occupation of the Cape of Good Hope. Seditious Meetings Act forbids public lecturing and meetings in England.
1796	Barrington commended by Governor Hunter for performing his duties commendably as Chief Constable at Parramatta, and receives a full pardon.	Sir Joseph Banks's *Catalogus Bibliothecae Historico-Naturalis, Scriptores Generales*, published, London. *A Treatise on the Police of the Metropolis, ...* by Patrick Colquhoun, is published in London, suggesting that transportation may only be effective for the 'more atrocious, young and vigorous offenders ... as they are most likely to	

Date	Events in Barrington's life	Publications	Historical events
1796 (cont'd)		eventually advance the fortunes of the settlement and render it eventually self-supporting.'	
1797	Barrington is linked in popular memory in various publications with Major Semple, alias James George Semple-Lisle, who is charged with organizing the only successful mutiny on board a convict ship, the *Lady Shore*. It was alleged in 1791 that Barrington foiled a mutiny on the *Albermarle*. This false rumour was perpetrated by London publishers.		The *Lady Shore* is seized by her military guard and is sailed to Montevideo. Major Semple is implicated. Previously convicted, this adventurer was twice sentenced to seven years transportation to New South Wales, in 1786 and again in 1795. (On his eventual return to England he surrendered and was gaoled in Tothill Fields prison in 1799).
1798		*An Account of the English Colony in New South Wales*, by David Collins, Judge-Advocate and Secretary of the Colony, published in London by Debrett.

Voyage à Botany-Bay, published by Desenne, the political publisher, celebrating George Barrington's reformation, and the exercise of British justice and mercy. | |

Date	Events in Barrington's life	Publications	Historical events
1799	Barrington rents his house to Revd Rowland Hassall, of the London Missionary Society. Judge-Advocate David Collins records that Barrington's health is visibly declining.		Combination Laws passed to prevent the formation of trade unions in England.
1800	Governer Hunter recalled to England. Phillip Gidley King, previously Commandant of Norfolk Island, appointed Governor of New South Wales.	*History of the Otaheitean Islands* published, recording, among other information, the departure of missionaries for Port Jackson on board the *Nautilus*.	Passage of the Act of Union, incorporating Ireland into the United Kingdom.
1801	General Orders, 28 November, announce Barrington's retirement due to his 'infirmity'. Barrington provided with half-pension to live on his land at Brush Farm, Parramatta.	*Barrington's Voyage to Botany Bay, in New South Wales,* published in Newcastle (UK). *A Voyage to New South Wales, comprising an Interesting Narrative ... by George Barrington*, published in Dublin. *A Voyage to New South Wales ... by George Barrington,* published in New York. *A Sequel to Barrington's Voyage to New South Wales,* published in London.	The United Kingdom of Great Britain and Ireland comes into existence. Prime Minister William Pitt resigns.

Date	Events in Barrington's life	Publications	Historical events
1801 (cont'd)		*A Voyage to New South Wales,* published in Cork.	
1802	'Prologue' allegedly spoken by George Barrington, on 16 January 1796, at the opening of the Theatre at Sydney, in New South Wales, published in London. Pierre Bernard Milius, second in command of the *Naturaliste*, visits Barrington in Parramatta.	Jeremy Bentham's Letter to Lord Pelham giving a *Comparative View of the System of Penal Colonization, in New South Wales and the Home Penitentiary System,* published, London. *Barrington's History of New South Wales, including Botany Bay, &c. No. 1 ... by George Barrington, an Officer of the Peace.* *The History of New South Wales, including Botany Bay, Port Jackson, Paramatta, Sydney ... enriched with Beautiful Colour'd Plates,* published, London. *Governor Hunter's Remarks on the Causes of Colonial Expense for the Establishment of New South Wales, &c. Hints at the reduction of such expense, and for reforming the prevailing abuses,* published in London.	The first book printed in the colony appears. *New South Wales General Standing Orders: selected from the General Orders issued by Former Governors,* produced at the Government Press, Sydney.
1803		*Puteschestivie w Botani-Bai,* published in Moscow,	The first editions of the *Sydney Gazette and New South Wales*

Date	Events in Barrington's life	Publications	Historical events
1803 (cont'd)		attributed to George Barrington.	*Advertiser* appear in the Colony, published by George Howe, Government Printer.
1804			Castle Hill uprising, March 1804. 350 armed convicts met at Parramatta shouting the United Irishmen's slogan, 'Death or Liberty', demanding ships back to Britain. Authorities quelled the uprising. Major George Johnston caught up with the rebels near Toongabbie. Refusing to surrender to the NSW Corps, Johnston opened fire and nine convicts were killed. The Garrison for superintending the convicts on the government farm, where Barrington had begun his career in New South Wales, had been withdrawn by Governor King in the previous year.
	George Barrington dies on 27 December, at Parramatta.		
1805	Barrington's death registered at St John's Parish Church. Auction of Barrington's land, goods and chattels announced in the *Sydney Gazette*.	Announcement of Barrington's death published in the *Sydney Gazette*, January 1805.	Battle of Trafalgar. William Bligh appointed Governor of New South Wales.

Plate 1 'Barrington tried in a Cause of Outlawry, &c, taken by stealth in Court', engraving by T. Darby, No. 25 Blackman Street, Borough (1790).
Source: Rex Nan Kivell Collection (NK 1941), by permission of the National Library of Australia, Canberra.

INTRODUCTION

My Lord and Gentlemen of the Jury, it may, perhaps, be expected by many persons, in this place, that I should say a great deal about the prepossession and newspaper reports; and, if I had the ability to do it, perhaps I should not be blamed, for, he who has been the unhappy object of much defamation has surely the right to depracate [sic] its baneful effects. *George Barrington, London, 17ᵗʰ September, 1790.*[1]

With these rueful words, George Barrington (1755–1804), England's and Ireland's most celebrated gentleman thief and pickpocket, reflected bitterly on the role of the press. Declaiming from the dock of the Old Bailey for the last time, he blamed newspaper reports for his conviction for picking the pocket of Henry Hare Townsend, Esquire, for which he had just received a sentence of seven years' transportation 'beyond the seas' to Botany Bay. Taking into account his previous convictions, he was fortunate not to have been hanged. The presiding judge, Baron Eyre, reminded him that he had been treated with more favour than he deserved: 'If ever there was a man in the world that abused and prostituted great talents to the most unworthy and shameful purposes, you are that man.'

George Barrington was a man of conspicuous, if wayward, talents, and his celebrity in the late eighteenth century was without precedent. While in England highwaymen such as Dick Turpin, Jack Sheppard and Jonathon Wild occupied a minor place in the annals of crime, as did in France the picaresque thieves Cartouche and Vidocq, or in Germany, Schinderhannes, the Robber of the Rhine, it was Barrington, with his clandestine career as Europe's most renowned 'genteel' pickpocket, who secured the most prominent place in the criminal chronicles. Even his slightest exploits were widely reported. Although this finally assisted in his downfall, it also helped to create a legend. Accounts of Barrington's daring thefts and his frequent arrests, trials and speeches, were popular publishing fare throughout the metropolis, across the countryside and much further afield. He was, without doubt, a most notorious and popular celebrity.

An aspiring actor, an elegant confidence trickster and a pickpocket *extraordinaire*, 'The Prince of Pickpockets' was one of the eighteenth century's most talked-about lawbreakers. For a man who had benefited vicariously from constant press attention throughout his nefarious career, his belated and mournful observation on the perfidy of the press rang true. In court, Barrington was forced to face reality; those hacks and journalists who had saluted his disguises and pilfering skills and reported with salacious delight his depredations on London's wealthy, also had the power to inflict great harm on his 'gentleman's' reputation. Every word and excuse Barrington uttered in court was transcribed, his acts of thieving bravado had been exposed and each elegant suit of clothes he donned was described in careful detail. While this harmed his defence in court, another dramatic result was that he attained an almost mythic quality as a rogue hero of eccentric and ingenious talents.

Eager readers had learned of Barrington's exploits in newsprint and magazines, in colourful poetry and ballads, in bold engravings depicting the 'Prince of Pickpockets' at work, or by hearing elaborate gossip about Barrington's illegal and *bona fide* accomplishments. This exposure instinctively encouraged literary artifice as well as 'genuine accounts', and Barrington was often drawn larger than life. What the press of the day argued was that there were differences in *quality* between a thieving beggar and a genteel pickpocket. In some versions he was touted as a well-mannered and talented rogue, while in others his tricks and disguises served to forewarn and deter.

A deliberate blurring made it difficult for contemporaries to separate the imagined from the real man. Barrington's emerging mythological persona was well served by his own theatricality and conscious 'presentation of self' and furthered by the liberties taken by various writers and publishers.[2] His criminal career had already ensured him an unrivalled position in the history of crime; he was a favoured subject of publishers. Then, in 1791, Barrington's involuntary and well-publicized voyage of transportation to New South Wales allotted him a unique place in the literature of travel and convictism. From this creative collision of fact and fiction, and utilizing the reality of Barrington's transportation, an invented travel narrative appeared in late 1793 or early 1794 entitled *An Impartial and Circumstantial Narrative of the Present State of Botany Bay, in New South Wales ... by George Barrington, now Superintendant of the Convicts at Paramata*.[3]

In the same way in which Barrington's masquerade and artifice inspired writers to create the 'Prince of Pickpockets', publishers now drew on a transformed Barrington to present readers with the 'Superintendant of Convicts'. The infamous pickpocket had undergone a conversion. Once removed from his familiar stamping grounds in London and landed in New South Wales after a sobering period on a convict ship, Barrington had changed radically. He rapidly became a respected and contributing member of colonial society, a law-abiding and law-upholding citizen. In exile, Barrington's life in 'Botany Bay' was still recorded, but this time only in convict returns, administrative reports and formal observations. Official reports were verifiable and unemotional, and the penal colony had no press to hound or 'invent' him. The reinforcing triangle of criminal, press and audience was fractured. Confounding expectations, including those of the presiding judge who had summed up at Barrington's trial with the pronouncement, 'I cannot entertain the least hope that you will in any manner reform', Barrington did truly convert. As soon as this confirmed intelligence filtered through a changed picture of George Barrington emerged, suggesting that fame was an inescapable fate.

The skilfully manufactured *An Impartial and Circumstantial Narrative* introduced George Barrington in his new role of superintendent of convicts and as author of an authoritative travelogue. The text is of significant interest both as an outcome of the public's fascination with celebrities and as a product of its day, part of the invigorated genre of travel writing fuelled by exploration in the South Seas and the Antipodes. In this respect *An Impartial and Circumstantial Narrative* points strongly towards the mythic quality of travel writing. The opportunity for a dynamic combination of celebrity and voyaging presented itself, and publishers could not allow the powerful selling attraction of Barrington's name to slip away.

An Impartial and Circumstantial Narrative was a direct result of Barrington's spectacular conversion, and yet it was a publishing forgery over which he had no control. Despite courtroom protestations to the contrary, in London he had enjoyed a modicum of control over his own image, skilfully inventing alibis and concocting his own version of events for the dubious benefit of juries. Once exiled in New South Wales, this control was gone. Publishers in London and elsewhere were able to take complete advantage of his absence. Parading the former pickpocket's new and legitimate position in the title of the work was an inspired move, invoking legitimacy of authorship and pointing to the truthfulness of the narration. Barrington had been elevated and administrators with no pecuniary interest in promoting his activities confirmed his position in written records. His exploits, with the series of antipodean travel narratives and histories attributed to him, remained inextricably entwined. Yet another version of the Barrington legend had been created.

George Barrington's Voyage to Botany Bay

I. The man behind the legend

Who was the man behind the historical legend? And how did his gradual transformation into a mythical hero come about? One leading contemporary account, *The Life of George Barrington, containing every Remarkable Circumstance, from his Birth to the Present Time*, written in 1792, illustrates the abounding misinformation which surrounded the man that publishers called 'our hero'.[4] The legend begins thus: 'George Barrington, alias Waldron, otherwise Jones, the hero of these memoirs, was born at Rush in 1758, in the kingdom of Ireland'. Such equivocation was then common, but it is now generally accepted that George Barrington was born in 1755 in Maynooth, Country Kildare, to artisan parents, a silversmith and a mantua-maker whose family name was Waldron. Educated first in Maynooth by John Donelly, an apothecary, then by a Dr Driscol, George showed promise as a scholar and came to the attention of a Church of Ireland dignitary who arranged formal grammar schooling at the Blue Coat School in Dublin.

As tradition has it, George was a bright and energetic youth and absorbed enough of a classical education to stand him in good stead. However, instead of completing his schooling, in 1771 at the age of sixteen, he fell foul of the school authorities. During a violent quarrel he stabbed a fellow pupil with a penknife. Soundly flogged for his crime he decided that it was necessary to abscond and to finance his escape he stole his headmaster's gold hunter watch and twelve guineas. Hoping to find fame and fortune on the road utilizing his evident good looks and education, he was quickly taken up by a troupe of travelling players who offered him the opportunity to act in a production of Otway's drama, *Venice Preserved*. Barrington's debut as Jaffeir took place on a hastily erected stage in a barn in Drogheda. Here, in this thespian environment, he learned his trade, a combination of acting and stealing.

The golden-haired youth's talents were quickly recognized by John Price, the troupe's entrepreneurial master, who regularly supplemented his theatrical income by picking the pockets of patrons and other innocent bystanders at local fairs, races and social gatherings. Taking his new leading man aside, Price persuaded George to become his partner in crime and taught him the finer points of 'stealing from the person', the legal definition of picking pockets. By this time, a change of name was required and George Waldron became George Barrington. The name Barrington was a wise choice with decent connections – John Barrington was a notable Irish actor also known on the London stage, and Admiral Barrington, of His Majesty's Royal Navy, had served with honour.

Disguised as master and servant, with John Price dressed as the servant, the pair proceeded to enrich themselves. Well-staged incidents allowed Price and his willing apprentice to make handsome profits until Price was arrested in Dublin in 1773. It was said that he was transported to America.

Fearing arrest himself, the newly-made Barrington was forced to make a hurried exit and flee his homeland on a packet ship. This was a provident move. In Dublin, Barrington had already captured the imagination of the local press. An anonymous Irish hack had noted in 1772 that he had affected to lead the life of a *Bon Ton* in Cork:

> A young fellow of fashion, [following] the usual career of amour, intrigue, and debauchery, of gaming, drinking and fighting; indispensable requisites in the character of a man of the *Ton* in Ireland; in short to gratify all the suggestions of vanity, profligacy and whim.[5]

On his way from Ireland he apparently gulled some aristocrats on the same ship, including the Earl of Leinster and his friends, who believed Barrington's plausible explanation that he was on his way to make his fortune on the London stage. They provided him with some useful introductions. In London, Barrington was absorbed into the crowds until ready to re-emerge a fully-fledged young gentleman of Anglo-Irish ancestry. At first the veneer was thin, but his appearance was convincing enough to carry him into fashionable metropolitan society. Using all his guile and skills to profitable effect, he soon found that supplementing his income by theft was the surest way to make a living. Well dressed and well versed, and armed with the tools of the trade – a key with a hook and joints, a knife with three joints, a ring with springs and a whalebone drag – Barrington set to work picking pockets. He made friends, some noble, others wealthy and, not a few, well-known rakes. Drawing on his education he may have also dabbled in writing. The legend states that Barrington composed several poems and odes and, later, at the height of his infamy, publishers attributed a number to his hand.

Invited to social levées and to the pleasure grounds and theatres of the metropolis, with little effort the elegant Barrington helped himself to the contents of purses and pockets, all the while cleverly avoiding detection and attention. For seventeen years in London, from 1773 until 1790, Barrington continued to affect the image of a gentleman of fashion and made a considerable living by relieving the well-to-do of their valuables. He did not always get off scot-free, but he managed to avoid detection on countless occasions. Unreported thefts kept Barrington in fine tailoring and, for the most part, in entertaining company. He used a

Plate 2   Barrington Mug, *c.* 1790, Staffordshire, Great Britain. 'Barrington picking the pocket of J. Brown, Esqr.'
Source: Collection, National Gallery of Australia, Canberra.

network of fences and pawnbrokers to dispose discreetly of stolen items, while keeping up the pretence of being a 'gentleman'. Although disguise was his strength, secrecy was not, and the print media – newspapers, magazines and broadsheets – began to write about him. Snippets of gossip regularly circulated, followed by published accounts of his exploits, reports of his arrests, celebrations of his street prowess, descriptions of his elegant attire and, not least, his legend-making performances in court. Rumours about him spread like wildfire around London's taverns and coffeehouses, and even rival criminals admitted to a grudging sense of admiration. Barrington's panache and ability constantly to outwit the law, his adroitness and haughty remonstrances, rather than provoking an outcry, turned him into a celebrity and provided a sharp reminder to all that the law was often powerless to act when manipulated by a virtuoso.

One incident after another aroused the press, but perhaps Barrington's most daring performance, and one which received much exposure, occurred in London in October 1775. He attempted to steal the Russian Count Gregory Orloff's diamond snuff-box 'from his person', while the Count was seated in his box at the Covent Garden theatre. The diamond-encrusted box, allegedly a gift given to him by the Russian Empress Catherine, was said to be worth a fortune, some estimated £30,000. The Count felt Barrington's hand upon him and seized him, but while he was doing this Barrington slipped the glittering box back into his victim's pocket. Barrington was arrested and held in custody at Bow Street for two days, appearing before the magistrate, Sir John Fielding. But the Count did not come forward to prosecute and without the Count's testimony the magistrate had to acquit. Sir John soundly admonished Barrington for his illicit attempt and *Lloyd's Evening Post*, the *Morning Post* and the *Morning Chronicle* reported the trial's failure with unashamed glee. Illustrators recreated the scene in memorable and lively engravings that appeared all over town.

This narrow escape did nothing to deter an emboldened Barrington who, buoyed by his luck, went on to steal the Earl of Mexborough's diamond Order at a social levée. Although suspected, he went undetected. He stole money and a watch from a Miss Hurst and was arrested but again avoided prosecution before Sir John Fielding for lack of evidence. Some time later, Mrs Anne Dudman had her purse stolen by Barrington at the Drury Lane Playhouse and she had him arrested. For a third time, Barrington appeared before Sir John who, although blind, recognised the fluent testimony and cultured voice of the accused. This time, Barrington was confined to Tothill Fields Bridewell where he was forced to await trial at the Old Bailey.

Plate 3 Engraving by Barlin, 'Barrington detected picking the Pocket of PRINCE ORLOW in the Front boxes of Convent Garden Theatre, of a Snuff Box set with diamonds supposed to be worth £30,000' (1790).
Source: Pictorial Collection, Rex Nan Kivell Collection (NK 1752/11), by permission of the National Library of Australia, Canberra.

The press was on full alert. Before his court appearance Barrington took a great risk and wrote to Mrs Dudman, appealing to her to withdraw her accusation against him. The letter survives, written in an elegant hand with an equally elegant plea.[6] She ignored his supplications and Barrington appeared before Justice Amhurst on 16 January 1777. The jury, although confused by Barrington's gentility and plausible explanations, could not ignore the evidence. Glowing character testimonials provided by friends were of no help. Found guilty of stealing, Barrington was sentenced to three years' hard labour heaving ballast at the Woolwich hulks. Reporting the trial, the *Morning Chronicle* noted that Barrington was 'dressed *a-la-mode*, genteel, gold taper cane and elegant Artois buckles ... the genteelest thief ever remembered seen at the Old Bailey'.[7] Good fortune soon visited Barrington on the prison hulk *Justitia*. A prison visitor, possibly a reverend gentleman, agreed to forward a letter of supplication to the authorities in which Barrington pleaded his deteriorating health and also admitted deep contrition for his acts. As a first offender, he received a pardon in late 1778,[8] but Barrington was beginning to understand the pain of hard labour and incarceration.

By now a firm favourite of booksellers (though not his unfortunate victims), news of Barrington's release soon spread. His skilful depredations continued to amuse readers who were regaled with details of disguises and possible whereabouts. In time, such reports were so widely published that Barrington complained that even if tempted into lawful work, he was excluded, his reputation left in tatters. However, although he protested against his public and somewhat dangerous fame, he did not change his ways. Having no formal qualifications and only a brief apprenticeship as an actor – which stood him in good stead in the dock – Barrington continued to choose the easiest solution and his success rate was high. His characteristic ploy was always to drop a stolen item when he feared detection, but he only did this at the last moment. Barrington thus ensured that vital evidence was not found upon his own person. His freedom did not last long.

Arrested again soon after his release, again for stealing, he was sentenced to another five years ballast-heaving on the *Justitia*, but received a remission in 1781 in consideration of his good behaviour, his evident illness and through the intercession of another influential sponsor. He was instead 'banished from the kingdom', a sentence designed to keep him out of England's major cities. He moved around, travelling between Ireland and Scotland still making a living from picking pockets dressed variously as a 'Quack Doctor', a 'Clergyman' and, one presumes, as a quality gentleman of independent means. In 1783 he returned quietly to

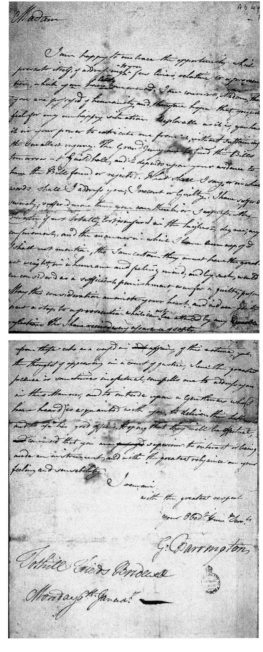

Plate 4   Letter from George Barrington to Mrs Dudman, written from Tothill Fields Bridewell, Monday 6 January 1777. Mitchell Library (Ms. Ab 4912).
Source: By permission of the Library Council of New South Wales, Mitchell Library, State Library of New South Wales, Sydney.

London but was spotted and arrested for having breached the continuing banishment order. Barrington pleaded that he had misunderstood that banishment was a perpetual punishment but, on this occasion, his famous oratory failed him. He was forced to serve out the remainder of his sentence, this time in Newgate Gaol. By 1785 he was free once more to plunder and it is said that he operated in York, Carlisle, Derby and then back in London.

In January 1787 Barrington was arrested for stealing twenty-three guineas and the pocket watch of Mr Havilard Le Mesurier at the Drury Lane theatre, and was again before the court at the Old Bailey accused of robbery and outlawry. After some extraordinarily circumlocuted pleading, insisting that his well-known identity made it easy for victims of theft to accuse him, the jury found Barrington not guilty.

In the meantime, well removed from London, events were advancing that were to have great bearing on his future. In May 1787 the First Fleet, under the command of Captain Arthur Phillip, R.N., sailed for Botany Bay. With a handpicked contingent of naval officers, a platoon of marine guards and the first muster of 750 convicts, the prison Fleet had weighed anchor for the 'new colony of thieves and ruffians'.[9] A revised scheme for dealing with crime aimed at ridding Britain's byways and gaols of petty thieves and criminals was well under way. For habitual offenders such as Barrington, being exiled was only a matter of time.

At the sailing of the First Fleet, when Barrington was still at large, some alleged that he was not picking pockets at all but was instead playing in *The Beggar's Opera*, in Glasgow. Whether in fact he was playing Macheath, the gentleman highwayman hero, is not recorded. He was absent from the metropolis, but was he in the north of England or in the south? In the midst of the mingling crowds who came to witness the Fleet's departure from Portsmouth, thieves and pickpockets attracted to the easy pickings worked quickly on spectators' pockets. Barrington, often well-disguised as 'a rider to a manufacturing house in Birmingham',[10] may well have been amongst the crowds. In truth no one was ever completely sure of his next move or location and, conceivably, he may deliberately have been attempting to avoid attention.

When he was arrested and reconvicted in 1790, Barrington was sentenced to exile, forced to join the prison flotilla on its voyage to New South Wales. Thus began a new phase in his career.

II. Sentences from the Court

In the past, and particularly at his memorable trials, Barrington had evidently presented himself with an air of great confidence. Although arrested more than a dozen times, he had cleverly avoided conviction seven times, and on all occasions it was his own defence that saved him. The law finally caught up with the master pickpocket and it seemed that he was unable to persuade the jury of his innocence; the witnesses were adamant that they had seen the pickpocket at work, and the evidence was too strong. Barrington was duly convicted of the simple felony of stealing, though not 'stealing from the person' which remained a capital offence.

While enjoying a high profile during the 1770s and 1780s, Barrington had taken the press with him and the use of his name guaranteed publishers high sales. There were copies of *The Genuine Life of George Barrington ...*, *Memoirs, An Account of the noted Criminal, George Barrington*, *The Famous Speech of George Barrington*, *The only Authentic Edition of the Memoirs of George Barrington*, *The Trial at Large of George Barrington*, *The Life, Amours, and Wonderful Adventures of that most Notorious Pickpocket, George Barrington*, *A New Flash Song, made on the noted George Barrington*, and *A New Edition, Greatly Improved, The Life of George Barrington*. The variety was impressive as one publisher after another claimed that 'every remarkable circumstance' of Barrington's life was faithfully reproduced. But even a thief such as Barrington could lose his attraction if caught once too often.

The trial was a turning-point for Barrington in more ways than one. When faced with the real possibility of the death penalty, his desire for fame, riches and popularity appeared to desert him. Despair and solemn observations replaced the usual haughty denials and, either admitting defeat or confessing his sins, Barrington spoke to the court:

> I am convinced, upon the whole, there is no joy but what arises from the practice of virtue, and consists of the felicity of a tranquil mind, and a benevolent heart ... It will be my study to possess them; nor will the heaviest affliction of poverty, pain, or disgrace, cause me to part with resolutions founded upon the deepest reflections and which end but with life: I will perish on the pavement before I will deviate from them.

Not unexpectedly, the newspapers turned on their hero, the Prince of Pickpockets. Reversing their usual admiration, they now sought negative opinions from London's criminal subculture in the hope, perhaps, of accelerating his exit from the public stage. Celebrities must not fail: the *St. James Chronicle* of September 1790, was typically harsh in its judgement:

> Pickpockets, we hear, no longer acknowledge any subordination, to their former superior, Barrington: They consider him as a *bungler* in

Plate 5   Etching, 'George Barrington drawn from the life during his trial at the Old Bailey on Friday Sept. 17, 1790' (artist unknown).
Source: Rex Nan Kivell Collection (NK 4848), by permission of the National Library of Australia, Canberra.

the operative part of the profession, by his being so often detected; whereas many others, employed on an equal number of years on *active service*, have never yet been taken.

Yet, surprisingly, hypocrisy from the press did nothing to diminish the pickpocket's aura for the public at large. Whether incarcerated in Newgate Gaol or landed in New South Wales, Barrington managed to retain public attention and, one might argue, even its affection.

Barrington recognized that the press loved nothing more than pursuing public figures and controversial trials, and knew that he could never escape what he termed 'the envenomed tooth of calumny'. He had claimed innocence on too many occasions and escaped the death penalty, but when he was finally brought to book in September 1790, the judge, Baron Eyre, applied a sentence that guaranteed that Barrington would be taken well away from the temptations of the metropolis to serve his time in the remote wilderness of New South Wales. The Recorder stated it plainly:

> George Barrington, the sentence of the Court is upon you is, that you be transported for the term of seven years to parts beyond the seas to such place as his Majesty, with the advice of his privy Council shall think fit to declare and appoint.

It was a fate which Barrington accepted with eloquence and equanimity.

The departure of Barrington and other convicts from England was often referred to 'satirically' as beneficial to the nation. The famous 'Prologue', for example, taken from *The Revenge*, the first play performed in Sydney in 1796 and reworked in the *Annual Register* of 1801, targeted pickpockets, thieves and fakers of London town, and gleefully identified 'Barrington, the topper [who] left his country, patriot, he, All for his country's good'. Altruism had little to do with Barrington's destiny or destination. Accepting exile as an alternative to hanging seemed sensible even if, for most, the departure was undertaken with reluctance.

Now publishers relished Barrington's misfortune and come-uppance; his change in circumstances provided grist for them to work with. Quickly published in a famous but fictitious letter written to his 'wife and child' (though Barrington was unmarried), the pickpocket was made to lament his fate. As improbable and inaccurate as the letter was (Barrington allegedly wrote from the *William and Ann* transport in Plymouth, whereas he was on the *Active* which had sailed from Portsmouth),[11] the sentiments nevertheless cleverly echoed Barrington's resigned state of mind as expressed during his final trial. As he well knew, his prospects in New South Wales were open to fate. Addressing the court, he was contrite:

With respect to the prospect before me, sad and distressing as it may appear, all may ultimately be for our good. With the best of hearts and best of dispositions there is, God knows, an overbearing fate that counteracts our best designs, and makes us act (that is, pickpockets) in spite of ourselves.[12]

Barrington avowed that if given another chance in another land, he would reform his ways. His words were as dramatic as they were prophetic:

If I am acquitted I will quickly retire to some distant land, where my name and misfortunes will be alike unknown ... I do now assure you, Gentlemen of the Jury, that I feel a cheering hope, even at this awful moment, that the rest of my life will be so conducted, as to make me as much an object of esteem and applause, as I am now the unhappy object of censure and suspicion.[13]

Like death-bed pronouncements and gallows speeches, editions of verbatim reports of Barrington's trial subsequently sold in great quantities. His words once more provided elegant fare for those publishers of chapbooks, broad sheets and other ephemeral publications. Within a couple of years or so of his leaving England under guard and being deposited unceremoniously in Port Jackson, the former pickpocket's name was part of the standard currency of unscrupulous London and provincial publishers who used his continuing celebrity to invent an 'authentic' narrative and attribute it to him. He had become a mythology in the sense of Roland Barthes' definition; his name had become a thing in itself, uncoupled from any referent in reality and open to multiple meanings.[14] Barrington was recast as an observer and authoritative commentator relating the affairs of the new colony for those left wondering or languishing 'at home'.

George Barrington's ignominious voyage to New South Wales was to provide eighteenth- and early nineteenth-century readers with a tangible marker, an emblematic proof, that transportation had the power to reform even the most artful thief. Wearing the new cloak of responsibility and enjoying the fresh airs of the emerging colony, Barrington was transformed, almost overnight, from a nimble-fingered London thief into a valued member of colonial society. In Sydney, his conduct was noted by the governors to be 'irreproachable' and his knowledge of men 'eminently useful'. This was a far cry from London where the judge had accused him of wasting his evident talents.

III. 'The Convict's Farewell'

While transportation was not new, New South Wales and Botany Bay had quickly become popular synonyms for a distant criminal haven. Warnings were issued by disappointed doomsayers such as Alexander Dalrymple (1737–1808), who had recommended the island of Tristan da Cunha as a more suitable penal settlement. He had already published *A Serious Admonition to the Publick, on the Intended Thief-Colony at Botany Bay*, in London in 1786. In 1787, in a Newgate tavern, carousers blared out the ballad, 'The Convict's Farewell to Old England', referring to the unlikelihood of return. The jest played with the idea of a personal fate in Botany Bay far better than incarceration, and echoed precisely Dalrymple's fear that Botany Bay held out too good a prospect for the criminal classes:

> Labour apart – where every day
> Nature is kindly giving,
> Plenty to have, and nothing to pay,
> That is the land to live in!
>
> Over the waves our course we'll bend,
> Glad the fond hope to cherish,
> Better to range in a foreign land,
> Than in prison perish.[15]

Between 1787 and 1789 the First and Second Fleets sailed from England and Ireland taking more than two and a half thousand convicts to the coast of New South Wales.[16] In 1791 the Third Fleet, including the *Active* on which Barrington sailed, deposited another eighteen hundred or so unquiet souls in the colony. For the great majority of those condemned to serve out sentences 'beyond the seas', New South Wales was feared almost worse than death. Unimaginable to all but explorers and navigators, and largely undescribed until the mid-1790s, the new territory of New South Wales was popularly dubbed 'Botany Bay' by those unfamiliar with the new geography. This name came from the voyage in 1770 by Captain James Cook, who had made a brief anchorage in the shallow, wide and sandy bay a few nautical miles south of Port Jackson. Initially, he named it Sting Ray Harbour, then Botanists Bay and finally, Botany Bay. No voyager saw the bay again until 1788 and the arrival of the First Fleet.

The penal settlement's first governor, Captain Arthur Phillip, R.N., quickly rejected Botany Bay as a site for permanent settlement in early January 1788. This was because of its shortage of fresh water, although the name Botany Bay 'stuck', becoming synonymous with exile and banishment. Port Jackson, further north, with its plentiful fresh water and safe anchorages became Phillip's well-considered choice. He was elated at this discovery: 'We got into Port Jackson early in the afternoon, and had the satisfaction of finding the finest harbour in the world, in which a thousand sail of the line may ride in the most perfect security.' Accordingly, the First Fleet voyagers and captives disembarked at Sydney Cove on 26 January 1788.

Back in Britain, the unexplored land and wary native Aboriginal inhabitants remained largely fantastic figments of popular imagination until published accounts became widely accessible, and even then only the most optimistic could envisage the colony's potential, or any long-term benefits which might befall the convicts forced to subsist there. Carving out new lives and achieving prosperity was not the original intention of a desperate government. It sought an immediate solution for crowded gaols in a distant site which might accommodate incorrigible prisoners and thereby remove an inconvenient problem from 'any county, riding, division, city, town, borough, liberty, or place within that part of Great Britain called England': well out of sight if not out of mind.[17]

King George III, in his speech at the Opening of Parliament at Westminster in 1787, announced that a plan had been formulated: 'by my direction, for transporting a number of convicts; in order to remove the inconvenience which arose from the crowded state of the gaols in different parts of the kingdom'.[18] New South Wales was duly established in legislation under an Act of Parliament, expressly to remove, house and reform felons transported from Britain. The prospect for the penal colony was that it was to be 'reciprocally beneficial' for both convicts and the State. Only later were any real expectations raised of extending British influence; initially the penal colony was intended to provide 'a remedy for the evils likely to result from the late alarming and numerous increase of felons in this country, and more particularly in the metropolis'.[19]

Lord Sydney, then Secretary of State, Sir George Young, a distinguished officer of the Navy (Admiral of the White) and the Lords of the Treasury agreed in 1786 in the Heads of a Plan, that 'the fertility and salubrity of the climate, connected with the remoteness of its situation (from whence it is hardly possible for persons to return without permission), seems particularly adapted to answer the views of the Government'.[20] Survival was possible, escape was inconceivable and prison reform was eminently desirable. Despite the extreme difficulties encountered by those who undertook the First and Second sailings, transportation was to continue. Furthermore, as Prime Minister William Pitt reported later to the House of Commons in 1791 in defence of the penal settlement, no cheaper mode of disposing of the convicts could be found. The settlement thus soon became popularly dubbed 'the colony of thieves'.

Ten vessels were contracted for the Third Fleet in early 1791 by the Commissioners of the Navy to convey the next shipment of felons, including the pickpocket Barrington.[21] The *Mary Ann* departed first in February. Another vessel, the *Queen,* sailed separately directly from Cork carrying Irish prisoners under the command of the naval agent, Lieutenant Samuel Blow, who was ordered to rendezvous with the rest of the Third Fleet at St Jago in the Cape Verde Islands. Meanwhile the major part of the Fleet sailed in two divisions departing on 27 March 1791. Under the command of Lieutenant Richard Bowen, the first division comprised the *Atlantic, Salamander* and the *William and Ann* which departed in convoy from Plymouth, while the second division, with the *Active, Albemarle, Admiral Barrington, Matilda* and *Britannia* sailed from Portsmouth under the command of Lieutenant Robert Parry Young.

Lieutenants Blow, Bowen and Young were appointed officially as naval agents for the Fleet, although each vessel had a private master in charge engaged separately by the official contractors, Messrs. Camden, Calvert & King. The Fleet sailed via Tenerife and Rio de Janeiro. There the Plymouth division parted company with the Portsmouth convoy to take a different route, sailing directly from Rio to Port Jackson, missing the usual interlude of re-victualling at the Cape of Good Hope. These hardy vessels were the first convict ships to take the foreshortened route.[22]

George Barrington was confined on board the *Active*, a vessel of around 300 tons under a private master, John Mitchinson.[23] According to *An Impartial and Circumstantial Narrative*, Barrington's fellow prisoners were ordered immediately into the hold and were encumbered with leg irons. Together with 'want of fresh air ... their situation was soon deplorable'. According to the invented account, Barrington was given better accommodation, but in reality this was most unlikely. With his convict companions, Barrington sailed in convoy with the Portsmouth division and was one of the 175 convicts who eventually landed from the miserable vessel that quitted England's shores in early spring. It transpired later that under the direction of the master, official rations were reduced and prisoners, including Barrington, were grossly underfed, leading to twenty-one deaths at sea. In An *Impartial and Circumstantial Narrative* Barrington was made to speak lightly of his conditions, the implication being that he had received the gaoler's special consideration prior to the voyage, and had benefited from the exertions of the boatswain during the voyage due to the generous intercession of a benefactor. Avoiding the harsh realities and actual circumstances that eventually came to light,

THE PEAK OF TENERIFFE.

Plate 6 'The Peak of Teneriffe', from *An Account of a Voyage to New South Wales, by George Barrington, Superintendant of the Convicts* (1803).
Source: Rare Books Collection, The Library, Australian National University, Canberra.

publishers were already romancing readers with a pleasant travelogue featuring Barrington as the light-hearted narrator.

Before the final departure from England – the Old Dart – while other felons had languished in gaol all but forgotten, Barrington's incarceration and enforced exit from London was documented in official papers and announced in a variety of unofficial sources. For months after his conviction Barrington awaited his fate in Newgate Gaol while the Third Fleet was assembled. Finding suitable vessels took time. Chartered vessels needed conversion to conform to exacting standards, and all had to be stowed to the gunwales with provisions and supplies in readiness for the long voyage. It was a major logistical exercise. Barrington, meanwhile, was allowed visitors who, according to *An Impartial and Circumstantial Narrative*, brought him 'necessaries' for the voyage: 'The news of my speedy departure brought several of my acquaintances to bid me adieu, and, with gratitude, I recollect that not one of them came empty handed; for before the time of locking up, I had such a collection of ventures, that I doubted whether I should be permitted to take them all on board'. In fact, space was at a premium on the ship and it is unlikely that even 'gentlemen' convicts were given much in the way of special consideration on board, although this practice still pertained in gaols on dry land. But creative publishers fed the legend.

Official records of transportation were scrupulously kept and Barrington was listed plainly without any fanfare against the terms of his sentence. But although the authorities afforded him no status, his personal fame and notoriety preceded him to Port Jackson, as to other parts of the globe. While in gaol, news had seeped out suggesting that his famous golden locks had been shorn and his clever hands shackled to prevent escape and any further *legerdemain*. It was rumoured, too, that Barrington always had friends in high places willing to vouch for him. According to contemporary accounts, he was permitted to walk without chains between the Sheriff and Newgate's gaoler, Mr Ackerman, who escorted him and the other convicts to Blackfriars Bridge to board the lighters used to transfer prisoners to the *Active* for embarkation.

Undoubtedly, the 'Prince of Pickpockets' considered himself well above the common criminal. He apparently found sharing close quarters with 'felons of all descriptions', brutes intoxicated with liquor, swearing and cursing, a punishment 'more severe than the sentence of my country'. Illustrators were fond of highlighting Barrington's patrician features, differentiating him in a few well-cut lines from more swarthy criminal stereotypes, and Barrington clearly enjoyed mixing with gentry and gentlemen, or at least he enjoyed being mistaken as one of them. One wonders whether on learning of the composition of the Fleet, Barrington relished the knowledge that his voyage was undertaken in company with an almost eponymous vessel, the *Admiral Barrington*.[24]

Associating the fortunes of a celebrated criminal such as George Barrington with the fortunes of the new penal colony 'beyond the seas' had a certain logic and symmetry, at least in publishing terms. Public interest in the success of the new settlement in New South Wales ran high. Some individuals and officials anticipated the commercial potential of the colony, and deserted relatives of transportees surely had vested interests in the ultimate success of transportation. Anxiously, many hoped that loved ones would earn tickets of leave and eventually return from long terms of distant penal servitude, while officials calculated that the threat of transportation would act as a real deterrent to crime and thus reduce the size of prison populations.

It was also believed that transportation, a punishment itself in the actual voyage, followed by years of honest hard labour, would have the potential to reform even the most incorrigible. Thus, news about whether there was indeed a civilizing effect was awaited with anticipation. Barrington's *An Impartial and Circumstantial Narrative* was to supply snippets of information about the customs and religion of the natives, but also referred to the necessary adaptations made by British natives toiling in the antipodean landscape. Civilization took some time to achieve, but in Barrington's narration he managed to express an optimistic note.

Yet even greater curiosity was expressed, and not only in Britain, in the ambition to develop and civilize an unknown land at the extreme ends of the earth by populating it with convicted men and women plucked from Britain's overcrowded prisons. Accepting the loss of the American colonies as a place to dump Britain's excess convicts had forced the need for alternatives, and while Africa's coasts seemed a potential destination, the realities of the dark continent presented insurmountable difficulties. It was hoped, for instance, that the Sierra Leone Company's experimental colony established in 1786 on the fevered coast of West Africa would successfully combine a philanthropic and commercial venture with free settlement for ex-slaves, but it struggled in its fragile infancy. There was a growing realization that Africa would provide no practical outlet or solution for convicts or their masters.[25] Still faced with the problem of excess prison populations and the rising incidence and prosecution of crime, the government continued to look at transportation 'beyond the seas'. Botany Bay had its distinct attractions.

Crime and its just punishment preoccupied reformers and adminis-trators, although there were those who decried experiments in human transportation. Alexander Dalrymple argued that the 'East-Side of NEW HOLLAND ... the intended Thief Colony', would become a desirable destination, encouraging rather than deterring felons: 'to place them, as Their own Masters, in a temperate Climate, where they have every object of comfort or Ambition before them!'.[26] Another notable objector was Jeremy Bentham (1748–1832) who presented a theoretical alternative, the 'Panopticon' penitentiary regime, as an efficient solution to the festering and temporary prison hulks. However, building special-purpose prisons was expensive and he was ignored. The overriding rationale and political momentum for 'solving' the convict problem by transportation was unstoppable. Bentham's essay, *Panopticon Versus New South Wales*, arguing the case against using New South Wales as an outdoors prison, did not appear until 1802, by which time the settlement in Sydney was well-established and even showed some signs of flourishing.

Arguments that equated transportation with slavery were also confidently rejected; convicts were spared from death and presented with opportunities for honest work and a chance to better themselves. They were fed, clothed and housed, and, if granted a ticket of leave, were free to earn some income. Emancipation was within reach and with hard work many could share in the fortunes of the colony; no slave ever enjoyed such prospects. It was not long, too, before the governors did actively encourage small numbers of skilled free settlers; the administration found itself desperate for the practical abilities of experienced farmers, builders, craftsmen and others with trade skills. While convicts could be forced to work, significant numbers remained debilitated and a burden, and many were without any practical skills for developing the colony. Not a few, of course, were accused of being vicious, idle and a drain on essential resources. Living off the stores was an easy option, a spectre identified by both Dalrymple and satirists. To some Botany Bay signified – 'Plenty to have, and nothing to pay, That is the land to live in'.[27]

While some of the public's curiosity about the penal colony's development was pedagogic, others maintained a more prurient interest in the gothic horrors of punishment, transportation and convictism. Furthermore, these were revolutionary times. News of deep unrest in France was starting to alarm the British establishment, particularly in Ireland. The Third Fleet carried a small number of individuals from Ireland accused of insurrection. Although Irish by birth, Barrington himself was always at pains to claim falsely an aristocratic Anglo-Irish ancestry. There are no signs that he was ever considered a revolutionary figure, but this did not deter newspaper satirists from taking opportunistic advantage of his familiar name and Irish connection.

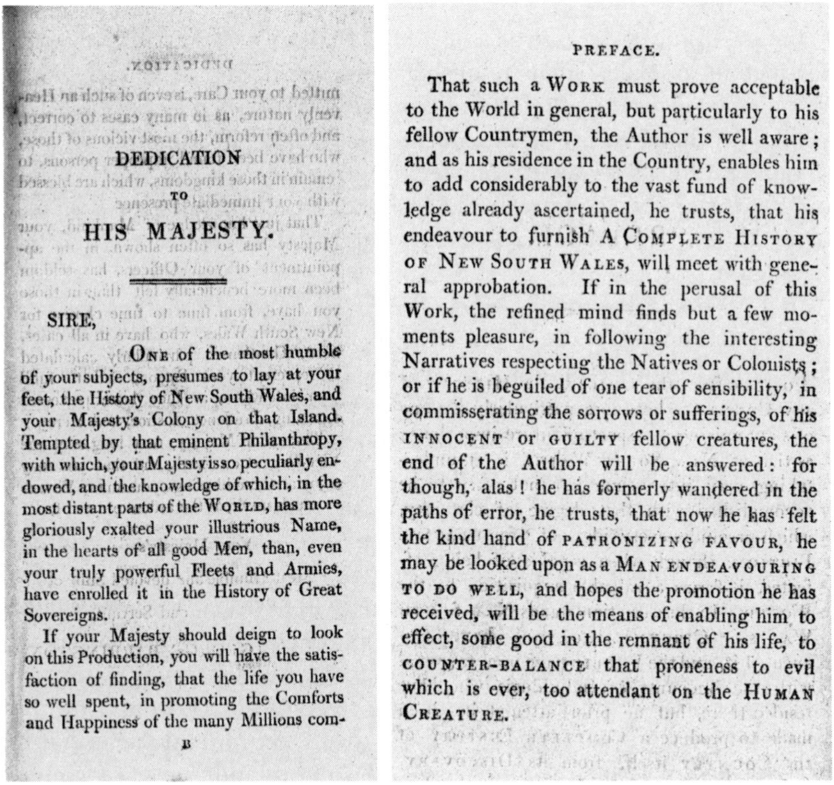

DEDICATION

TO

HIS MAJESTY.

SIRE,

ONE of the most humble of your subjects, presumes to lay at your feet, the History of New South Wales, and your Majesty's Colony on that Island. Tempted by that eminent Philanthropy, with which, your Majesty is so peculiarly endowed, and the knowledge of which, in the most distant parts of the WORLD, has more gloriously exalted your illustrious Name, in the hearts of all good Men, than, even your truly powerful Fleets and Armies, have enrolled it in the History of Great Sovereigns.

If your Majesty should deign to look on this Production, you will have the satisfaction of finding, that the life you have so well spent, in promoting the Comforts and Happiness of the many Millions com-

B

PREFACE.

That such a WORK must prove acceptable to the World in general, but particularly to his fellow Countrymen, the Author is well aware; and as his residence in the Country, enables him to add considerably to the vast fund of knowledge already ascertained, he trusts, that his endeavour to furnish A COMPLETE HISTORY OF NEW SOUTH WALES, will meet with general approbation. If in the perusal of this Work, the refined mind finds but a few moments pleasure, in following the interesting Narratives respecting the Natives or Colonists; or if he is beguiled of one tear of sensibility, in commiserating the sorrows or sufferings, of his INNOCENT or GUILTY fellow creatures, the end of the Author will be answered: for though, alas! he has formerly wandered in the paths of error, he trusts, that now he has felt the kind hand of PATRONIZING FAVOUR, he may be looked upon as a MAN ENDEAVOURING TO DO WELL, and hopes the promotion he has received, will be the means of enabling him to effect, some good in the remnant of his life, to COUNTER-BALANCE that proneness to evil which is ever, too attendant on the HUMAN CREATURE.

Plate 7   Preface, 'Dedication to his Majesty', from *The History of New South Wales including Botany Bay, Port Jackson, Parramatta, Sydney, and all its Dependancies from the Original Discovery of the Island: with the Customs and Manners of the Natives; and an Account of the English Colony, from its Foundation, to the Present Time. By George Barrington: superintendant of the Convicts* (1802).
Source: Rare Books Collection, The Library, Australian National University, Canberra.

In an ironic twist, given that His Majesty's law had consigned Barrington to exile, some publishers magnified his allegiance to the Monarch by dedicating Prefaces of Barrington's invented 'histories' to His Majesty in the most fawning manner: 'One of the most humble of your servants presumes to lay at your feet, the *History of New South Wales*, and your Majesty's Colony on that Island'. The Dedication was signed, 'Your Majesty's Most Humble and devoted Subject and Servant, George Barrington'.

In 1799 a satirical publication, *The Spirit of the Public Journals for 1798*, containing essays and 'Jeux D'Espirits', published a spoof entitled 'The Botany Bay Resolutions Regarding Public Allegiance to the King emanating from Port Jackson'.[28] Published by the radical James Ridgway, himself a former prisoner in Newgate for sedition, it reported on a 'very numerous and respectable meeting of His Majesty's faithful and loyal Subjects at Botany Bay ... with George Barrington Esquire in the chair', implying to the uninformed that he was part of a vocal loyalist group in the colony.[29] Among the resolutions proposed by the Chairman was that the inhabitants of Botany Bay pledge themselves to defend the constitution and laws of the colony and the mother country against 'all men of French or Jacobinical principles with their lives and fortunes'. It was stated that 'whatever opinions there might be of Ministers [of Pitt's government], the meeting knew him [Barrington] too well to suspect for a moment that he had any design upon their *pockets*'. The information was, of course, uncorroborated, the pamphlet's purpose being to satirize John Reeves, a fervent loyalist who had been unsuccessfully charged with libel by the radicals in the House of Commons. Meantime, oblivious to his continued notoriety, Barrington was keeping watch at the government farm at Toongabbie, near Parramatta.

Years after he had been transported on the *Active*, Barrington and Botany Bay were linked again in another spoof, this time the anti-Jacobin *The New Times*. Here he was styled 'Citizen Barrington, Representative of Botany Bay at the British National Convention'. His legendary skills were used to poke fun at French revolutionary claims of liberty, equality and fraternity:

> Citizen Barrington, Representative from Botany Bay, was yesterday detected picking the pocket of the President of the National Convention, of a gold snuff box. He was reprimanded, but defended what he had done on principles of equality.[30]

Further afield, Desenne, an entrepreneurial Parisian bookseller–publisher, carefully prepared a Preface to Barrington's 'history', *Voyage à Botany Bay* (published in 1798), to insert propaganda on the concepts of justice and mercy then circulating in France. In 1794 Desenne had pleaded, together with Desmoulins and the Dantonists, to relax the Terror reigning there. Barrington provided a perfect example of a man allegedly treated with redemptive humanity by his captors. '*Citoyen*' Barrington became an international figure, a malefactor made good, a subject of His Majesty's largesse and a grateful recipient of the far-sighted system of British justice. Desenne waxed lyrical about the opportunities given to Barrington and other felons serving time under the punishment of transportation:

> Barrington, having seen the Error of his Ways, does not display himself in this account as a Malcontent in Declamation against the Laws of his Land; nor does he accuse those who must needs invoke against him of Arbitrary Despotism: he knows that Tyranny, in whichsoever Colours it clothes itself, is nothing but Injustice Armed; Inequity Empower'd; the Will of the Mightier supplanting the Wish of All; ... By confessing his Guilt, he justifies his Judges; in depicting his Remorse, he gives Grounds to those to have heretofore entertain'd a Doubt, for believing that, after many a Long Year, and many Days spent in the Vicinage of Felony and the Derangement of Evil-doing, there may come, even in the Life of a Great Delinquent, a Moment of Regret.[31]

Unusually, Desenne had interpolated sentiments that Barrington is recorded as expressing at his trial in 1790. Speaking not in any anticipatory sense of revolution either in Britain or France, but on personal reflection (and extensive experience of the court system), Barrington had declared his faith in British juries:

> Life is the gift of God; and liberty is its greatest blessing: the power of disposing of both, or either, is the greatest man can enjoy. It is also adventitious that, great as that power is, it cannot be better placed than in the hands of an English Jury; for they will not exercise it like tyrants, who delight in blood, but like generous and brave men, who delight to spare rather than destroy; and who, not forgetting they are men themselves, lean, when they can, to the side of compassion.[32]

IV. Barrington in New South Wales

Incarcerated in Newgate in 1790–91 without access to news of the penal colony, Barrington could not have been aware that the arrival of the next consignment of convicts was more than anxiously awaited at Port

Jackson. This was because the ships of the Third Fleet, carrying convicts to Port Jackson, were also to bring out vital supplies and, in 1791, these were most urgently required. Every person in the colony – officers, troops and convicts alike – was by now suffering distress from reduced rations and the colony was in desperate need of basic provisions. Starvation loomed as a possibility as the crops failed and nothing arrived to supplement the stores.

Captain-Lieutenant Watkin Tench, of the Marines (?1758–1833), who had arrived with the First Fleet in 1788, wrote, 'The dread of perishing by famine stares in the face … gloom and dejection overspread every countenance'.[33] Watkin Tench was to write the first published account about the penal settlement, *A Narrative of the Expedition to Botany Bay,* published *in absentia* in 1789, and his further volume, *A Complete Account of the Settlement of Port Jackson*, was published in 1793. Tench was a careful observer who took a vital interest in all events in the colony.

In December 1789 the supply ship *Guardian*, whose mission had been to bring thirty-one hand-picked convicts with a knowledge of farming, along with the desperately needed supplies, was wrecked off the Cape of Good Hope. This meant that no relief had arrived from England for more than two years. Once the bad news reached England, another vessel was despatched. The *Gorgon*[34] man-of-war sailed midway between the departures of the Third Fleet's two divisions and arrived within days of the *Active*. The *Gorgon* was to bring eighty-five marines as relief troops, and enough food to stave off starvation. Exhausted by waiting and hoping, and with eking out the dwindling provisions, Watkin Tench hailed the *Gorgon*'s arrival on 21 September 1791 with 'rapture and exultation'.[35]

The first vessel of the Third Fleet to leave England had been the *Mary Ann* and she was first to arrive through the Heads on 9 July 1791. To Tench's great despair, having 'rowed in a boat six miles out to sea, beyond the harbour's mouth, to meet them,' he discovered that although the vessel brought 140 or so relatively healthy female convicts, there were no significant supplies, not a single journal or newspaper on board, and only a few official letters for the governor.

Isolated from the outside world, Tench had no knowledge of King George's porphyria-induced madness, the French Revolution, publication of Edmund Burke's counter-revolutionary polemic *Reflections on the Revolution in France* (1790), and Thomas Paine's democratic manifesto reply, *Rights of Man* (1791–2). When the *Active* disgorged its convicts, it too was disappointingly barren of news and, unlike the *Mary Ann*, the *Active*'s prisoners had been grossly underfed and were incapable of labour.

Eyewitness accounts confirmed that many were permanently debilitated. George Barrington was amongst that number and he was observed.

Watching the arrivals, Tench noted critically that the state of the convicts, 'although infinitely preferable to what the fleet of last year had landed, was not unexceptional'.[36] The transports of the Third Fleet carrying naval agents suffered the fewest deaths, and indeed the physical condition of the convicts disembarking was infinitely better than the unfortunates who had survived the horrors and privations of the Second Fleet. During that notorious voyage in 1789, 267 convicts died and 500 were landed sick. According to Governor Phillip's information provided to the Home Secretary, Lord Grenville,[37] 198 deaths had occurred during the Third Fleet's voyage, and it was officially recorded that overcrowding and lack of nourishment accounted for most of these. The *Active* had no naval agent on board and, as we have seen, twenty-one convicts died during its voyage.

Tench's *Narrative of the Expedition*, a shrewd and humane documentary record, contained much intelligence on the state of the Fleet, its commanding officers, the controls exercised by the naval agents and the 'distressful state of the colony for provisions'. Amongst those disembarking whom Tench watched with great interest and found worth recording with an 'honourable mention', was '*Barrington*, of famous memory'.[38] Tench's comment that Barrington was 'of famous memory' was a telling phrase. Though he had been away from England for more than two years, and had no access to current magazines or newspapers, Tench was well aware of Barrington's exploits and, it would seem, carried a formed picture of him in his imagination. As he disembarked, Tench perhaps recalled something of the famous illustration of Barrington lifting Count Orloff's diamond snuff-box.

In England, one of Barrington's visible trademarks had been his attire and even crude woodcuts managed to convey that elegance. His likeness had also been painted in oils by the young portraitist, William Beechey, in 1785, rendering him on canvas as a young gentleman wearing a silk cravat, dressed in a stylish, dark, gold-braided and buttoned jacket and waistcoat. He then appeared for all the world to see, not as a thief, but as a professional man or, perhaps, a modest nobleman. Circumstances dictated very differently for him after his arrival at Port Jackson. Tench noted in December 1791:

> Of that elegance and fashion with which my imagination had decked him (I know not why), I could distinguish no trace. Great allowances should, however, be made for depression and unavoidable deficiency in dress.[39]

Plate 8 Portrait of George Barrington (*c*. 1785), by Sir William Beechey (1753–1829).
Source: Pictorial Collection, Rex Nan Kivell Collection (NK13), by permission of the National Library of Australia, Canberra.

Barrington, like other common convicts, had only the clothes issued by the gaol authorities. The official clothing allowance estimated to be sufficient to cover a male convict's needs for one year was set out in the 'Plan of Transportation'. It consisted of two jackets, four woollen drawers, one hat, three shirts, four pairs of worsted stockings, three frocks, three trousers and three shoes, worth the total sum of £2.19.6d. 'Deficiency of dress' as Tench put it, was depressing – Barrington was used to finer garb. Beyond rations and the barest necessities, there was nothing to be found in Port Jackson and here theft was out of the question. In the penal settlement, theft was punishable by death without any opportunity for special pleading. Thus Barrington was forced to start from scratch, to transform himself. Yet another reinvention took place and the narrative of Barrington's life now became inextricably linked with the rising fortunes of the colony.

V. *Respectable publishing and plagiarizing pirates*

The powerful attraction of fresh information conveyed by 'Complete Accounts', 'Narratives' and 'Records' of the penal colony drawn directly from the pens of participants and eyewitnesses cannot be underestimated. The time lag between observing or 'being there' and reporting events often represented only the intervening months taken for the return sea voyage of a vessel to England. Publishers there were at the ready, set to print any material delivered to them, and thus, in relative terms, the rapid turnaround of intelligence provided fast news of the settlement. The publishers Stockdale and Debrett, both of Piccadilly, and Cadell and Davies located in the Strand, had each undertaken to make the first expensive printings for subscription sales. Initially copies of these exclusive publications went into private hands and private libraries, but soon information about the contents spread and, for the most part, this went unchecked and uncontrolled.

While official letters and reports sent by Governor Phillip and those in positions of authority in the colony to the Secretary of State in London, explained the great difficulties under which the infant colony laboured, public news of the fortunes of Port Jackson and Botany Bay remained sporadic. Parliament was silent on the expedition and rumours, although colourful, were usually unfounded, with no actual news to impart. There was widespread curiosity about the southern continent, particularly in the scientific world, and publishers had been assiduous in securing rights to the first accounts produced by high-ranking officers in charge of the venture. Contracts for subscription publications were signed in advance with Governor Phillip and Lieutenant-Governor John Hunter before they departed.[40] Illustrated editions were anticipated by Cadell and Davis in the Strand, and by John Stockdale of Piccadilly.

Accounts from 'First Fleeters' appeared in rapid succession. The earliest published account was from the lower-ranked observer, Captain-Lieutenant Watkin Tench, and appeared as a modest and pocket-sized 'interim report', published by Debrett of Piccadilly in April 1789. Governor Arthur Phillip's *Voyage of Governor Phillip to Botany Bay*, published by J. Stockdale, appeared in late 1789, and Surgeon-General John White's *Journal of a Voyage to New South Wales*, published by Debrett, arrived in 1790. *Extracts of Letters from Arthur Phillip, Esq. Governor of New South Wales, to Lord Sydney* followed in 1791 (also published by Debrett), and Lieutenant-Governor John Hunter's *An Historical Journal of the Transactions at Port Jackson and Norfolk Island*, was published in 1793 by J. Stockdale. Tench's second volume, *A Complete Account of the Settlement at Port Jackson*, also came out in 1793, published by G. Nichol of Pall-Mall. David Collins' *An Account of the English Colony in New South Wales ... By David Collins, Esquire, late Judge Advocate and Secretary of the Colony*, appeared some years later in 1798, published by T. Cadell Jun. and W. Davies. (It was from this edition that a number of illustrations were plagiarized and used in Barrington's 'sequel' editions.)

In the midst of this publishing flurry stimulated by the colony's establishment *An Impartial and Circumstantial Narrative of the Present State of Botany Bay, in New South Wales ... By George Barrington, now Superintendant of the Convicts at Paramata*, emerged in late 1793 or early 1794. *An Impartial and Circumstantial Narrative* evidently relied upon large fragments lifted straight out of John Hunter's *Historical Journal,* and it was Hunter's authoritative tone that provided *An Impartial and Circumstantial Narrative* with its ring of authenticity. Most readers were not able to recognize the origins of *An Impartial and Circumstantial Narrative* without access to Hunter's original. *An Impartial and Circumstantial Narrative* was concise and given the new credentials of its author, rang true. In publishing terms, both the length and timing of the product was perfect.

Not long after, the first published account written by a woman of stamina and quality, Mrs Mary Parker, *A Voyage around the World in the Gorgon Man of War: Captain John Parker. Performed and Written by his Widow,* was published in 1795.[41] This was in the same year that re-vamped versions of Barrington's *An Impartial and Circumstantial Narrative* became available to the public. Sold under two titles, either as *A Voyage to Botany Bay* or *A Voyage to New South Wales*, with more stolen information, hand-tinted illustrations and two entirely fictional chapters about Barrington's stay at the Cape of Good Hope, the price for the new versions had risen from sixpence to two shillings and sixpence. These hard-backed versions were reviewed by respected journals.

Both the *Gentleman's Magazine* and the *Monthly Review* perused the writing of this 'well-known character', the former questioning authorship and authenticity, the latter convinced that it really was 'the performance of that ingenious adventurer'. To accept Barrington's account as genuine was not necessarily a sign of intellectual laziness; there were precious few sources against which to check Barrington's 'facts' and readers, many only semi-literate, had also to grapple with the confusion expressed publicly by literary professionals. The *Monthly Review* began its comment on *A Voyage to New South Wales* with a charitable observation:

> We confess that we took up this performance with prejudice and suspicion, arising from the name which appears in the title page as being that of the author. Not that we supposed Mr George Barrington to be incapable of writing a very readable book; but the well-known character and exploits of a man at once brought to our minds such a recollection of past imposture and depredation on the public, that is was impossible for us to read a line of such a production without caution and distrust – On perusing, however, a few pages of the work, our suspicion abated; and, before we arrived at its conclusion, not a doubt remained of its authenticity.[42]

This must have been a pleasing comment for printers such as Lowndes and Symonds, who had both speedily cut extensive sections from others' published observations and deftly reworked them into the plagiarized 'Barrington' manuscript.

Not all were as easily fooled. The sharp-eyed *Gentleman's Magazine* for September 1795 was dismissive in one curt paragraph, and the reviewer exercised well-known and understandable prejudices:

> Whether this be a genuine work of the celebrated convict or not, it contains nothing that has not been seen before on the subject; and if it gives a genuine account of Mr. B's reformation, we are glad to find that his distance from his native country has put him beyond the reach of temptation to violate her laws and the laws of society in general.[43]

Such opposing views notwithstanding, and with liberal doses of scepticism and questions of authenticity abounding, the popularity of

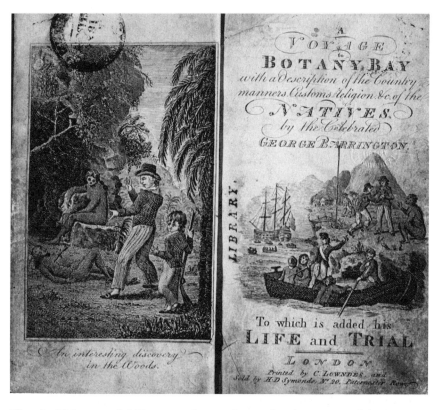

An interesting discovery in the Woods.

A VOYAGE to BOTANY BAY with a Description of the Country manners, Customs, religion, &c. of the NATIVES by the Celebrated GEORGE BARRINGTON. To which is added his LIFE and TRIAL LONDON

Printed by C. Lowndes, and Sold by H.D Symonds, No 20. Paternoster Row

Plate 9 Title page of *A Voyage to Botany Bay with a description of the Country, manners, Customs, religion, &c. of the Natives by the Celebrated George Barrington. To which is added his Life and Trial.*
Source: Rare Books Collection, The Library, Australian National University, Canberra.

Barrington's accounts was unprecedented. Such was the rage for curiosity that the original unillustrated and unbound pamphlet was still being circulated as the bound and elaborated versions left the presses and hit booksellers' shelves.

VI. Transformations and translations

The renewed Barrington publishing phenomenon began with the text reproduced here, *An Impartial and Circumstantial Narrative of the Present State of Botany Bay,* and continued in many forms. This was a first, a unique publication – seemingly the first literate convict's view of the colony in the southern hemisphere. Paradoxically, Barrington's writerly fame occurred at a great distance and apparently without his knowledge or consent; it was reported later that he was greatly disturbed at the unauthorized use of his name on the narrative. Canny readers may have been alerted to the possibility of deception, but the old advice *caveat emptor* (let the buyer beware) appeared not to have been heeded as publishers rushed out one version after another and willing readers paid for them.

Despite the ubiquity of this work and others that allegedly flowed from Barrington's pen, he received no handsome royalties. Publishers had a field day cashing in on the public's curiosity at his expense. Unlike the small number of official 'foundation accounts' written by those in authority – highly priced reports of the settlement that reached a chosen few subscription readers[44] – Barrington's pastiche accounts reached a diverse reading public in a variety of editions, enough to fascinate the untravelled as well as prospective travellers. These became the most widely available popular texts about the colony and copies could be found in gentleman's libraries, circulating libraries and on the shelves of Mechanics' Institutes well into the nineteenth century. In 1827, more than twenty years after Barrington's death, *Blackwoods Magazine* recorded the belief that most English people – ninety-nine out of one hundred – if asked to describe New South Wales, 'would think only of ropes, gibbets, arson, burglary, kangaroos, George Barrington and Governor Macquarie'.[45]

Announcing that England's most talked-about pickpocket had become a highly respected superintendent of convicts was guaranteed simultaneously to attract tantalized disbelief *and* a wide readership. The rapid printing of a publication under Barrington's already-famous name became bait for retailing details of the ambitious colony and its development. Significantly, such publications aroused more interest than the official accounts published in the 1790s and later. Readership was probably drawn equally from those hungry for new knowledge and those eager for novel entertainment and clues as to Barrington's whereabouts. Many were anxious to read the first-hand accounts produced by the reformed thief from the convict settlement. Barrington's famous oratory had the power to impress judges and juries and thus there was no reason to doubt that his writing would not similarly impress. Scandal seekers, however, found little to please in *An Impartial and Circumstantial Narrative* although references to contact with the Aborigines, especially to the young women and to courtship rituals, may have caused a frisson or two.

The account presents Barrington making amends for his past existence. Refigured in a sanctioned position of trust, he addressed readers as an officer of the peace, older and wiser, compelled by necessity and duty to dress simply, to obey the law and uphold it. This was a distinctly new chapter. Transported and transformed, remade through honest toil and converted to respectability and civil behaviour, Barrington, the superintendent of convicts, provided an excellent example of a deeply reformed character.

The official records note that Barrington arrived at Sydney Cove in Port Jackson on 26 September 1791, dishevelled, weakened and humbled after an extended ordeal in the dark and stinking holds of the *Active*. Though he had endured disease, foetid air, short rations, severe discipline and physical restriction, he had at least survived. The journey was a kind of epiphany for Barrington. As we know, others of his fellow convicts had perished under the harsh conditions. Yet, unlike his compatriots on board, Barrington's inelegant arrival was unusually heralded. Apparently, news of his changed and exemplary behaviour on board the *Active* had reached England even before he had reached New South Wales.

The publishers of *An Impartial and Circumstantial Narrative*, S. & J. Bailey of Paternoster Row, seized the day by opening the first page of their invented narrative with a letter guaranteed to launch Barrington back into the public eye. With a customary flourish it read:

DEAR SIR, I embrace the earliest opportunity of performing the promise I made you upon my quitting ENGLAND: and should the contents of the accompanying sheets, collected chiefly from personal observation, aided by the best local inquiries, acquit me, in your mind, of a breach of that promise, I shall feel myself more than happy ...
SIR, Your obedient, and obliged, Humble Servant, George Barrington.[46]

The scene was set – Barrington was honouring a promise. This evidence presented at the outset confirmed that he had undergone a conversion. The following narrative is jaunty, with events recounted as seen through the eyes of the intelligent beholder of his circumstances, allegedly Barrington, who takes the voyage of transportation and penal colony in his stride. His first utterance exudes a confidence that is typical of the whole: 'It was with unspeakable satisfaction that I received a summons to be ready early the next morning for my embarkation, agreeable to my sentence'. The conclusion of this first shortish version is, however, abrupt, in keeping with its supposed convict origins: 'There being a ship lying in the harbour ready for sea, I took the opportunity to remit the foregoing pages, hoping they will meet approbation and by the next conveyance will send a further account of the progress of the settlement, &c.,'.

All information supplied appeared under an impressively worded title that claimed to inform on all counts; on the state of the country, the 'natives', the convicts, the general conditions and the prospects. There was no one better qualified to impart this information than one so well known to the public at large.

As a literate and educated man, Barrington was always a likely candidate for promotion in the colony where such qualifications were in short supply. He was advanced speedily, first to watchman, then to constable and finally to superintendent of convicts at Parramatta. Here was a convicted criminal appointed to a responsible position as a result of his exemplary behaviour and for his 'humble, not servile' demeanour. For the reading public, this rapid elevation was startling news but, in the struggling colony, the need to identify capable convicts for use in supervisory roles was paramount. From the outset, the military establishment was stretched to its limits and furthermore, its officers were reluctant to provide extra men to act as prison guards. Somewhat short-sightedly, the Treasury had not made appropriations for free individuals to act in these positions. Men like Barrington soon found themselves in demand for supervision of the penal settlement.

Considerations of time, distance and accuracy notwithstanding, any news of the colony was coveted, even Barrington's. Rosy pictures of progress might have been desired initially, but realists expected hardships at the outset of settlement. Official but unreported requests to the Treasury indicated shortages, the bitter disappointment following successive crop failures, an obvious lack of needed skills and the increasing number of conflicts between the convicts and the Aborigines. Barrington's 'impartial' account, while not ignoring the difficulties, added a finer and more confident gloss. Portrayed in an aloof and confident mode, he moved among the convicts at one remove: 'I proceeded through the different gangs of people, observing their occupations; and found them much more attentive to their business, and respectful to those over them, than I could possibly have imagined'.

An Impartial and Circumstantial Narrative must have taken off in leaps and bounds in London because, within a very short time, a longer version appeared published by a Manchester printer, A. Swindells of Hanging Bridge. The aptly-named Swindells, true to his name, cavalierly extended the narrative from forty-four to forty-eight pages to include a melodramatic and romanticized 'finis', containing a description of an Aboriginal maiden, Yeariana. The young Aboriginal woman in one of the later versions attributed to Barrington has her indigeneity lessened, '[she] may have been taken for a beautiful Oriental Creole'. Barrington is claimed to have rescued this young woman who may have been based in fact – taken from a description of Gooredeeana, a young Aboriginal woman described glowingly by Watkin Tench in his *A Complete Account of the Settlement at Port Jackson* published in 1793. Other borrowings came from Tench's first account, *A Narrative of the Expedition to Botany Bay*, published in 1789.

Whole paragraphs, or edited versions of paragraphs, taken from official accounts of the colony published in 1789, 1790, 1791 and 1793, appeared in *An Impartial and Circumstantial Narrative*. The publication claimed to have been 'Entered at Stationers' Hall', but no record exists, probably because claiming registration of work with the Worshipful Company of Stationers was a common publishing ploy. Trade 'pirates' hoped to deter each other without going to the expense of the entering fee and legal deposit procedures. Such a deception also imparts a note of pseudo-authenticity. Ironically, the Barrington simulacrum actually contains no basic untruths. The imposition of the personal pronoun throughout to give the impression of Barrington 'being there' was a compelling and clever ruse. Yet much of the information can be cross-referenced back to official accounts and many incidents indeed came from the records of eye-witnesses.

Narratives such as those attributed to Barrington – imagined histories and sagas – were part of a longer and larger tradition generated by Defoe, but contemporary exploration of the Pacific and South Seas heightened possibilities for publishers of authentic, invented and constructed accounts. From the 1770s onwards, following the publication of Captain Cook's and other voyaging narratives, the public's hunger for Pacificana proved insatiable, particularly for accounts relating to the customs and rituals of 'natives', noble and ignoble 'savages', and encounters between

Europeans and hitherto undiscovered 'races'. Imaginations were fired by colourful ethnographic narratives such as George Keate's *Account of the Pelew Islands* (1788), which went into numerous editions and was pirated and translated into French, German and Spanish. Thomas Gilbert's *Voyage from New South Wales to Canton* (1788), the popular chapbook, *An Authentic and Interesting Narrative of the late Expedition to Botany Bay ... by An Officer* (1789), and William Bligh's *Narrative on the Mutiny on Board His Majesty's Ship Bounty* (1790), all added further excitement. Voyaging, new geographies, voluntary explorations or involuntary transportations to the Antipodes, provided the stuff of both new knowledge and utopian dreams.

Audiences immediately engaged with *An Impartial and Circumstantial Narrative* which supplied enough convincing ingredients to feed established tastes: criminality, danger, racial encounters, social inter-course, progress, exotic flora and fauna, punishments and rewards, and the southern hemisphere's new vistas were all represented. The alleged author also offered readers a novelty: the spectacle of a notorious criminal now working in a new role as a presenter of the austral world. Barrington's account presented a different perspective. His views complicated the stereotypical scene; not all criminals were depraved and ignorant, not all officers were inhumane, not all Aborigines were 'savages'. Barrington's voyage combined transportation *and* discovery. For readers, the named officers, gaolers, convicts and Aborigines were all objects of ethnographic curiosity, all practising customs, some familiar, some seemingly incredible. Barrington's faintly mocking superiority when describing the rituals of the 'natives', was extended to officers attempting to maintain British civility and taste in a wild land bereft of comforts and sociable institutions.

The retitled, hard-backed, expanded versions of *An Impartial and Circumstantial Narrative*, with the inclusion of two further chapters referring to the Cape of Good Hope, followed in 1795. These enhanced editions made no reference to the recent British occupation of the Cape, but declaimed against the drinking habits and 'atrocious behaviour' of the Dutch colonists and Cape merchants, the 'indolence' of the Hottentots (the Khoikhoi peoples), the 'wars of the Caffrees' (an anglicized version of 'Kaffirs', or the Bantu people of the Cape), and inserted adventures hunting lions, hyenas and elephants. Retitled *A Voyage to Botany Bay* by the publisher, C. Lowndes of Drury Lane, the work had now grown in length to 120 pages and featured two illustrations. The title page carried a much reduced heading, *A Voyage to Botany Bay with a Description of the Country, manners, Customs, Religion &c. of the Natives by the*

Celebrated George Barrington. To which is added his Life and Trial', and it was illustrated with a view of prisoners landing at Sydney Cove and an engraved frontispiece bearing the caption, 'An interesting discovery in the Woods'. This illustration showed a male European figure, 'Barrington', with his youthful European helper, 'Tim', discovering a prone figure, an injured Aboriginal man (shot with an unlikely arrow), alongside a young and distressed Aboriginal woman, presumably 'Yeariana', looking on.

After 1795, further liberties were taken with the text, illustrations were added as they came to hand, and what began as a forty-four page pamphlet-like publication swelled into a mammoth production, hard-backed, illustrated and dedicated to His Majesty, George III. All information was carefully manipulated to suit the times and the availability of current information. In 1810 a reprint of *An Account of a Voyage to New South Wales* was extended to 472 pages with nine coloured prints and a rudimentary map of New South Wales. A succeeding *History of New South Wales* was even more extravagant, containing sixteen prints and over 500 pages. Both versions sported engravings of George Barrington in the frontispiece. The frontispiece to the 'History' showed him wearing a tailored coat and cravat, accentuating his elegant hands and supple fingers. Having more lately turned to writing, he holds a quill in one hand and a copy of his 'History' in the other. The caption announced 'George Barrington, Late Officer of the Peace at Paramatta'.

Following the publication of *An Impartial and Circumstantial Narrative*, a run of successful 'Histories' attributed to George Barrington appeared, including renamed epitomes, translations and sequels. 1795, however, was the bumper year when publications peaked, with nine revised and embellished versions of *An Impartial and Circumstantial Narrative*, retitled either as *A Voyage to Botany Bay*, or *A Voyage to New South Wales*, each version selling at a different price ranging from 'only Six-pence', to 'Half-a-Crown'. Two editions of *A Voyage to New South Wales*, priced at 'Half-a-Crown', were published in 1796, with a further unpriced version published in Philadelphia. *Voyage à Botany-Bay ... Par le célèbre George Barrington. Traduit de l'Anglais, sur la troisième édition* appeared in Paris in 1798. Probably in the same year or a little later, a Spanish version appeared in Madrid, *Viaje y Translaccion del Famoso Barrington a Botani-Bay en la Neuva-Holanda*. The last year of the eighteenth century was unaccountably silent, but in 1800 *A Sequel to Barrington's Voyage to New South Wales* was printed incorporating *'an Interesting Narrative of the Transactions and Behaviour of the Convicts'*, and this included an 'Official Register of Crimes in New South Wales'. By this time, Barrington was promoted to 'Principal Superintendant of the Convicts'.

The year 1801 witnessed further versions of Barrington's Voyage to Botany Bay, and *A Voyage to New South Wales*. In 1802 *The Frauds and Cheats of London detected ... with an account of George Barrington,* appeared in London, with an epitome of *The Voyage to Botany Bay* re-titled as *The History of Botany Bay*. This was accompanied by alternative versions, as *Barrington's History of New South Wales* and *The History of New South Wales ... by George Barrington*. In 1803 *The Life and Trials of George Barrington* did the rounds again, along with *Select Criminal Trials at Justice Hall in the Old-Bailey* referring in detail to Barrington's last trial, while *An Account of a Voyage to New South Wales, by George Barrington ... Enriched with beautiful Coloured Prints,* arrived brightly illustrated and embellished with yet more 'facts'. In Moscow in 1803 a translation of *A Voyage to Botany Bay, Puteschestvie v Botani-Bai: s opisaniem strany, nravov, obychaev i religii prirodnykh zhitelie – Georgiia Barringtona,* was published by V Universitetskoi Tipografii u Liubiia i Popova, with a preface devoted to Barrington's infamous career in London prior to his remarkable reformation in the Antipodes. In 1804 *Fairbairn's Edition of the Life, Amours and Wonderful Adventures of that Most Notorious Pickpocket, George Barrington,* featured a romantic and roguish interpretation of Barrington's early life.

The historical records tell us that Barrington died in December 1804, allegedly insane, in Parramatta, but this did not prevent the publication of *Barrington's New London Spy or the Frauds of London Detected ... By the celebrated George Barrington, Principal Superintendant of the Convicts at Botany Bay*. In 1805 *Barrington's New London Spy for 1805* was published 'by the celebrated George Barrington', and in 1807 yet another version of *Barrington's London Spy* followed. In 1808 *The History of New Holland*, wrongly attributed to Barrington with a 'Discourse on Banishment', arrived along with the 1808 edition of *Barrington's New London Spy*. In 1809 came *The London Spy ... By the Celebrated George Barrington, Superintendant of the Convicts at Botany Bay*, and 1810 witnessed recycled versions of Barrington's histories and accounts, namely *An Account of A Voyage to New South Wales* and *The History of New South Wales*. In 1812 *Barrington's New London Spy* returned to print, still with a mention of Barrington's work as 'Superintendant of the Convicts'. The final fresh printing of *The Life, Times and Adventures of George Barrington* was published in 1820 by John Wilson of Oxford Street and 'sold by All Booksellers'. Barrington's name still had currency and retained value in the publishing world for thirty or more years.

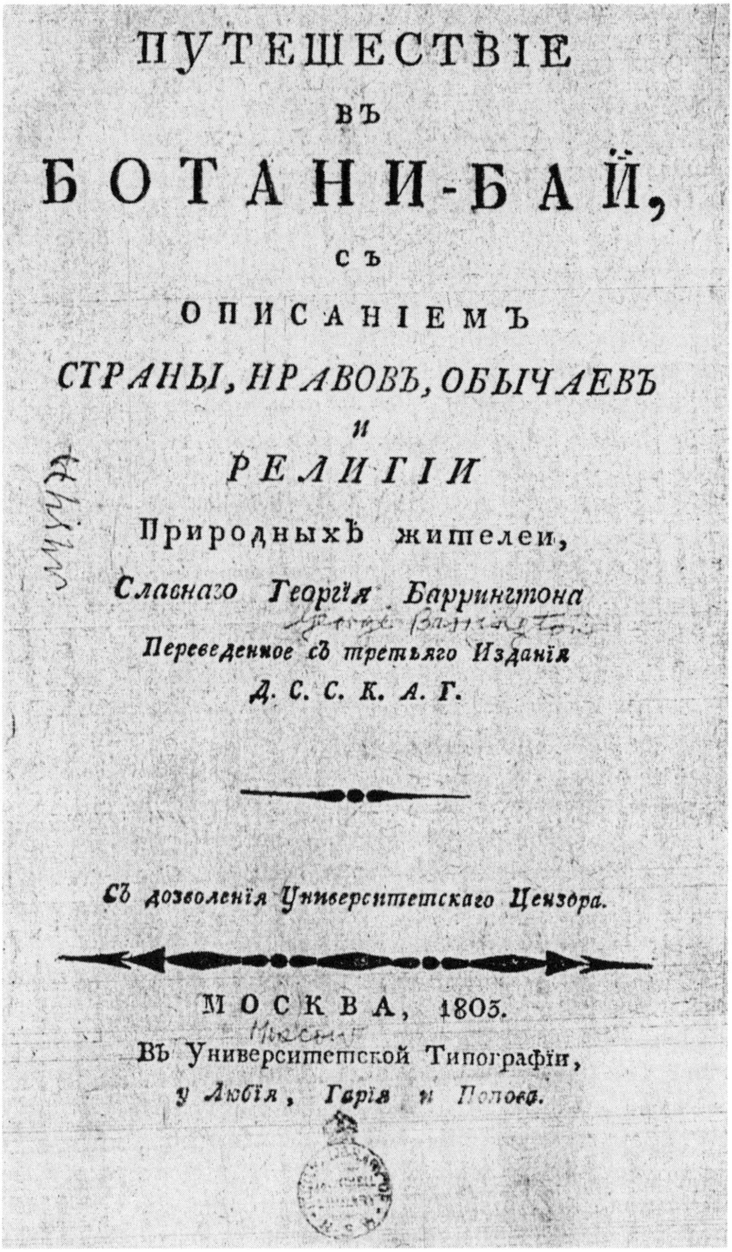
ПУТЕШЕСТВІЕ

ВЪ

БОТАНИ-БАЙ,

СЪ

ОПИСАНІЕМЪ

СТРАНЫ, НРАВОВЪ, ОБЫЧАЕВЪ

И

РЕЛИГІИ

Природныхъ жителей,

Славнаго Георгія Баррингтона

Переведенное съ третьяго Изданія

Д. С. С. К. А. Г.

Съ дозволенія Университетскаго Ценсора.

МОСКВА, 1803.

ВЪ Университетской Типографіи,

у Любія, Гарія и Попова.

Plate 10 Title page of Russian edition of *A Voyage to Botany Bay: Puteshestvie v Botani-Bai: s opisaniem strany, nravov, obychaev i religii prirodnykh zhitelei – Georgiia Barringtona.*
Source: By permission of the Library Council of New South Wales, Mitchell Library, State Library of New South Wales, Sydney.

VII. *The convict's eye*

What may be said of the content of Barrington's *An Impartial and Circumstantial Narrative*? Was it consistent to the eye in terms of narrative flow and the choice of language? Did it appear to have internal integrity and hold together? For contemporary readers without access to alternatives, the answer was resoundingly in the affirmative. All within *could* have been true. With the benefit of hindsight, and now with a wealth of material to scrutinize, modern readers are able to discern the less reliable from the official accounts, but in the 1790s information was harder to obtain and differentiation difficult. If publishers deliberately set out to deceive by manipulating contemporary accounts, making grand assertions as to veracity, emblazoning title pages with extraordinary lists of contents, promising to provide the public with the very latest news, it was likely that the gullible and even the less-gullible would fall for the trick. Subscription readers seeking authenticity developed a taste for personal accounts produced by authorized officials. The wider public, enticed by inexpensive or cheap versions, pamphlet and chapbook editions, developed broader tastes, unknowingly or even deliberately eschewing the views of the governors in favour of those like Barrington's which were far more accessible.

Barrington's *An Impartial and Circumstantial Narrative* played with figures to a small extent (for example, by changing ages, distances, or measurements but only to avoid direct charges of plagiarism). The narrative concentrated primarily on descriptions of events relating to the regular contacts between the governor, other officers and the Aborigines, individually naming men and women and dignifying, to an extent, the exchanges of language and gifts. Adopting a stance similar to Watkin Tench who sensibly terminated his account of the settlement by leaving to others, 'the task of anticipating glorious, or gloomy, consequences, from the establishment of a colony, which unquestionably demands serious investigation, 'ere either its prosecution or abandonment be determined',[47] Barrington's publishers refused to be drawn on the future of the colony by putting words into Barrington's mouth. There was no indulgence in prognostications about the future of the colony, details only provided the numbers of acres cleared, the span of acres under cultivation, the poor state of the soil, and sudden 'vicissitudes' of the weather which rendered 'our harvests very precarious'. Future prospects for the colony followed later in the sequels to Barrington's first histories.

There were bonuses in Barrington's account for the common reader as well as naturalists and botanists, ethnographers and cultivators, penologists and reformers, who all wanted printed information on climate, natural resources, rainfall, flora, fauna, the progress of settlement and, of course, 'the natives'. The gaze of *An Impartial and Circumstantial Narrative* was directed towards a panorama of exotic descriptions guaranteed to stimulate further inquiry. Condensed for popular consumption but without illustration, the first text had sufficient vocabulary to kindle the imagination, and as coloured illustrations were added to later editions, readers found themselves offered the same benefits as those sold by subscription at higher prices.

Readers of *An Impartial and Circumstantial Narrative* had first to exercise their imaginations vigorously to conjure up a 'Mocock from the East Indies', or the 'Native Dog' said to resemble 'the Pomeranian breed'. They had to visualize a settlement little more than a village patrolled by soldiers, with few roads or solid buildings and dark-skinned visitors who exchanged fresh fish for baked bread. Illustrations helped to illuminate in more ways than one; not content with stealing the words of others, hack engravers stole illustrations flouting the Engravers Copyright Act in much the same way that hack publishers had flouted copyright of the texts.

Drawings of the settlement originally by Edward Dayes (1763–1804), water colour sketches by the convicted forger and transportee, Thomas Watling (b. 1762), and crudely copied engravings originally by James Heath (1757–1834), that had appeared first in David Collins's *Account of the English Colony* (1798), all found their way into Barrington's histories.[48] They were plundered by V. Woodthorpe, Esquire, a London engraver whose work figured exclusively in the attributed histories, *The History of New South Wales* (1802), and *An Account of a Voyage to New South Wales* (1803). Many images were reversed with the effect of reorientating the position of landmarks, trees, dwellings and people. Freely removing detail, Woodthorpe added his own touches. The 'South View of Sydney' (1803) has, incorporated into the lower right-hand corner, an Aboriginal woman fishing from a canoe. Woodthorpe added this 'native' icon to exoticize the almost European vista.

Landscapes presented one type of illustrative opportunity, while flora and fauna presented even more attractive possibilities. Again, complete veracity to the original was of little concern to hack engravers. Lifting illustrations from the *Journal of a Voyage to New South Wales with Sixty-Five Plates of Nondescript Animals, Birds, Lizards, Serpents, curious Cones of Trees and other Natural Productions* (1790) by John White, Surgeon-General to the Settlement, Woodthorpe managed to re-assign features of birds, plants and animals that did not pertain in life. Completely strange to European eyes, in the 1802 version of Barrington's

SOUTH VIEW of SYDNEY.

Published by M. Jones, Paternoster-row Mar. 1 1803.

V. Woodthorpe fc.

Plate 11 'South View of Sydney', from *The History of New South Wales. By George Barrington* (1802).
Source: Rare Books Collection, The Library, Australian National University, Canberra.

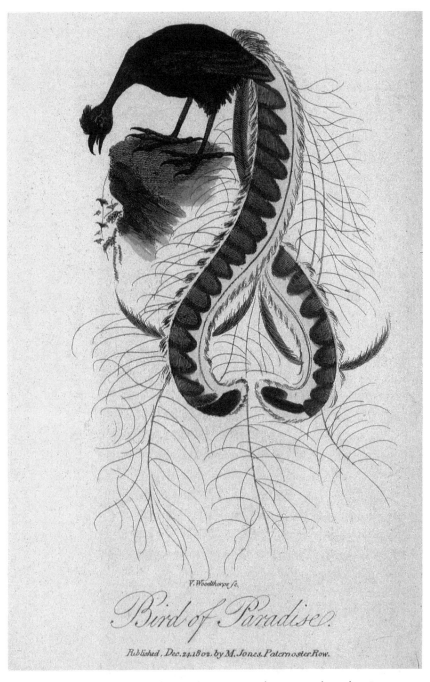

V. Woodthorpe sc.

Bird of Paradise.

Published. Dec. 24.1802. by M. Jones. Paternoster Row.

Plate 12 'Bird of Paradise', from *The History of New South Wales. By George Barrington* (1802).
Source: Rare Books Collection, The Library, Australian National University, Canberra.

History, the kangaroo ate oak leaves and acorns and carried two joeys in its marsupial pouch. The lyrebird (*Menura superba*), known then as the Bird of Paradise, according to Woodthorpe's interpretation displayed a depressed set of tail-feathers. Woodthorpe was probably confused; two eminent ornithologists in England, Major-General Davies and Dr John Latham, had depicted the lyrebird's spectacular tail plumage dipping from the horizontal, while Judge-Advocate David Collins and the Frenchman, L. P. Vieillot, sketched the bird with its magnificent lyre-shaped tail in the ascendant. Woodthorpe played safe and drew the male bird with its tail folded and in dipped repose.[49]

Plants were equally targets of Woodthorpe's inaccuracies which were lifted from *The Voyage of Governor Phillip to Botany Bay* (1789) and *The Naturalist's Pocket Magazine; or, Compleat Cabinet of the Curiosities and Beauties of Nature* (1799), as well as from White's *Journal of a Voyage to New South Wales* (1790). On one illustrated page, Woodthorpe managed to bring together the *Banksia Serrata* and *Banksia Pyriformis*, the Tea Tree (*Leptospermum pubescens*), the Peppermint Tree (*Prosenthera aspalathoides*) and the Yellow Gum Tree (which, to modern eyes, is clearly the Blackboy (*Xanthorrhoea*)), all depicted with a free hand and a degree of flourish which could easily deceive anyone unfamiliar with antipodean botany.

Where Woodthorpe excelled was in demonstrating his ability to cut and rework other's engravings; this shone out particularly in a range of ethnographic illustrations. To prevent a charge of plagiarism, Woodthorpe removed figures and landscape elements from illustrations of Aboriginal men and women depicted in various situations, in rituals, in 'Courtship', in 'Burying the Dead', in 'Manhood' (showing tooth avulsion) and in 'A Male and Female Native' (a family portrait). These illustrations, almost certainly stolen from Collins' *Journal*, were recast figures crudely drawn in almost burlesque fashion, taken from those that had been elegantly engraved for the original publication. Making copies from copies, reversing plates, excising figures, creating palimpsests, was all part of the pirating trade but, in spite of the inaccuracies, these highly coloured plates were irresistible to those who rarely had access to hand-coloured books.

This material, textual and illustrative, contributed to new science, new knowledge, new interpretations and new possessions. The land itself was claimed with European names: the Carmarthen Hills, the County of Cumberland, Richmond, the Hawkesbury River, the Nepean River, places celebrating familiar British men and favoured places in the mother country. Tentative maps suggested *Terra nullius*, since Aboriginal place

Plate 13 'Botany', from *The History of New South Wales. By George Barrington* (1802).
Source: Rare Books Collection, The Library, Australian National University, Canberra.

names were not noted on the first maps (with the exception of Parramatta named by Governor Phillip). The crude map in Barrington's 1802 *History* was almost featureless. Yet in spite of this, Barrington's narrative, like all the other foundation accounts, gave ample testimony and descriptions of the Aborigines' well-established habitations and efficient use of the land and sea. No one reading these could doubt the regularity of contact between the European settlers and the Aborigines, a contact evidenced by the newcomers' halting attempts to understand Aboriginal languages and customs, and by the clumsy and often violent methods used to 'capture' and convert Aboriginal informants. If nothing more, Barrington's account was a novel attempt to personalize the first contacts with Aborigines and to render such contact comprehensible to the untutored.

VIII. Barrington's exile and redemption

Familiarity may breed contempt, but the proverb never did apply in Barrington's case. After his exile in New South Wales, continual mention was made of him in Britain as if he was still active in the neighbourhood. To haunt him or heighten memory, depending upon one's point of view, in 1792, not long after his arrival in Port Jackson, readers in England were reminded of Barrington's misdemeanours. Publishers presented *The Life of George Barrington, containing every Remarkable Circumstance, from his Birth to the Present Time.* This forty-page booklet recounted details of his trials for robbing Mrs Dudman, Elizabeth Ironmonger, Sir G. Webster, Mr Bagshaw and Mr Le Mesurier, and contained 'the whole of his Celebrated Speeches'. For those who might have missed the opportunity to marvel at his oratory, Barrington's courtroom virtuosity was paraded once more in print. A butt of satire and clever legal jokes, references turned up in expected and unexpected places.

The Home Secretary learned of Barrington's accelerated promotion from watchman to principal superintendent of convicts through official channels as a matter of course. Convict musters, watchman's warrants, notification of land grants and good conduct reports relating to Barrington were relayed to London in government despatches. Circulating rumours, however, were still serving good purpose for publishers. Anti-Jacobin papers used references to Barrington to criticize any tendency towards French-styled democracy, and tavern-room poets enjoyed characterizing Botany Bay by referring to the pickpocket and his new-found respectability. While hack publishers and booksellers were making money from histories attributed to Barrington, others with even more in the bank could still find a use for the famous Barrington name.

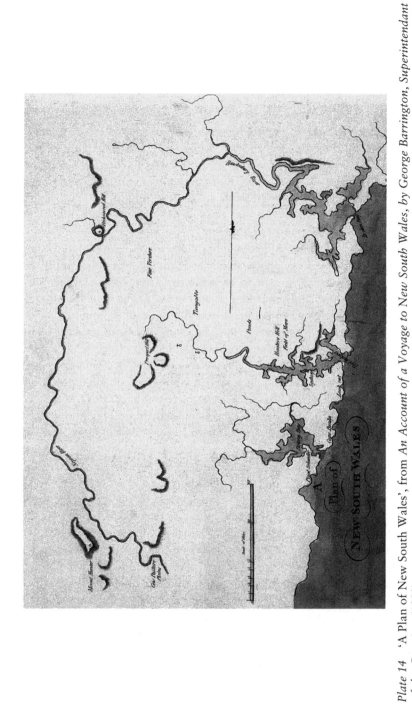

Plate 14 'A Plan of New South Wales', from *An Account of a Voyage to New South Wales, by George Barrington, Superintendant of the Convicts* (1803).
Source: Rare Books Collection, The Library, Australian National University, Canberra.

James Lackington, for example, the prosperous bookseller of Finsbury Square,[50] made free in 1794 with Barrington in a reference to James Turpin, a Methodist preacher found guilty of stealing church silver plate and sentenced to be hanged at the Exeter Assizes. Turpin was reprieved to be sent to Botany Bay, where, as Lackington suggested, 'perhaps he may have address enough to get himself made chaplain to Barrington, as on his trial he told the judge, that if he would send him to Botany Bay, he would do much towards the glory of God.'[51] Sly references were common, and this ubiquity helps to explain why men such as Watkin Tench and others often felt that they 'knew' of Barrington well before they saw him. All were prey to his legend.

Tench had made it his purpose to see Barrington and described him with surprising respect. Knowing in late 1791 that his departure from the colony was imminent, he noted anxiously in his journal that 'Barrington had been in the settlement between two and three months, and I had not [recently] seen him'. Tench wanted to look at the legendary Barrington again in the flesh before he left the colony:

> I saw him with curiosity. He was tall, approaching six feet, slender, and his gait and manner, bespeak liveliness and activity ... His face is thoughtful and intelligent; to a strong cast of countenance he adds a penetrating eye, and a prominent forehead. His whole demeanour is humble, not servile.[52]

Tench had rapidly gained a practical respect for the man who had once only inhabited part of his imagination. A further comment from Tench provides another clue as to Barrington's conversion:

> [Barrington] is appointed high-constable of the settlement of Rose Hill, a post of some respectability, and certainly one of importance to those who live here. His knowledge of men, particularly of that part of them into whose morals, manners and behaviour he is ordered especially to inspect, eminent fit him for office. I cannot quit him without bearing testimony that his talents promise to be directed in future to make reparation to society for the offences he has heretofore committed against it.[53]

What outsiders did not know of Barrington was the extent to which he had prospered in the colony. Governor Hunter, as well as others in authority, complimented his work and he was rewarded with a conditional pardon followed by a full pardon, and then with grants of land. Barrington moved up in society, where his opinion was evidently respected. He was called upon to give references as well as a testimonial for the colonial magistrate, Richard Atkins, joining in an unlikely alliance with the evangelical 'flogging parson', Reverend Samuel Marsden (who had arrived in Sydney in 1794), against the litigious landowner, John Macarthur. According to the historical records, in 1799 Barrington loaned his house to the Reverend Rowland Hassall, one of the London Missionary Society's missionaries in Sydney who arrived in 1798 from the Society Islands. Hassall became Revd Marsden's business manager, and Marsden eventually bought a parcel of Barrington's land at auction after his death in 1804.

So integrated into the commerce of the colony did Barrington become that envious and less prosperous settlers complained of his dealings; a number of ex-convicts including Barrington, Simeon Lord, James Larra, Isaac Nichols and Henry Kable were mentioned disparagingly in a petition from the settlers of the Field of Mars (a small division in the county of Cumberland), for their profitable dealings, which suggests that, for some, Barrington was far too close to the officer class.[54]

In 1800 Barrington had one hundred acres of land of which sixteen acres had been cleared and were productive, under wheat and maize. He had three horses, eight hogs and twenty-five sheep, a small dwelling and one assigned convict working for him. As superintendent of convicts, he earned £50 per annum, and, on his retirement in 1802, this was reduced to £25. He enjoyed the confidence of his masters and many others in the community and his reputation in the colony reached heights that he could have only dreamed about when standing in the dock at the Old Bailey in 1790. Even then, there was some curious prescience in his words: 'I do now assure you, Gentlemen of the Jury, that I feel a cheering hope, even at this awful moment, that the rest of my life will be conducted, as to make me as much an object of esteem and applause, as I am now the unhappy object of censure and suspicion'. A decade later, Barrington had redeemed himself and achieved a pleasing status, a reward for his sobriety and capable judgement.

But his health was beginning to decline, a legacy of his past life perhaps, or the long-term result of the debilitating voyage to Botany Bay on board the *Active*. Whatever the cause, this decline was noted in the official gazette. Barrington was pensioned-off to live on his farm, part of the larger Brush Farm Estate located close to Parramatta, where he was comfortable. There, in 1802, he was visited by Pierre Bernard Milius (1773–1829), who had evidently read much about him. Milius was second in command of the *Naturaliste*, the vessel commanded by Nicolas Baudin that was despatched by Napoleon on a scientific investigation to the Pacific and Antipodes (1800–1804).

Milius was landed sick in Sydney in 1802 when the *Naturaliste* called into Sydney. After his return to health he sailed from Sydney on an American ship for China, and thence to France in 1803. He was then appointed to command the *Geographe* and returned to the Orient in 1804. While in Sydney, once recovered, he took every opportunity to travel within the colony where an interesting opportunity presented itself. Sufficiently prey to the legend to want to travel to Parramatta, he provided a graphic description of the man, 'the celebrated Barrington', who was now in his last years. Milius recorded his visit to Barrington,[55] and sketched a sad and illuminating scene which is here quoted in full:

> Among the curious things offered in Paramatta, the celebrated Barrington, known in all Europe as the most quick-fingered of his century, must be among the first order. This extraordinary man, condemned to deportation, was appointed Chief Constable of the town. He carried out over several years the functions of position with all the integrity of an honest and upright magistrate. He won the affection of the governor and the esteem of all the most distinguished persons of the colony: he was at the same time the scourge of wrong-doers and the protector of the weak. When I visited him it seemed to me that all his intellectual faculties were extinguished. He was in the bath. When he got out of it, I believed that I was looking at a mummy from Teneriffe. His legs were so thin that I didn't know how they could support the weight of his body. His eyes were fixed on me without appearing to see me. Somebody served him with a cup of chocolate which it was necessary to make him take like a baby of 15 months, so diminished were his energies. I was shocked at the length of his fingers. He seemed destined by nature to draw from them the whole role that he had played almost all his life ... I was assured that he had not yet reached 45 years; but I would have given him 60, so weak and bowed down he seemed to me. He had a woman close to him to serve him whom it seemed was taking the greatest care of him.[56]

We know almost nothing of Barrington's last two years in the colony. Clearly, he was unwell, losing his faculties and suffering from dementia and wasting, and certainly he was in no position to contribute any information to the histories attributed to him. His affairs were eventually placed in the hands of commissioners: the Revd Samuel Marsden and the surgeon, Thomas Arndell. Milius reported that Barrington had studied for the law and was not without talent; that much had always been recognized by scores of well-placed observers, from British judges to colonial governors. Milius also reported that he had been told that Barrington had 'extremely charming manners' and had a 'great deal of spirit and finesse'. While his imagination may have been coloured by romanticized accounts of the celebrated Barrington, Milius' description of Barrington's physical state in 1802 was stark, and he frankly rehearsed his own theory as to the cause of Barrington's 'langour'. It must, he reported, 'be attributed to the remorse that tore at his soul and to the poisoned memories of his past life'. Remorse may have well contributed to Barrington's malaise, but the description offered was of causes more physical. Aged only forty-nine, his customary elegance and eloquence had deserted him and he was fortunate, as Milius remarked, to have a woman to care for him.

In his final unknowing state, Barrington was clearly in no position to dispute facts with publishers who took his name in vain. Seven years after Barrington's death, David Dickenson Mann, a former convict who published his views in *The Present State of New South Wales* in 1811, insisted that Barrington 'expressed a very considerable degree of displeasure when he was in a state of sanity at his name being affixed to a narrative which he knew only by report as being about to be published'.[57] If he had chosen to earlier, Barrington could have claimed some virtue in involuntarily assisting in the dissemination of knowledge of the colony of New South Wales, and of the customs and habits of its European and indigenous inhabitants. He remained unaccountably silent.

The notice appearing in the *Sydney Gazette* announcing Barrington's death was brief. Barrington, 'late Superintendant of Convicts at Parramatta', had died 'a lunatic' on 27 December 1804 and was buried on 29 December. His estate was advertised as up for auction by Simeon Lord, including his household furniture, a flock of sheep constituting 124 ewes, lambs and wethers, and an excellent farm on the banks of the Hawkesbury River, opposite the village of Cornwallis, consisting of fifty acres. Next of kin were advised soon after to make their claims on Mr William Wilson, a brandy merchant in London's Monument Yard, where 'he or she may hear something to their advantage'.[58] Perhaps there were unheralded connections with the mother country but the links were tenuous. After death, Barrington could continue to exist only, in Tench's words, in 'famous memory'.

IX. Impartial and counterfeit histories

For all that eighteenth- and nineteenth-century readers may have chosen to believe or disregard from *An Impartial and Circumstantial Narrative* attributed to Barrington, it is clear that the original text withstood the test of time. It would seem that for many Barrington's version of the history of New South Wales was the 'real' history. To some eyes the account seemed to offer a perversity, an inversion of the expected perspective, an unauthorized account and a completely different view from that of the governor and officials. And yet, closely examined, it was nothing of the sort. Plagiarized, manipulated and reordered, the essential information came from authoritative sources not easily disguised nor wholly distorted.

Those who could afford to purchase expensive subscription copies were in a privileged position to add to their own knowledge through the accumulating published information on the colony. Others had to rely upon other sources and for a number of crucial years, Barrington's history was the only popular interpretation readily available. Sixpence was a small price to pay to receive the latest information from the southern hemisphere, a world away.

Publishers in London, the provinces and overseas made certain that Barrington's 'voice' was clearly heard. Almost every paragraph contained the personal pronoun and, like any good storyteller, Barrington took readers with him to experience events, beginning with his transfer from dry land to the swaying decks of a transport ship. Subsequent attributed editions, although prefaced with extravagant explanations, all began with the famous and insouciant lines, 'It was with unspeakable satisfaction that I received a summons to be ready early the next morning for embarkation ...'

Barrington, the elegant convict observer, invited all to embark with him on a voyage to Botany Bay. He allowed readers to sample the delights of Orotava, to share the hospitality of the burghers of Cape Town and then to receive the approbation of the governor and officers of New South Wales. *An Impartial and Circumstantial Narrative* was generous in its information and in the way it appeared to make such extraordinary transitions comprehensible. The narrative did not attempt to be learned, or ape the form of official reports, but it offered a simplified and abridged version for mass consumption. Of course, this was never the production of a single author but a team of players, clever and devious editors and illustrators who skilfully cut, précised, pasted and copied, working quickly without the benefit of first-hand knowledge themselves. Little wonder that certain spellings were at variance or that events were taken out of context, or that illustrations were sometimes more than inventive. The emphatic and imaginative stroke of genius in all this production and conversion of knowledge was to take Barrington up as author.

Unfortunately, during Barrington's lifetime the same inspired publishers failed honestly to share with readers an account of his actual circumstances, beyond the fact that he was 'Superintendant of the Convicts at Parramatta'. More often than not, Barrington's name was taken in vain and his identity used callously for profitable or satirical purposes while he was unable to make his own contribution. After his death, his 'brilliant talents' were acknowledged in the most elaborate versions which trumpeted the publication of second, third and further editions by virtue of public demand: 'Instead of continuing to *degrade*, Mr Barrington has become an *ornament* and an improvement to society'.[59] In some strange paradox, accounts of the penal colony attributed to Barrington may have encouraged free settlers as well as criminals to voyage to Botany Bay. The views offered were essentially optimistic and Barrington's conversion and elevation was proof indeed that even the most notorious had a chance of redemption.

An Impartial and Circumstantial Narrative was one version of many, and although claiming to provide a 'description' of the country of New South Wales, it mapped only the smallest portion of European settlement. It also claimed to provide an account of the treatment of convicts during their passage and after their arrival, but this information was brief especially when compared with the lavish detail of the almost daily contact with the Aboriginal inhabitants of the Sydney region. Revealing an unfamiliar world of native custom and ritual and a wealth of curious information about flora and fauna only to be imagined, this rival and unofficial account retained a simplicity and directness that ensured the widest appeal.

Offering kernels of truths, peripheral visions, and an ingenious interpretation, the contribution that Barrington's counterfeit history made to increasing public knowledge cannot be estimated. Silhouetted against the backdrop of contemporary writings and read with or against the foundation accounts, *An Impartial and Circumstantial Narrative of the Present State of Botany Bay, in New South Wales ... by George Barrington, now Superintendant of the Convicts at Paramata*, added an imaginative dimension to the grand visions and aspirations of the Lords of the Treasury and the governors of New South Wales.

Notes

1. *The Genuine Life and Trial of George Barrington, from his birth in June, 1755, to the time of his conviction at the Old Bailey in September, 1790. For robbing Henry Hare Townsend, Esq., of his gold watch, seals, &c.* (London: Robert Barker, August 1791), p. 44.

56

2. Erving Goffman, *The Presentation of Self in Everyday Life* (London: Allen Lane, 1969).

3. *An Impartial and Circumstantial Narrative of the Present State of Botany Bay, in New South Wales: With a Description of the Country; Treatment of the Convicts on their Passage, and after their arrival. Also the Manners, Customs, Religion, &c. of the Natives, Truly Depicted. Containing among a variety of entertaining subjects The Particulars of the Voyage; a description of the Buildings and Soil at Sydney Cove; Journey to Paramata; Convicts Houses and daily Occupations; their Emoluments from Government on the Expiration of their Term; Birds; Animals; Vegetables; manner of taking one of the Natives, who dies of the Small-Pox; entrap two others, who escape with much Ingenuity; their Retaliation upon the Governor, who very narrowly escapes Death; a reconciliation takes place; &c. &c. &c. &c. By George Barrington, Now Superintendant of the Convicts at Paramata.* (London: S. & J. Bailey, *c.* 1793–4).

4. *The Life of George Barrington, containing every Remarkable Circumstance, from his Birth to the Present Time ... With the whole of his Celebrated Speeches, Taken from the Records of the King's Bench, Old Bailey, &c.* (London: Printed for the Booksellers, 1792), p. 1.

5. *The Genuine Life and Trial of George Barrington, from his birth in June 1755, to the Time of his Conviction at the Old-Bailey in September 1790, For robbing Henry Hare Townsend, Esq., of his gold watch, seals, &c.* (London: Robert Barker, August 1791), p. 13.

6. Letter from George Barrington to Mrs Anne Dudman, 6 January 1777 (Ms. Ab 49, Mitchell Library, State Library of New South Wales, Sydney).

7. *Morning Chronicle*, 16–17 January 1777.

8. John Howard (?1726–90), prisoner reformer and writer of the influential tract, *State of the Prisons* (1777), visited the *Justitia* on a number of occasions in 1776–77 and found conditions on this prison hulk deeply shocking.

9. Sir Nathaniel Wraxall, MP (1751–1831), poured contempt upon the transportation venture in these derogatory terms. (See N. W. Wraxall, *A Short Review of the Political State of Great Britain* (London: J. Debrett, 1787, 8th edition), pp. 78–83.)

10. In 1790, when an account of Barrington's celebrated speeches was published, each of his known disguises was reported. See *The Memoirs of George Barrington, containing every Remarkable Circumstance, from his birth to the Present Time, including the following Trials – 1. For robbing Mrs. Dudman. 2. Elizabeth Ironmonger. 3. Returning from Transportation. 4. Robbing Sir G. Webster. 5. Mr Bagshaw. 6. Mr Le Mesurier. 7. For Outlawry. 8. For robbing Mr Townsend. With the Whole of his Celebrated*

Speeches, Taken from the Records of the King's Bench, Old Bailey, &— London, Printed for J. Bird, No. 22, Fetter Lane, Fleet Street; and Simmonds, No. 20, Paternoster Row. [Price One Shilling]

11. Letter attributed to George Barrington, in *Historical Records of New South Wales,* vol. 2 (1793–95) (Sydney: Charles Potter, Government Printer, 1892), p. 771 (henceforth *HRNSW*).

12. *The Whole Proceedings on the King's Commission of the Peace, Oyer and Terminer, and Gaol Delivery for the City of London; and also The Gaol Delivery for the County of Middlesex, held at Justice Hall in the Old Bailey, on Wednesday, the 15th of September, 1790, and the following Days: Being the Seventh Session in the Mayoralty of the Right Honourable William Pickett, Lord Mayor of the City of London.* Taken in Shorthand by E. Hodgson, Professor of Shorthand; and Published by Authority. Number VII. Part I. London : Printed for E. Hodgson (the Proprietor); And Sold by him, at his House, No. 14, White Lion Street, Islington. Sold also by T. Walmsley, No. 35, Chancery Lane; S. Bladon, No. 13, Paternoster Row; and J. Marsom, No. 183, High Holborn. MDCCXC. (London: 1790). See also, *Universal Magazine,* 1790, p. 62, for an account of Barrington's trial.

13. *Ibid.*

14. Roland Barthes, *Mythologies* (New York: Noonday Press, 1972).

15. 'The Convict's Farewell to Old England', Windmill Tavern, Newgate-street, 6 January 1787, cited in *Australians to 1788,* D. J. Mulvaney and J. Peter White (eds) (Sydney: Fairfax, Syme & Weldon Associates, 1987), p. 401.

16. Order for Transportation, 1786 (*HRNSW,* vol. 1, pt. 2 (1783–92), pp. 30–1).

17. 'Heads of a Plan', 18 August 1786 (*HRNSW,* vol. 1, pt. 2 (1783–92), p. 17).

18. *27 George III,* 1787.

19. 'Heads of a Plan', 18 August 1786 (*HRNSW,* vol. 1, pt. 2 (1783–92), p. 17).

20. *Ibid.*

21. Transport vessels were provided by Messrs. Camden, Calvert and King on a contract made with the Commissioners of the Navy for the conveyance of convicts to New South Wales, 1 February 1791: the *Queen* (Ireland), *Atlantic, William and Ann, Britannia, Matilda, Salamander, Albemarle, Mary Ann, Admiral Barrington, Active.* Convicts embarked: 1875 males and 175 females. Return, 15 February 1791 (*HRNSW,* vol. 1, pt. 2 (1783–92), p. 463).

22. 'These vessels worked their way down to the latitude of the Cape, and then without calling at Table Bay or False Bay, ran down their easting in about 40 degrees South' (Charles Bateson, *The Convict Ships 1787–1868* (Sydney: A. H. & A. W. Reed, 1969), p. 133).

23. The *Active* left Portsmouth on 27 March 1791 and made the passage to Port Jackson in 183 days.

24. The *Barrington* was named after Admiral Samuel Barrington (1729–1800), a distinguished naval hero who fought against the Spanish and the French.

25. For a detailed explanation of the British penal settlement in Sierra Leone, see Introduction, *Maiden Voyages and Infant Colonies: Two Women's Travel Narratives of the 1790s*, ed. Deirdre Coleman (London and New York: Leicester University Press, 1999).

26. Alexander Dalrymple, *A Serious Admonition to the Publick, on The Intended Thief-Colony at Botany Bay. etc.* (London: J. Sewell, 1786). This was also reprinted, including *Memoir*, by George Mackaness (Sydney: Ford, 1943), pp. 17–30.

27. 'The Convict's Farewell to Old England', Windmill Tavern, Newgate-street, 6 January 1787, cited in *Australians to 1788*, D. J. Mulvaney and J. Peter White (eds) (Sydney: Fairfax, Syme & Weldon Associates, 1987), p. 401.

28. 'The Botany Bay Resolutions: at a very numerous and respectful meeting, His Majesty's faithful and loyal subjects of Botany Bay, held a meeting in October, 1792, George Barrington in the Chair.' In *The Spirit of the Public Journals for 1798. Being an Impartial Selection of the Most Exquisite Essays and Jeux D'Espirits, Prose, that appear in the Newspapers and Publications, with explanatory notes*, vol. 2 (London: J. Ridgway, 1799), pp. 397–9.

29. *Ibid.*, p. 398.

30. *The New Times*, 10 June 1800 (First Year of the Republic, One and Indivisible, price One Shilling in Specie, or, Five Shillings in Paper) (Petherick Collection, National Library of Australia, Canberra).

31. Preface, *Voyage à Botany-Bay, avec une Description du Pays, des Moeurs, des Coutumes et de la Religion des Natifs. Par le célèbre George Barrington. Traduit de l'Anglais, sur la troisième édition.* À Paris, Chez Desenne, Libraire, Palais-Egalité, Nos 1 et 2. An. VI (Paris: Desenne, 1798). (English translation was kindly provided by Professor James Grieve, Australian National University, Canberra.)

32. *Memoirs of George Barrington, from his Birth in MDCCLV, to his Last Conviction at the Old Bailey, on Friday, the 17th September, MDCCXC.— London: Printed for M. Smith, opposite Fetter-lane, in Fleet-Street. MDCCXC* (London: M. Smith, 1790), p. 106.

33. For reasons of accessibility, all references to Captain Watkin Tench's publications have been taken from the most recent edition of his works, entitled *1788 Comprising A Narrative of the Expedition to Botany Bay* and *A Complete Account of the Settlement at Port Jackson, Watkin Tench,* edited and introduced by Tim Flannery (Melbourne: The Text Publishing Company, 1996). Henceforth, references will read either Tench, *A Narrative of the Expedition* (Flannery edition) or Tench, *A Complete Account of the Settlement* (Flannery edition). Tench's comment on 'gloom and dejection' is

taken from Tench, *A Complete Account of the Settlement* (Flannery edition), p.119. Tench's first work was entitled, *A Narrative of the Expedition to Botany Bay; with an account of New South Wales, its productions, inhabitants, &c. to which is subjoined, A List of the Civil and Military Establishments at Port Jackson.— —By Captain Watkin Tench, of the Marines* (London: J. Debrett, 1789). His second work was entitled, *A Complete Account of the Settlement at Port Jackson, including an accurate description of the Situation of the Colony; of the Natives; and of its natural productions: Taken on the spot, By Captain Watkin Tench, of the Marines* (London: G. Nicol, 1793).

For readers who wish to consult an earlier and extensively annotated edition of Tench's accounts, see, *Sydney's First Four Years: being a reprint of A Narrative of the Expedition to Botany Bay and A Complete Account of the Settlement at Port Jackson by Captain Watkin Tench*; with an introduction and annotations by L. F. Fitzhardinge (Sydney: Angus & Robertson, in association with the Royal Australian Historical Society, 1961). Watkin Tench (?1758–1833) returned to England from New South Wales in 1792. He served in the war against the French in 1793–4, and was taken prisoner from his ship, the *Alexander*. He was exchanged by the French in 1795 and continued serving in the Marine Corps until 1802.

34. Mary Ann Parker, wife of Captain John Parker (1749–94), captain of the *Gorgon*, expressed delight in being able to bring relief and succour to the colony. See Coleman, *Maiden Voyages and Infant Colonies*, pp. 2–3.

35. Tench, *A Complete Account of the Settlement* (Flannery edition), p. 210.

36. *Ibid.*, p. 206. A detailed account of the Third Fleet and descriptions of the ill-treatment of convicts and their later debilitation is found in *HRNSW*, vol. 2, pp. 172–88.

37. William Wyndham Grenville (1759–1834) succeeded Lord Sydney at the Home Office on 5 June 1789, and was raised to the peerage in 1790.

38. Tench, *A Complete Account of the Settlement* (Flannery edition), pp. 204–6.

39. *Ibid.*, p. 224.

40. The first writers after settlement in 1788 were all commissioned officers of the Royal Navy, the military establishment or the Marine Corps. Captain Arthur Phillip (1738–1814) was appointed the first Governor of New South Wales and Commander in Chief in 1786. David Collins (1756–1810) was Judge-Advocate and Secretary of the Governor. John White (1756–1832) was Surgeon-General to the First Fleet and the Settlement at Port Jackson and John Hunter (1737–1821) was appointed Second Captain to Phillip on the *Sirius* and became second Governor of New South Wales. Captain-Lieutenant Watkin Tench (?1758–1833) commanded a company of Marines.

41. *A Voyage around the World in the Gorgon Man of War: Captain John*

Parker. Performed and Written by his Widow for the advantage of a numerous family. [Mary Ann Parker], (London: J. Nichols, 1795). For the fully annotated edition, see Coleman, *Maiden Voyages and Infant Colonies.*

42. The *Monthly Review*, vol. XVIII (September–December 1795), pp. 474–5.

43. The *Gentleman's Magazine and Historical Chronicle for the Year MDCCXCV*, vol. LXV, p. 760.

44. For example, Tench's *A Complete Account of the Settlement at Port Jackson* (1793) was published by subscription and 502 names were noted on the first edition, including members of England's intelligentsia, former Marines, members of the Militia and army regiments and high-ranking clergymen. Copies went to university college libraries including the University of Cambridge, and to the Chester Library. Subscribers included the political economist, David Ricardo, and Captain John Hunter, whose own account was also published in 1793 by Stockdale of Piccadilly.

45. *Blackwoods Magazine* (London: T. Cadell & W. Davis, November 1827), p. 686. See also *Riley Papers*, ML A110 (Mitchell Library, State Library of New South Wales, Sydney), p.15. For this information I am indebted to Richard Neville, whose lively perspectives on many of the issues and influences which shaped the creation of images about Australia from the time of European settlement appeared in an exhibition 'A Rage for Curiosity: Visualising Australia 1788–1830', at the Mitchell Library in 1998. Neville makes a number of textual and illustrative references to George Barrington's 'histories' in his publication, *A Rage for Curiosity: Visualising Australia 1788–1830* (Sydney: State Library of New South Wales Press, 1997), and also in his essay 'Eager Curiosity: Engaging with the New Colony of New South Wales', in *The World Upside Down: Australia 1788–1830* (Canberra: National Library of Australia, 2000), pp. 7–12.

46. *An Impartial and Circumstantial Narrative of the Present State of Botany Bay, in New South Wales: With a Description of the Country; Treatment of the Convicts on their Passage, and after their arrival. Also the Manners, Customs, Religion, &c. of the Natives, Truly Depicted. Containing among a variety of entertaining subjects The Particulars of the Voyage; a description of the Buildings and Soil at Sydney Cove; Journey to Paramata; Convicts Houses and daily Occupations; their Emoluments from Government on the Expiration of their Term; Birds; Animals; Vegetables; manner of taking one of the Natives, who dies of the Small-Pox; entrap two others, who escape with much Ingenuity; their Retaliation upon the Governor, who very narrowly escapes Death; a reconciliation takes place; &c. &c. &c. &c. By George Barrington, Now Superintendant of the Convicts at Paramata.* (London: S. & J. Bailey, c. 1793–4).

47. Tench, *A Complete Account of the Settlement* (Flannery edition), pp. 273–4.

48. For a detailed discussion of the 'Barrington Panorama', see Tim McCormick, Robert Irving, Elizabeth Imashev, Judy Nelson and Gordon Bull, *First Views of Australia 1788–1825: A History of Early Sydney* (Chippendale, NSW: David Ell Press, Longueville Publications, 1987), p. 276.

49. For an informative and amusing account of the history of illustrations of Antipodean flora and fauna, including the plagiarized illustrations of the lyrebird, see Alec H. Chisholm, *The Romance of the Lyrebird* (Sydney: Angus & Robertson, 1960), pp. 4–5 and pp. 38–41.

50. James Lackington was one of London's most successful booksellers, specializing in 'remaindering'. In the 1790s, his bookshop, 'The Temple of the Muses', was the largest in London and possibly in the world. From the bookselling perspective, Lackington would have had a professional interest in publications attributed to Barrington due to the great sales potential and frequency of reprints and new editions. What is notable is that he chose to cite George Barrington as an interesting character in his memoir. By 1794, Lackington's memoir was in its seventh edition. See *Memoirs of the first forty-five years of the Life of James Lackington, written by himself* (London: J. Lackington, 1794).

51. *Ibid.*, p. 188.

52. Tench, *A Complete Account of the Settlement* (Flannery edition), pp. 224–5.

53. *Ibid.*

54. Barrington may have elicited emotions of jealousy from less fortunate settlers who complained about entrepreneurial officers and 'dealers, peddlars and extortioners'. See 'Field of Mars Petition', *Historical Records of Australia,* vol. 2 (Sydney: Library Committee of the Commonwealth Parliament, 1915), p. 137. The historian A. G. L. Shaw suggests that substantial fortunes were made by military residents, in which some ex-convicts shared. A. G. L. Shaw, *Convicts and the Colonies: A Study of Penal Transportation from Great Britain & Ireland to Australia and other parts of the British Empire* (Melbourne: Melbourne University Press, 1998; first published 1966), p. 68.

55. Pierre Bernard Milius, *Voyage aux Terres Australes par Pierre Bernard Milius, second sur le 'Naturaliste' dans l'expédition Baudin (1800–1804).* Transcribed by Jacqueline Bonnemains and Pascale Hauguel (Le Havre: La Société Havraise d'Etudes Diverses, 1987).

56. *Ibid.*, p. 46.

57. David Dickenson Mann, *The Present State of New South Wales* (London: John Booth, 1811), p. 110.

58. *Sydney Gazette and New South Wales Advertiser*, 6 January 1805, p. 1.

59. *The History of New South Wales, including Botany Bay, Port Jackson,*

Parramatta, Sydney, and all its Dependancies, from the Original Discovery of the Island: With the Customs and Manners of the Natives, and an Account of the English Colony, from its Foundation, to the Present Time, By George Barrington: Superintendant of the Convicts (London: M. Jones, 1810), Introduction, p. 4.

Note on the Text

An Impartial and Circumstantial Narrative of the Present State of Botany Bay, In New South Wales ... by George Barrington, now Superintendant of the Convicts at Paramata (c. 1793–4)

The copy text here presents one of the first undated editions of a narrative attributed to George Barrington, published probably in late 1793 or early 1794 by S. and J. Bailey of Bishopsgate Street Within, London. With its fashionably objective title, it is an outstanding version among many although, according to the distinguished Australian bibliographer, J. A. Ferguson, it was likely to have been an abridged version. Which pirated version could lay claim to be the 'original' remains open to question, and which was the completely unabridged version cannot be readily judged. *An Impartial and Circumstantial Narrative* was published under alternative titles such as *A Voyage to New South Wales*, *A Voyage to Botany Bay*, or *Barrington's Voyage to New South Wales*. The text of *An Impartial and Circumstantial Narrative of the Present State of Botany Bay, In New South Wales ... by George Barrington*, differs little in style and vocabulary from similar versions of approximately the same length. Most ran from forty-four to forty-eight pages, while a shorter version contained a mere eight pages. The longest ran to 140 leaves.

I have produced the edition's orthography and typographical errors, usually mis-spellings or variations in spellings of place names such as 'Sidney', or 'Paramata'. Most obvious is the spelling of 'Superintendant', following the eighteenth-century form. The original text was set with no line space between paragraphs, and long dashes, colons and semi-colons have been preserved with other forms of punctuation. The original text used the elongated 's' which has been replaced in this annotated edition. All numbers in the original text were Arabic in style. Printery pagination codes present at the base of the original leaves have been excised. The quality of the original versions varied but copies of the extant versions were printed on thin paper and often bound in light wrappers. Prices also varied, versions being priced from 'six-pence' to 'half-a-crown'. Most versions were 8 *verso* editions, while a few were 12 *duodecimo*.

Dating the text of *An Impartial and Circumstantial Narrative* is an imprecise undertaking, and expert bibliographic opinions have varied over the years. Internal evidence, taken with the earlier publication dates of authorised accounts published from late 1789 to 1793, permits the suggestion that the most probable date lies somewhere between late 1793 and early 1794. The distinguished British bibliographer, E. Duff Gordon, suggested that the pamphlet was probably printed in 1790. In the 1970s, staff of the *English Short Title Catalogue* suggested a date of 1791. These dates are clearly too early. J. A. Ferguson clustered all the versions noted above *c*. 1795. Only one printer, styled 'The Proprietor', dated his version at 1795; all the other versions are undated.

Printers, booksellers or publishers advertised their names on the versions referred to above. 'The Proprietor', C. Lowndes, T. Sadler, T. Walker, H. D. Symonds, M. Clements, J. Eves, T. Thomas, A. Swindells, as well as S. & J. Bailey, all produced variations of the same text. Who the writers or compilers were remains a mystery. In 1969, the Brummell Press of London produced *A Voyage to Botany Bay, by George Barrington: together with his Life and Trial and the sequel to his Voyage*. This, a limited edition of 350 copies, combined reprints of *A Voyage to Botany Bay* (*c*. 1795) published by C. Lowndes, together with *A Sequel to Barrington's Voyage to New South Wales* (1801), also by Lowndes.

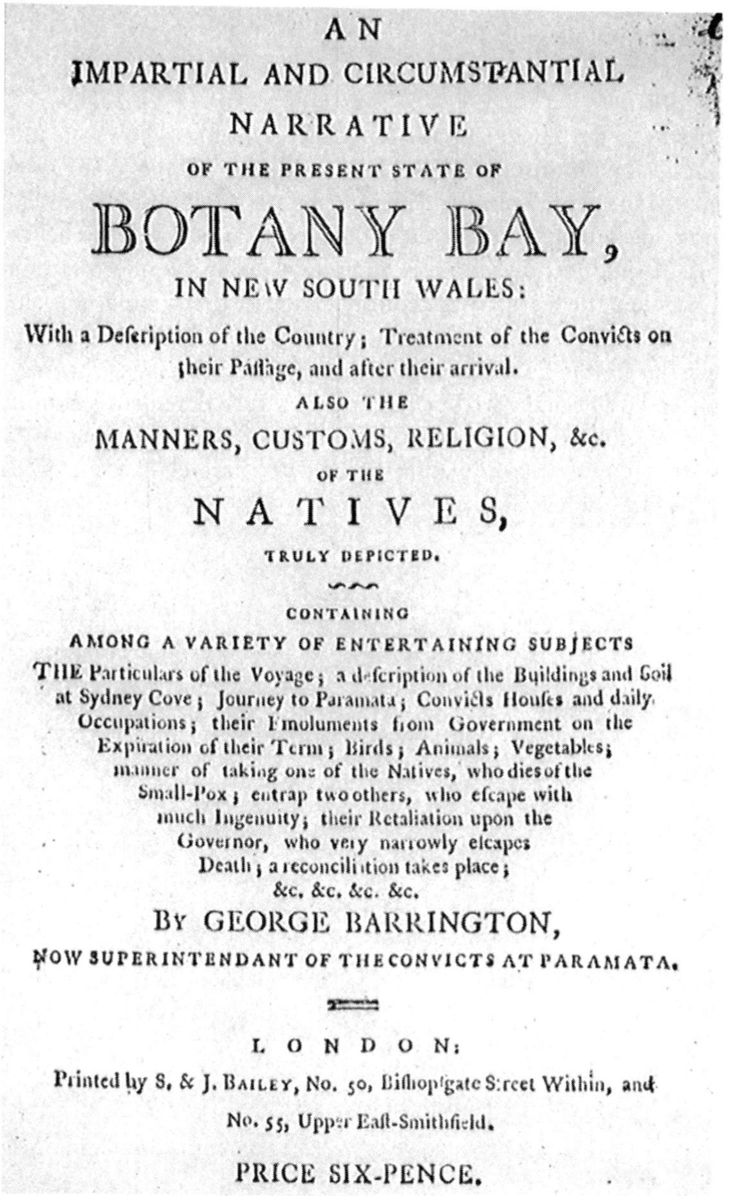

AN
IMPARTIAL AND CIRCUMSTANTIAL
NARRATIVE
OF THE PRESENT STATE OF

BOTANY BAY,

IN NEW SOUTH WALES:

With a Defcription of the Country; Treatment of the Convicts on
their Paffage, and after their arrival.

ALSO THE

MANNERS, CUSTOMS, RELIGION, &c.

OF THE

NATIVES,

TRULY DEPICTED.

~~~

CONTAINING

AMONG A VARIETY OF ENTERTAINING SUBJECTS

THE Particulars of the Voyage; a defcription of the Buildings and Soil
at Sydney Cove; Journey to Paramata; Convicts Houfes and daily
Occupations; their Emoluments from Government on the
Expiration of their Term; Birds; Animals; Vegetables;
manner of taking one of the Natives, who dies of the
Small-Pox; entrap two others, who efcape with
much Ingenuity; their Retaliation upon the
Governor, who very narrowly efcapes
Death; a reconciliation takes place;
&c. &c. &c. &c.

By GEORGE BARRINGTON,

NOW SUPERINTENDANT OF THE CONVICTS AT PARAMATA.

━━━

LONDON:

Printed by S. & J. BAILEY, No. 50, Bifhopfgate Street Within, and

No. 55, Upper Eaft-Smithfield.

PRICE SIX-PENCE.

Plate 15 Title page of *An Impartial and Circumstantial Narrative of the Present
State of Botany Bay, in New South Wales ... by George Barrington, Now
Superintendant of the Convicts at Paramata* (c. 1793–4).
Source: Ferguson Collection (F214), by permission of the National Library of Australia,
Canberra.
The Editor's Notes 1, 2 and 3 (p. 121) provide a detailed explanation of this title page.

Entered at Stationers' Hall.[4]

To Mr.

DEAR SIR,

I EMBRACE the earliest opportunity of performing the promise I made you upon my quitting ENGLAND: and should the contents of the accompaying sheets, collected chiefly from personal observation, aided by the best local inquiries, acquit me, in your mind, of a breach of that promise, I shall feel myself more than happy: they had been more ample, but I was impatient to pay a debt of gratitude, that would not brook the loss of an opportunity; consequently you will find the conclusion rather abrupt; but by the next ship, I shall, I trust, make amends, having nearly transcribed some letters from my friend Mr. Wentworth,[5] containing a pleasant narrative of the rise and progress of the settlement at Norfolk Island,[6] together with some further particulars relative to, SIR, Your obedient, and obliged,

Humble Servant,
George Barrington,

GEORGE BARRINGTON'S VOYAGE TO BOTANY BAY.

It was with unspeakable satisfaction that I received a summons to be ready early the next morning for my embarkation, agreeable to my sentence.[7] I instantly made the most of my time, and by the assistance of a friend, procured some necessaries for my voyage: government allowance being extremely slender,[8] to one like me, who had hitherto been accustomed to most of the luxuries of the table. The news of my speedy departure brought several of my acquaintances to bid me adieu, and, with gratitude, I recollect that not one of them came empty handed; for before the time of locking up, I had such a collection of ventures, that I doubted whether I should be permitted to take them all on board.

About a quarter before five a general muster took place; and having bid farewell to my fellow prisoners, we were escorted from the prison to Blackfriars-bridge, by the city guards, where two lighters were waiting to receive us. This procession, though early, and but few spectators, made a deep impression on my mind; and the ignominy of being thus mingled with felons of all descriptions, many scarce a degree above the brute creation, intoxicated with liquor, and shocking the ears of those who passed with blasphemy, oaths, and songs the most offensive to modesty, inflicted a punishment more severe than the sentence of my country, and fully avenged that society I had so much wronged.[9]

Absorbed in the most humiliating meditating meditation, the objects we passed going down the river were totally unnoticed by me; nor was I roused from my lethargy till looking around me I found we were along side of the ship. In my turn I ascended the ship's side, and to my great satisfaction, the first person I cast my eyes upon was my particular friend,[10] whose generous exertions not only procured me stowage for my packages, but prevailed on the boatswain to admit me to his mess, and also the liberty of walking the deck, unencumbered by those galling and ignominious chains, which my past conduct had consigned me to.[11] My benefactor, having rendered my situation thus comfortable, bade me farewell, and left me; my heart swelling with gratitude, was too full, to admit of verbal acknowledgment; but the remembrance of it is too strongly engraven thereon, for the most distant time to effect the slightest eradication.

My fellow prisoners to the amount of upwards of two hundred, were all ordered into the hold which was rendered as convenient as circumstances would admit, battens being fixed fore and aft for hammocks, which were being hung seventeen inches apart from each other; but being encumbered with their irons,[12] together with the want of fresh air, soon rendered their situation truly deplorable.[13]

My messmate, the boatswain, had provided me with a neat snug hammock, and gave me a berth next to his own, not only for my hammock, but a place also for my little property, which I could have immediately under my eye.

We lay about a week at Long Reach, when we dropt down to Gravesend, and soon after arrived from thence at the Mother-bank,[14] where lay several other transports for the same destination; and it coming on a stiff easterly breeze, we ran through the Needles. It was delightful weather, and the prospects on each hand must have afforded the most agreeable sensations to every beholder, and is, perhaps, as rich and luxuriant as is any where to be met with; but, alas, it only brought a fresh pang to the bosom of one who in all probability was bidding it adieu for ever.[15]

A most violent gale took place the third day after we lost sight of the land, and which for near ten hours baffled the skill of all hands: two men were blown from the main topsail yard, and the sail split in ribbands, and I not being capable of any service upon deck, retired to my hammock until the storm had subsided, the wind perfectly fair, and the ship jogging on under an easy sail, at the rate of about seven miles an hour.

The danger we had just escaped was succeeded by one that had nearly proved much more fatal: the captain with great humanity, had released many of the convicts who had been in a weakly state from their leg irons, and they were allowed alternately, ten at a time to walk upon deck. — Two of them, Americans, who had some knowledge of navigation, prevailed upon the majority of their comrades to attempt seizing the ship, and carry her to America.[16] —These arguments had the desired effect, and were put in execution with equal spirit and audacity. A favorable opportunity presented itself, the captain and most of the officers being below examining the stowage of some wine, a cask having leaked out in the spirit room, I was the only person on deck excepting the man at the helm; hearing a scuffle on the main deck, I was going forward, but was stopped by one of the Americans, followed by another convict who made a stroke at me with a sword he had wrested from one of the centenials, which was put aside by a pistol which the other had just snapped at me; I snatched up a handspike in my reach, and brought the foremost to the ground; the man at the helm had quitted the wheel, and called up the captain. I still kept my situation, guarding the passage of the quarter deck, my antagonists having retreated a few paces, but being joined by many others were rushing at me, when the discharge of a blunderbuss from behind me, among them, wounded several, they retreated, and I was immediately joined by the captain and the rest of the officers, who, in a few minutes, drove them all into the hold, and two of the ringleaders were instantly hung at the yard-arm.[17]

As soon as the conspirators were re-ironed, the captain paid me many handsome compliments,[18] and assured me, when we arrived at the Cape, he should on the part of the owners think it his duty to reward the service I had, by my courage and presence of mind, rendered them; and seldom a day past but some fresh meat or poultry was sent me by the captain, which raised me in the estimation of my messmates, who were no ways displeased at the substitution of pies made of fowl or fresh meat to a dish of salt junk.[19]

With a settled north westerly breeze we gradually preceded to the southward, at the rate of between eighty and one hundred miles in twenty-four hours: we soon reached the island of Teneriffe,[20] and came to anchor in the bay of Santa Cruz. Some of the officers having obtained leave from the agents of transports to visit the town of Ortava,[21] a few miles from Santa Cruz, and on my expressing a desire to see the town, I was permitted to be of the party. The country is exceedingly beautiful and fertile, notwithstanding the frequent convulsions of the neighboring volcanoes.[22] We arrived at Ortava about noon, and by signs, for none of us were masters of the language, we got a few eggs and plenty of small wine. We had scarcely taken our seats, when we were relieved from the inconvenience attending our not being acquainted with the language, by the arrival of an old Spanish soldier, who had been some time a prisoner in England, and spoke our language tolerable well. We informed him we had come from Santa Cruz to take a nearer view of the Peak, and if the time would admit, to ascend it. He said it was impossible at this season of the year, as no guides would undertake to accompany us, but that he would take us as far as was prudent for us to venture, and we walked about a league from the town into the plain where we had a full view of the stupendous mountain.[23] Our time being short, and the weather being intensely cold, we returned to Ortava, and got some salt fish, with a few hard eggs for supper; to which the old soldier invited himself, but amply repaid us for his intrusion, by a lively and humourous description of the squabbles of his neighbours, and knavery practised by the mountaineers on the curious and exploring stranger; the intervals were supplied by several songs from a company of mountaineers, who, by their extreme vociferation, intirely discomposed the serenity of our loquacious guest, and, but for my meditation, would have produced a serious quarrel between them. At noon on the second day of our absence from the ship, we began to think of returning, so taking leave of the old soldier, reached Santa Cruz by sunset; and one of the boats being luckily on shore, we immediately went out on board, highly gratified with our excursion.[24]

The ships having completed their watering, the signal was made for every person belonging to the fleet to repair on board their respective vessels, and the next morning the signal to get under weigh.[25] We shaped our coarse to the southward, and as we crossed the Equinoctial Line,[26] the ceremony of shaving and ducking, was punctually observed:[27] – at noon a hoarse voice hailed the ship, as from the sea, with 'Ho! The ship ho!' which was answered by one stationed for the purpose, with 'Hallo? what ship's that?' 'The Albermarle',[28] 'I don't recollect her passing this way before, I shall come on board and examine her.' Upon which half a dozen most grotesque figures entered the ship, as from the bottom of the deep; having previously slung a grating under each bow, as a stage to ascend from; with great solemnity they proceeded to the quarter deck; the principal personages were Neptune and Amphitrite,[29] attended by their nymphs and mer-maids, personated by the oldest seaman in the ship, but so disfigured with red ochre, robes, and wigs, made of raveled spun-yarn, that it was a difficult matter to recognize their persons. After receiving a double toll from the captain, (it being the first time of the ship's crossing the line,) consisting of half a gallon of liquor and two pounds of sugar; they, in turn, questioned every person on deck. When any one said he had crossed before, and had not, his watery majesty, with great dignity, turned to one of his attendants, who held a large book, said, 'Look if you have this gentleman down in my log-book?' which was answered in the negative, and the rum and sugar was instantly demanded. When it came to my turn, my friend, the captain, desired them to put my quota down to him. —Having finished with the quarter deck, they proceeded to the examination of their own comrades, after having prepared for the ceremony of treating those who could not pay, with a view of Neptune's cellar: for this purpose they had made a tackle fast to the main yard-arm, through which they wove a rope, with an iron crow made fast to the end of a seat. The only exhibition was on the person of the cook, who not being of the most conciliatory disposition, most of the ship's company owed him a grudge; and as he peremptorily refused to pay, although in his power, they placed him on the crow, and brought the yard rope between his legs, making another fast round him, to prevent a possibility of his falling; they then swang him oft, and running him close up to the yard, soused the poor devil from the height of near 50 feet into the water; this was preformed thrice, but when they took him on board he was so exhausted that his life was thought to be in danger, which put an end to this part of the ceremony, and the other defaulters were let off with only shaving, performed by Neptune and his assistants; the party were seated on a piece of board placed across a large tub, the razor a part of an iron hoop, and for soap a composition of tar, tallow, and every filth they could collect—The disagreeableness of this operation, exclusive of the smart, the hand of the razor not being lightest, occasioned by a struggle to get from under it, in which the board whereon he is seated gives way and the poor pilgarlic is duck'd over head and ears in bilge-water. The forfeits made them all as merry as griggs[30] and the day closed with dancing and songs on the forecastle. Everyone (cook excepted) forgot their temporary mortifications and joined in the evenings conviviality.[31]

We had a series of fine weather till we arrived at the Cape of Good Hope on July the 20th, anchored about sunset in Table Bay.[32] This being the last port we could touch at for refreshments during the remainder of the voyage, all hands set to work to procure such articles as they might stand in need of, as well for their present consumption, as for their future comfort in the new colony. Early in the morning, the captain ordered the pinnace to be manned and went on shore, from whence he returned about noon, and sending for me aft gave me a draft on a merchant at Cape Town for two dollars; at the same time telling me that I might at any time take advantage of the boats going ashore to visit the town as often as I pleased, by speaking to the officer on deck.[33] The confidence reposed in me struck me more forcibly than the money, and I was really so confused that I could scarcely articulate my acknowledgements: during our stay here I visited the town almost every day, and brought such articles as were most in request in new Holland.[34]

Having completely stored the ship with provisions and water taken in 600 sacks of flour for the colony and other stores,[35] the signal was made for the transports to be in readiness to get under weigh, and the next morning we worked out of the bay.[36]

As nothing material happened during the voyage I shall not trouble you with our different bearings and distances but content myself with

T. Woodthorpe fc.

THE CAPE OF GOOD HOPE.

Plate 16 'The Cape of Good Hope', from *The History of New South Wales*. By *George Barrington* (1802).
Source: Rare Books Collection, The Library, Australian National University, Canberra.

informing you, we had, in general, pleasant weather, and about noon, Oct. 12th, found ourselves abrest of land called Red Point,[37] only 10 leagues distant from Botany Bay.—About 2 leagues to the southward of the bay is a chain of chalky hills o'ertopp'd by level land. On this land is a clump of trees something like Portsdown Hill, in the neighborhood of Portsmouth. The wind springing up to the east we stood from the land under an easy sail till day-light, when we were quite abrest of the bay: and at noon the 13th came to anchor in port Jackson.[38] At 10 o'clock the next morning the convicts were all ordered on shore; their appearance was truly deplorable, the generality of them being emaciated by disease, foul air &c. and those who laboured under no bodily disorder, from the scantiness of their allowance were in no better plight.[39]

The boats from all the ships in the harbour attended in order to land them: there were in all 250 men, 6 women, and one convict's wife and child, who had obtained permission to accompany her husband, and we lost during the voyage 32 men.[40] Upon their landing they were entirely new cloathed from the king's store, their old things were burnt to prevent infections that might have been in the ship being introduc'd in the colony.

From the report of the captain, I had a most generous reception with the Governor. His excellency said, he had long wanted a proper person as superintendant of the convicts at Paramata,[41] that he appointed me to that office,[42] and that I should take charge of the farm house. When I was dismissed, the serjeant took me to his house, where I partook of a fish dinner and it being some time ere we could set off for my future residence, we took a walk round the Cove, where some extensive buildings have been erected for the Governor,[43] Lieutenant-governor,[44] Judge-advocate,[45] and a great part of the officers.[46]

The Governor's house is of stone, near seventy feet in front, and makes a very handsome appearance.[47] The houses of the officers are of brick, the rest are generally log houses, plaistered, the roofs either shingled or thatched. Here is also an hospital, a good temporary building, and also barracks for the soldiers, and comfortable cabins for the officers, with gardens adjoining: but unluckily these gardens are not very productive,[48] as the soil is very indifferent, and to this inconvenience must be added the depredations of the rats[49] and thieves. A mile or two from the cove, the soil is considerably better, where the officers and others have little farms,[50] there are also brick-kilns[51] and a pottery, both of which articles they would bring to tolerable perfection, were they possessed of the materials to glaze their earthen ware. Not being able to proceed till morning, I flung my cot in a corner of the serjeants house, and spent the evening with him; we rose at day break and re-embarking my effects,

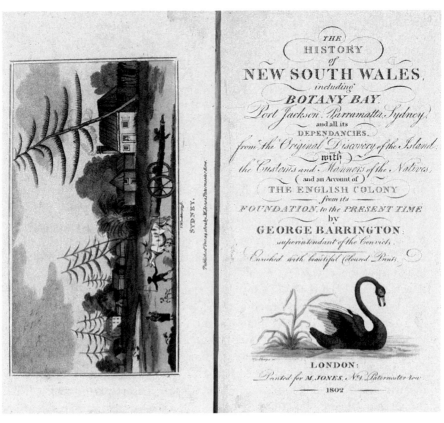

Plate 17   'Sydney', from *The History of New South Wales. By George Barrington* (1802).
Source: Rare Books Collection, The Library, Australian National University, Canberra.

TOWN & COVE of SYDNEY.

Pub. by M. Jones Paternoster Row March 16, 1803

Waithorpe, f.

Plate 18 'Town and Cove of Sydney', from *The History of New South Wales. By George Barrington* (1802).
Source: Rare Books Collection, The Library, Australian National University, Canberra.

left Sidney Cove about eight o'clock in the morning, and arrived at Paramata about noon.[52] We landed about a quarter of a mile from the town, and walked up to it; it is situated on an elevated spot, in the form of a crescent; a strong redoubt is constructed, where there are very good barracks[53] for a detachment of the military, which is always on duty here, as well as to preserve good order and regularity among convicts, as a check upon the natives, who from the distance to Sidney Cove,[54] might be tempted to molest the settlers, were there no armed force to protect them; they have little apprehensions from the natives, as they have never shewn any inclination to attack armed men; not that they are destitute of courage, but that they are perfectly convinced of the great and invincible superiority of our fire arms.[55] After a short walk we arrived at the house appropriated for me, it is a snug cottage with four rooms in it: the situation is delightful, being in the midst of pleasant gardens, the convicts houses form a line in front at a distance, they have each a small garden, and those who are industrious seem very comfortable, as their days work is not so hard as many working men's in England.[56]

A servant who kept the house gave us some refreshment, after which I waited on the commanding officer of the troops, on duty here, and presented a letter given me by the governor.

In the morning a general muster of the convicts took place, when the whole was assembled, to the amount of four hundred, they were informed by the officer of the trust of the governor had been pleased to repose in me,[57] and that any misbehavior or disobedience of orders issued from me, would be as severely punished, as though they proceeded from the governor himself: they were dismissed to their several employments. I proceeded through the different gangs of people, observing their occupations; and found them much more attentive to their business, and respectful to those over them, than I could possibly have imagined. Some were employed in making bricks and tiles; others building houses, huts, &c. a great number clearing the grounds, bringing in timber and making roads. Others at their different callings, such as smiths, gardeners, coopers, shoemakers, taylors, bakers, attendants on the sick, &c.[58]—The hours of work are from sunrise till half past seven, when they breakfast; at half past eight they resume their work 'till half past eleven, when they are rung to dinner; at two they recommence their labours, and the setting of the sun is the signal that terminates their daily toil, and which is announced by the drum beating a retreat.[59]—In order to encourage the cultivation of gardens, Saturday is appropriated to clear away and cultivate spots for themselves, and those who have been industrious feel the benefit, by having plenty of vegetables which now saves their salt provisions, and enables them to truck with the natives for fish. Independant of these advantages, those who rear the greatest quantity of vegetables and plants, receive premiums from the governor, who at the proper seasons of the year, distributes seeds among them for that purpose. The women sweep round the huts every morning, and cook the victuals for the men, collect all their dirty cloaths, and return each man his respective linen, washed and mended on Sunday mornings.[60] My business was chiefly to report the progress made in the different works carrying on at Paramata; for which purpose I was furnished with abstracts from a kind of overseers or head men of the various gangs: and in less than a week I was as much at home, and as perfectly master of my business, as though I had been coeval with the colony.[61] Having a good deal of time on my hands, my attendance and inspection being generally finished in the forenoon, I frequently visited the farms of settlers, these in general were convicts, whose term of transportation were expired, and had lands granted to them in the following proportions; thirty acres to any single man, fifty to the married ones, and ten more for every child, they receive provision and clothing for the first eighteen months; the necessary tools and implements for husbandry, with feeds and grains to sow the ground the first year; two young sow pigs were also given to each settler, and a pair or two of fowls. On these conditions twenty seven of them had commenced farming in the neighborhood of Paramata, Prospect Hill[62] and some ponds about two miles to the northward. At this time these settlements had little the appearance of farms; but as there were many very industrious and careful men amongst them, their stock began to thrive, and the face of the country shew evident signs of culture. In my walks I often fell in with the Kangaroo,[63] of which there are great numbers: they are about the size of a common deer, of a dark tan colour, its head, I think resembles that of a Mocock[64] from the East Indies. The hind legs are much longer than the fore, and with them they leap and spring forward with amazing rapidity, their forefeet seldom being seen to touch the ground, and indeed they are so very short, that it is not possible the animal can make great use of them in running; they have prodigious force in their tail, which is a principal part of their defence when attacked: they strike a blow with this weapon sufficient to break the leg of a man, or the back of a dog, it also assists them in their springs which is truly surprising.[65] The native dog is much swifter than the Kangaroo, and will attack them with great courage, the chace is seldom of long duration, the Kangaroo is soon tired, and is generally overtaken in 15 minutes. Having had several young native dogs given to me, from time to time, I take great delight in Kangaroo hunting, it is not only an agreeable exercise, but

Kangaroo.

Plate 19 'Kangaroo', from *The History of New South Wales*. By George Barrington (1802).
Source: Rare Books Collection, The Library, Australian National University, Canberra.

Plate 20 'A Native Dog', from *The History of New South Wales. By George Barrington* (1802).
Source: Rare Books Collection, The Library, Australian National University, Canberra.

produces a dish for the table, nearly as good as mutton, and in the present dearth of live stock is not an unacceptable present.[66]

The native dog greatly resembles the Pomeranian breed:[67] with their ears erect, they have a remarkable savage look, are not unlike a wolf, both in size and appearance. There is no getting the better of their native ferocity; for if you take ever so much pains in rearing them, they will at all times destroy the sheep, pigs, or poultry: I don't think it is possible to tame them so that they are of little or no use, except in hunting.[68]

I had many opportunities of getting acquainted with several of the natives; and as I seldom saw them without giving them some trifle or other, soon became a great favourite with them and mostly had 1 or 2 of them with me in my rambles. The men are in general from five feet six to five feet nine inches high; are rather slender, but straight and well made. The women are not quite so tall, rather lustier, but are mostly well made. Their colour is of a brownish black or a coffee cast, but many of the women are almost as light as a mulatto;[69] now and then you may meet with some of both sexes with pretty tolerable features, but broad noses, wide mouths, and thick lips, are most generally met with; their countenances are not the most prepossessing, and what renders them still less so, is, they are abominable filthy.—They know no such ceremony as washing themselves: and their skin is mostly smeared with the fat of such animals as they kill, and afterwards covered with every sort of dirt; sand from the beach, and ashes from their fires, all adhere to their filthy skin, which never comes off, except when accident or the want of food obliges them to go into the water. Some of the men wear a piece of wood, or bone thrust through the septum of the nose, which by raising the opposite side of the nose, dilates the nostril, and spreads the lower part very much.[70] Many of them want the two front teeth on the right side of the upper jaw;[71] and I have seen several of the women who have lost the two first joints of the little finger of the left-hand, a circumstance which I have not yet been able to discover the meaning of. They have in general good teeth; their hair is strong, short, and curly; and they have no method of cleaning it, it is always filthy and matted: the men's beards are short and curly like the hair of their heads. They all go entirely naked, men women and children, and seem to have no fixed place of residence, but lie down wherever night overtakes them. Cavities in the rocks on the sea shore, are places they usually seek to shelter them from the wind and rain; and they mostly make a good fire before they go to sleep, by which means the rocks round them become heated, and retain their warmth a considerable time, like an oven; and spreading a little dried grass they lie down and huddle together. The men are generally armed with a lance, and short stick, which they use in throwing it: this stick is about a yard long flat on one side, and a notch on one end, the other is furnished with a flat shell fixed into a split in the stick, made fast with a strong gum, which when dry, is as hard as a flint; on the flat side of the stick they place the lance, the but end of which rests against the notch in the throwing stick; poising the lance thus fixed in one hand, binding it with the fore finger and thumb to prevent it slipping off, keeping fast hold of the throwing stick, they hurl the lance with considerable force, to the distance of 70 or 80 yards.[72] Their lances are about ten feet long; the shell fixed on the throwing stick is intended for sharpening the point of the lance, and other uses. They throw their lances with great velocity, yet I should think it no difficult matter being on ones guard, either to parry or get out of the way.

When they are upon any hostile expedition,[73] they paint their faces and bodies with red and white streaks, as if they intended to strike terror with their death like appearance. The colours they use are frequently red and white, the first of which is a kind of ochre, or red earth, which is found here in abundance; the latter is a fine pipe-clay, great quantity of which are used in the potteries in the colony. The bodies of the men are much scarified, particularly about the breast and shoulders; and although not regular, yet are considered as ornamental.[74]

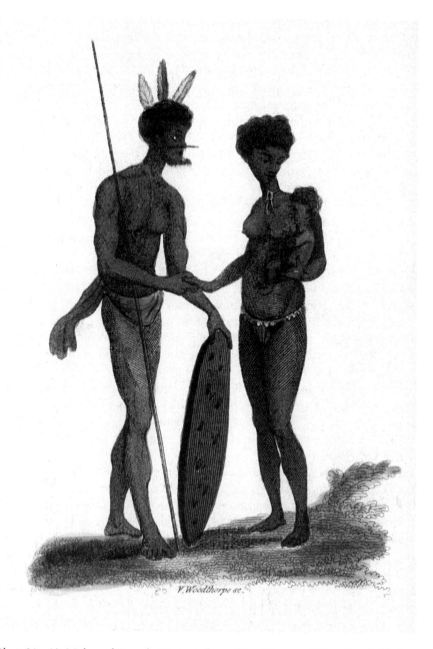

Plate 21 'A Male and Female Native', from *The History of New South Wales.*
By George Barrington (1802).
Source: Rare Books Collection, The Library, Australian National University, Canberra.

The warriors thus painted range in a line, with each a green bow[75] in their hand, as a token they do not mean to use force, unless obliged thereto, in their own defence, or in case their difference cannot be settled by an amicable agreement, a long parley often ensues, and concessions on both sides generally terminate their campaign.

Building themselves habitations never seem to have entered their imaginations,[76] or any place to have sheltered them from the weather though they have plenty of the most inclement; their indolence and want of foresight in this particular would be fatal to them, were it not for the liberal hand of nature, who has so abundantly supplied the sea shores with soft crumbly rocks which for the most part are excavated by the washing of the sea so as to form caves of considerable dimensions; sometimes fifty or more of them find a comfortable lodging in one of these caves. In the woods, where no rocks are, they strip the bark off several trees, and cutting them into slips, flatten and interlace them to four stakes drove into the ground, bending broad pieces of the bark over the top to shelve off the rain; these commonly hold a family; and as the weather is very cold in the winter months, they find it necessary to huddle close for the benefit of the warmth to which each individual contributes a share.— These huts are only used when they are out Kangaroo hunting for in that season they employ themselves wholly in the woods.[77]

Most of the large trees are hollow, by decaying at the heart and when the Opossum, Kangaroo, Rat, Squirrel, and various other animals which inhabit the woods, are pursued, they commonly take shelter in these trees.[78] In order therefore to make sure of them, wherein they seldom fail, when they find them in a tree, a man climbs to the top,[79] which is performed in the following manner, they cut notches in the bark, about an inch deep, which is a kind of rest for the ball of the great toe; the two first notches are cut before they begin to climb; they rest as they ascend, at such a distance from each other, that when both feet are in the notches, the right foot is raised nearly as high as the middle of the left thigh, and when they are raising themselves, the hatchet is held in their mouths, that they may have the use of both their hands; and when making the notch, the body rests on the ball of the great toe, the fingers of the left hand are placed in a notch cut on the side of the tree, should it be too large to admit their clasping it sufficiently with their left arm, to keep their body firm and close to it: in this manner they ascend, with wonderful agility, trees fifteen or twenty feet in circumference, sometimes sixty or seventy feet[80] before they come to a single branch. Being come to the top or the place he judges most convenient, he takes his seat with his club or stick in his hand, another person below makes a fire, and fills the hollow trunk with smoke, which obliges the animal to attempt its escape, either up or down, but which ever way it takes, it is almost certain destruction, as they very seldom escape.

Oppossumes[81] are very numerous here; and there are a variety of other animals of different sizes, down to our implacable enemy the Field Rat. One would almost conclude from the great resemblance of the different quadrupeds found here, that there is a promiscuous intercourse between the different sexes of all those various animals. This strange similarity does not attach solely to quadrupeds, for the finny inhabitants of the sea are in the same predicament, their variety is truly astonishing.[82] Nature seems equally playful in the feathered tribe; the Parrot is the most common, I have shot several,[83] with the head, neck, and bill of the Parrot, and with the same beautiful plumage of these parts, for which that bird here is distinguished; a tail and body of a different make and colour, with long delicate feet and legs, which is quite the reverse of the Parrot kind.

There is also a bird with the feet and legs of a Parrot, whose head, neck, make, and colour, are like the common Sea Gul, with the wings and tail of the hawk. The country abounds in birds of numberless species: those of the Parrot kind, such as the Macaw, Cockatoo, Lory, Green Parrot, and Paroquet's of different species and sizes, are ornamented with the most gay and luxuriant plumage that can be conceived.[84]—And there is also a very large bird, but that is not common, at first they were taken for the Ostrich, as they did not fly when pursued, but ran so exceedingly swift that a strong native dog could not overtake them; I shot one of them which measured upwards of two yards and a half from its feet to the upper parts of its head. Its flesh, though not the most grained, is far from being unacceptable: it resembles when raw, a neck of beef: and the side bone of this bird makes an excellent dinner for half a dozen.[85] The Crow, I think relishes equally as well here as the barn fowl of England.[86] A prodigious quantity of Bats have made their appearance during these last two years, they are generally seen about Rose Hill towards the close of the evening; the head of this Bat very much resembles that of a Fox, the wings of many of them extend four feet from tip to tip. I have one of them that eats out of the hand, and is as domestic in the house as a cat.[87] A great variety of beautiful plants and flowers abound in this country; and, we find wild spinage, parsley, and sorrel in abundance.[88] Exclusive of the plantain, banana, and other tropical fruits, here are some I believe peculiar to this country; and there is also a nut which acts as a violent purgative, and an emetic, if eaten unprepared; it must be soaked seven or eight days in water, taking care that the water be changed every day. When it has been thoroughly soaked, it is then roasted in the embers; and when done it is not unlike a chestnut and very palatable.[89]

V. Woodthorpe fc.

Plate 22 'Black Cockatoo', from *The History of New South Wales. By George Barrington* (1802).
Source: Rare Books Collection, The Library, Australian National University, Canberra.

V.Woodthorpe sc.

Plate 23 'Emu', from *The History of New South Wales. By George Barrington* (1802).
Source: Rare Books Collection, The Library, Australian National University, Canberra.

About a twelvemonth before my arrival, the small pox made its appearance, and occasioned a terrible havoc among the poor natives.[90] It was truly shocking to find the coves of the harbour, which were formerly thronged with numerous families in tempestuous weather, now strewed with the dead bodies of men, women and children. No vestige of this cruel disorder being visible in the countenances of any of the natives, it was reasonable to suppose that they were never before infected with it, and of course ignorant of treating this cruel ravager of the human species. The various attitudes which the dead bodies were found, afforded reason to believe that when any of them were indisposed, and the disorder assumed the appearance of the small pox, that they were immediately deserted by their friends, and left to perish, in this helpless situation, for want of sustenance. They have been found sitting with their heads reclined between their knees; others were leaning against a rock, with their heads resting upon it. Two children, a boy and a girl, the boy about nine, and the girl about two years older, were picked up during the prevalence of this disorder, labouring under its dreadful effects.[91] Two old men, who were supposed to be the fathers of these children, were picked up about the same time, and carried to the hospital, they were taken all possible care of; the men survived but a short time, the children both recovered, and appeared perfectly satisfied with their change of living.

About this time a native, whom I saw frequently at the governor's, and who was now as perfectly in his ease in company as if he had been bred in England, being decently clothed and managing his knife, fork, cup, and saucer with great dexterity, was entrapped from his friends.[92] —Some officers were sent down the harbour with two boats for the purpose of seizing any of the natives they could lay their hands on; the governor having found that no encouragement would induce them to pay a visit to the colony on their own accord; he therefore determined to get some of them in his possession, and by kind treatment prevail on them to bring their countrymen to repose more confidence in us. – Arabanoo, the name of the native above alluded to was taken in the following manner: Being enticed to draw near the beach, by the display of various articles calculated to excite his curiosity and desire, and busily employed in admiring the presents that were given him,[93] one of the seamen, stationed for that purpose, threw a rope about his neck, and in a moment dragged him to the boat; his cries brought a number of his friends to the skirts of the wood, from whence they threw several spears without effect—To pourtray the terror and dismay depicted in the countenance of this poor creature, would require the hand of an able artist; he believed he was to be put to instant death, but when he was assured by the officers his life was safe, and they at the same time casting off the rope that he had round his neck and fixing it to his leg, treated him with so much kindness, that he gradually became cheerful. On his arrival at the governor's house, he had an iron shackle put round his leg to prevent the possibility of an escape; this he was taught to consider as a Bang Ally,[94] a term in their language, used for a decoration of any kind; and it was no difficult matter to bring him into a belief of this, as it was not uncommon to see some of the convicts ironed in the same manner as a punishment for the crimes they had committed in the colony. Arabanoo from the kind treatment he had experienced, was soon reconciled to his situation, and the iron becoming troublesome, galling his leg, it was taken off, and he was permitted to go where he pleased. The names of the different gentlemen who took notice of him where soon familiar to him, and he could call them with great facility.[95]—He was a very good tempered fellow, about thirty years of age, well made, and on the whole, not an unhandsome figure.[96] The intentions of the governor was, however, frustrated for some time, Poor Arabanoo, ere he could bring about a good understanding with his countrymen, was attacked with the small pox, and he only lived to the crisis of his distemper. The children recovered from the small pox, and were perfectly happy in their situation, but were then too young to be of service in reconciling their countrymen to us; they very soon understood almost everything that was said, and could also make themselves tolerably well understood: but the governor was still determined if possible, to get a man or two in his possession who might be taught enough of the language to render themselves useful negociators.[97]

Accordingly some officers[98] and a party of men were sent upon this expedition, in an armed boat, they proceeded to the north side of the harbour, where they saw two natives walking on the beach: a plan was soon formed to entice them to conversation: a few large fish were held up, and an officer who spoke some few words in their tongue, hailed them, which had the desired effect. The men advanced unarmed, with much confidence, and readily took the fish that was presented to them. The boat was lying a-float, and five or six men on the beach nearly surrounded them, when the officer in the boat observing the opportunity favourable, made the signal to secure them; in a short time they were tripped up, and tumbled into the boat, ere they had time to look around them.—They called out to their friends the moment they recovered their recollection, and a considerable number appeared from the woods, and many spears were thrown, one of which pierced through the gunwale of the boat, the party pulled off instantly, and the people presented their fire arms, they halted, not daring any further attack. The two prisoners were made fast to the thwarts of the boat on being put on board; but having got a distance from the shore, their hands were loosed, and they were only secured by one leg. When they were landed at Sydney Cove, the residence of the governor, many people prompted by curiosity, went to see them; among them were Araboo and Nanbarra, the two children before mentioned; the moment they saw them their eyes sparkled with joy, they called them by their names, the children were also known to them: and by their apparently satisfied behavior tended greatly to calm their apprehensions.

They discovered that one of the men they had taken was a chief of the tribe of Cadigal,[99] name Coalby; he was about thirty five years of age; the other about twenty five, was named Banalong. He was a smart, active, good looking young man, of a lively pleasant disposition: they were treated with the utmost kindness; but least they should attempt an escape they wore each of them an iron on one leg, with a piece of rope spliced to it, and a man was ordered for each, who was responsible for their security.—Wherever they went they were accompanied by their leaders, holding one end of the rope.[100]

They had been taken near three weeks, when they had been so well satisfied with their treatment, that their keepers began to be under very little apprehension of their attempting to get from them; this security they did not fail to avail themselves of: accordingly one evening about dusk, their guards sitting within the door of their huts eating their supper: Banalong being also in the hut, in the like manner employed: Coalby seated without the door, pretending also to be eating his supper, unspliced the rope from the shackle, leaving the other end fast in the keepers hand, who had not the least suspicion of what was going forward; he was over the pailing of the yard in an instant. The noise he made in leaping the pailing roused those within, but too late; the fugitive gained the woods, in spite of an immediate pursuit, and joined his friends.

The kind treatment, and the air of satisfaction which Banalong manifested for the space of a year after Coalby's flight, determined the governor to trust him with his liberty. Accordingly the shackle was taken off his leg, nor did he in the least seem disposed to leave the governor's house, or desert his new friends: so that no person had the least suspicion of his leaving the colony; he, however, one evening, just as it was dark, stripped himself, and leaving the cloaths that had been given him behind, decamped into the woods.[101]

Both he and Coalby were frequently seen by the boats employed in fishing, and would even converse with the people, who earnestly invited them to return to Sydney; but no entreaties could prevail on them.

The governor having received information that they were seen in a

Cove at the entrance of the harbour, he went thither, attended by several of the officers, but they were all unarmed, which ill-judged piece of confidence had like to have proved fatal to the governor. The particulars of this expedition are nearly as follows:

The governor, with some of the gentlemen of the colony went down to the mouth of the harbour, in order to pitch on a spot proper to erect a landmark,[102] to enable strangers the more readily to ascertain the harbour's mouth when at sea; on their return they were met by a boat which had just landed a party of officers, who intended to take a survey of the shore as far as Broken Bay. The coxswain of the boat informed the governor, that one of the party (Mr. White, the surgeon) had seen Coalby and Banalong, and had some conversation with them; that they enquired after every person they had any knowledge of in the colony, and particularly the governor, and they would go up to Sydney if he would come for them.

In consequence of this information his excellency returned to the cove, got some presents for them, which he supposed would be acceptable, he also ordered four muskets into the boat, and immediately sailed to the spot where the men had seen them.[103] When they arrived at the place, they found a number of the natives sitting round a fire, and near them lay the remains of a dead whale, which had been thrown ashore in a hard gale, and on which they had been heartily feasting. As soon as they were within hail, the governor stood up in the boat, and called for Banalong, and in their language asked where he was—Banalong instantly answered, 'Here I am.' His excellency then said, 'I am the governor your father.' which title he always gave the governor when he was at Sydney. After desiring the two gentlemen to remain in the boat,[104] and to have the muskets ready, (upon examining which, two were found unprovided with flints,) his excellency landed and walked toward them with his arms extended, to shew him he was unarmed, that they might be under no apprehensions for their safety.[105]

They appeared very backward in coming to a near conference; however he continued approaching them till he entered the wood; one of them possessed more assurance than his comrades, after frequently repeating the words 'Governor, Father,' ventured to shake hands in a friendly manner. His excellency then returned to the boat, and ordered one of the people to bring some wine, beef, and bread, and a jacket or two, which had been brought on purpose, and returned to them with these presents. On showing a bottle, one of them called wine! wine! two of them immediately advanced, took the things and drank a little of the wine;[106] the governor also gave them two or three knives, he then returned to the boat, and told the gentlemen that remained in her, that he had not seen either Coalby or Banalong, and that his mind was not altogether satisfied with regard to their pacific intentions; at the same time desiring them to stay by the boat, and give a look out, and be ready in case of alarm. He then went forward accompanied by Capt. Collins. The officer in the boat frequently heard one of the natives call to Banalong, and acquaint him with the observations he had made upon those who were in the boat, which was kept upon her oars; presently one of the people came from the governor, and acquainted Mr. Waterhouse, the officer left in the boat, that both Coalby and Banalong were amongst them, had asked for him, and that Governor Phillips desired he would join them. He immediately accompanied the messenger to the governor, whom he found with Capt. Collins, in a close conversation with two natives who were unarmed.[107]

Mr. Waterhouse[108] went up, but did not recognize Banalong, till he was pointed out to him, he was altered so much, nor could he then persuade himself that he was the same.[109] On the question being repeatedly asked, where was Banalong, he grew rather impatient, and was going off: however a bottle being shewn him, and being asked the name of 'THE KING;' having observed, when at the governor's house, his *majesty's health drank* in the first glass after dinner, and he had been taught to repeat the word before he drank his own glass, he imagined the liquor was called the king: and when he afterwards came to know that it was wine, yet he would frequently call it king. This convinced the gentlemen[110] that it was no other but their old acquaintance Banalong; and every method was tried to induce him to go down to the boat, but he always retired when any one approached nearer to him than he wished, so that they gradually got out of sight of the boat, when about a dozen natives placing themselves in a situation to prevent any surprise, Banalong and Coalby came among the gentlemen, and asked various questions relative to different transactions which had occurred at the settlement during their residence there. Banalong laid hold of Mr. Waterhouse by the neck, Coalby shook them all by the hand; a jacket being given to him he was puzzled how to put it on, and begged one of the gentlemen to do it for him.[111] Banalong had a very fine spear in his hand, which the governor asked him for, but he would not part with it.[112] During all this time the most perfect harmony and friendship seemed to subsist among the whole party, but the governor perceiving upwards of twenty closing round his party proposed returning to the boat, telling Banalong that he would shortly return, and bring him and Coalby a couple of hatchets, which pleased them extremely. The governor then went down to the beach, and the officers in the boat came on shore; the crew with their arms remained in the boat, as the natives by continuing their position, indicated some remaining symptoms of distrust; his excellency was afraid of alarming them. Banalong was very cheerful, and appeared transported at the sight of so many of his dear friends as he termed them, incessantly shaking hands all round. He pointed out a small fire near them, and said he would sleep there till their return. They were merry on their escape, and told them how Coalby got rid of the shackle by which he had been secured when at the settlement, and that if they had meant to keep them they should never "Nangora," fall asleep.[113]

The party now began to move towards the boat, when a stout native[114] who had been standing at a distance, approached; at first he shewed strong indications of fear, which soon subsided on being treated in the same familiar manner as Coalby and Banalong, and he became tolerably conversable. He shewed a wound which he had received in his back with a spear; this also put Banalong upon shewing that he had also been wounded in several parts of the body since he had quitted the settlement; one dangerous, over the left eye, nearly healed: these wounds he said, were received in a recounter with a neighbouring tribe near Botany Bay.[115]

The party still proceeded towards the beach where detained by Banalong, who continued teazing them about the hatchets that were to be sent him; and he pointed out the stout native who had retired about thirty yards distance, whom he appeared anxious should be noticed. The governor advanced towards him, and upon the savage indicating that he would not be approached, he laid down his sword still going towards him with extended arms, to assure him that he was unarmed.

As the governor drew near, the native seized a spear that lay concealed in the grass,[116] fixed it in the throwing stick, and for some moments appeared to stand on his defence. There being not the least reason to suppose that he would throw it without provocation, his excellency continued to advance, calling out, "Weree, Weree,"[117] a term used by them when they [meet] with a thing not to be done which displeases them: notwithstanding which the native discharged his spear with surprising velocity, and immediately ran off. In their retreat to the woods many spears were thrown, but the only one which took effect was unfortunately the first, which struck our much beloved governor. It entered his right shoulder, just above the collar bone, and came out behind, about three inches lower under the blade bone.[118]

The gentleman[119] near the governor concluded that he was mortally wounded, and feared, from the number of armed men that began to shew themselves from the woods, that it would be impracticable for them to reach the boat. The governor holding up the spear which trailed on the ground, endeavored to make his way to the beach, but its great length frequently stopped him: in this situation he desired some one, if possible to draw the spear out of his body, but it being barbed, it was found impracticable; they then with great difficulty broke it, and disembarrassed him from the greater part; he then drew a pistol from his pocket and discharged it at them, and found the apprehension of there being more fire arms among the party, kept a respectable distance; and the governor carried between two people, reached the boat without any further molestation, immediately after their arrival at Sydney, the surgeon was sent for, Mr. Balmain,[120] the first who arrived at the governor's house, after examining the wound, relieved every body from the most painful suspense, by assuring them, that alarming as the situation of the governor might appear, he did not fear any fatal consequences from it, he extracted the point of the spear, dressed the wound, and to the admiration of every body, in six weeks he was enabled to go about.

Governor Phillips still desirous of being reconciled to the natives,[121] did not harbour any resentment against them on account of the late transaction, which he affirmed to have proceeded from a sudden impulse of fear rather than treachery, and had given the necessary directions that none of them should be fired at or any ways molested, unless they provoked it, by throwing spears or any other hostilities.—Nanbarre, the boy,[122] who had now become a tolerable interpreter; attended some of the officers, who were upon a shooting excursion, near the spot where the accident to the governor had happened, a number of the natives appeared on an eminence at a short distance; being asked who it was that threw the spear at the governor, they named a man of the tribe who dwelt to the northward; that his name was Carrigal.[123] Nanbarre who also desired to enquire after Banalong and Coalby, when they pointed to some people at a distance—One of them threw a spear but with no mischievous design taking care it fell where nobody was standing. The girl Araboo was in the boat, and pointing to one of the natives, said he was her father,[124] and was very desirous of going to them; she had arrived at the age when her inclination began to tend towards the sex, and with great naivete and innocence told the officers that she wanted to be married. As she had no opportunity of a connexion of that kind in the clergyman's house where she dwelt, and it would be a difficult matter to keep her against her will, it was judged most prudent to permit her to go where she pleased, and she was told that as soon as some new cloaths should be made she should go, with which assurances she was perfectly satisfied to stay some time longer; during which great pains were taken to instruct her in English, that she might be enabled to explain our intentions towards her countrymen.[125]

The governor being sufficiently recovered to venture in a boat, went to the place where Banalong and his wife lived[126]—he found several natives on the spot, who told him that they were out a fishing, Araboo was in the boat, and her father being amongst them, a hatchet and some fish was given him, and he gave the governor a short spear[127] in return; they then perceived four canoes paddling towards them, in the foremost they perceived Banalong; the boat then lay on her oars, and they landed from their canoes; as soon as Banalong had secured his, he approached the boat, holding up his hand to shew he was unarmed.

Upon which the party landed from the boat, and he very readily joined them; he asked the governor where he was wounded, and said that he had quarreled with and beat the man who wounded him—being told that he would be killed if he was caught, he seemed no ways concerned, but desired it might be done—several presents were made him, and he wanted some also for his wife; but being told if she wanted them she must come and fetch them herself—in about half an hour she made her appearance; she was called Barangaroo, appeared older than him; a petticoat and several little presents were given to the lady, and a red jacket with a silver epaulet, which Banalong used to wear when at the settlement,[128] was given him, which delighted him exceedingly; he was asked if he would come and dine with the governor the next day, which he readily assented, and said that he would bring his wife and some friends with him.

Notwithstanding Banalong did not visit the governor according to his promise, he frequently joined the different parties he fell in with, although they were all armed, and would without the least fear go to the long boat, though he always saw muskets in her. His wife was generally with him in a canoe, and he intimated that he still intended to pay the governor a visit, but his suspicion of being detained had not been intirely done away; however the governor did not chuse to take him by force, as he still entertained hopes, that he would be soon reconciled to pass some of his time at Sydney, when he could be assured of being his own master, to go and come when he chused.

At length his excellency's wishes were accomplished; as he was going to Paramata, a native was seen standing at one of the points of the land, and as they rowed past him, he was asked were Banalong was, when he pointed to an island called Momill,[129] to which they rowed; and as they rowed near the rocks he came down to the boat accompanied by his wife and friends without the least sign of fear and distrust. They greedily took some bread that was given them, and the boat soon after pushed off and left them; from the confidence now evinced by this man there was little doubt but he would shortly trust himself at Sydney—Accordingly a few days after, the governor was passing in his boat, Banalong called him repeatedly from the opposite shore where he was with some of the officers; the surgeon, in whom he placed great confidence, persuaded him to go to the governor; he took three natives with him and was exceedingly pleased with the presents made them. It seems that Banalong's wife opposed his coming, and finding her tears and entreaties of no avail, she flew into a violent passion, and broke a fine fish gig of her husband's, for which she would have received a hearty drubbing, had it not been for the interference of the surgeon, who took them back to their residence on the north shore. Banalong appeared quite at ease and not under the least apprehension of being detained; he promised when he went away to bring his wife over, which he did two days after, accompanied by her sister and two other natives, they were followed by a third.—Blankets and clothing were given them, and each as much as they could eat.—Banalong dined with the governor, and drank his wine and coffee as formerly: his excellency bought a spear of one of them, and gave them to understand that spears, lines, or birds, or any thing they brought should be purchased, and at the same time promised him a shield, for which he was to bring a spear in return. The next day they came over for the shield, but it was not finished; two of these men were owned by Araboo, as her brothers, and for whom she procured two hatchets, the most desirable thing that can be given them. Banalong came the next day for his present; his comrades who accompanied him went away in a short time, but he staid for dinner, and left Sydney Cove highly delighted with his shield, which being made of a good substantial hide[130] and covered with tin, was likely to resist the stroke of a spear.

The girl who had been near eighteen months[131] in the colony with the clergyman's wife, was so impatient to get away that at last it was consented to; and the day after she had left the settlement, she was seen in the canoe naked, however she put on the petticoat before she joined the clergyman and some others who went to visit her: she appeared much pleased with her liberty, and the boy Nanbarre, who was of the party, wished to stay with the natives all the night, he was accordingly left behind, but the next morning returned to the settlement, and having fared but indifferently, he did not think proper to repeat his visit. The natives now visited the colony daily; one morning Banalong came very early and breakfasted with the governor, and on taking his leave told him he was going a great way off, but should return in three days, with the two young men who were with him; and it was conjectured that they were going to fight with some other tribe.—When Banalong returned from his expedition, he immediately waited on the governor, with whom he dined according to custom: after dinner he related the cause of his absence: that he had been to fight a man who formally wounded him: he said his shield was a good one, and that his spear had pierced the shield and the arm of his antagonist:[132] he also said that the people he had been to fight with, had killed one of the convicts, who had been some time missing.[133] Araboo, the native girl, returned to the colony after a few weeks absence, with some officers who had been down the river, and seemed perfectly happy in the opportunity of getting from the party she had been with. She said she had lived three days with the young man she wished to marry, but that he had another wife who was jealous of her and beat her.[134]

The governor had built a small house at Paramata[135] (the one I now occupy) and was going to remain there some time when several of the natives were desirous of accompanying him.—His excellency took three of them in his boat; but Banalong going to fetch his cloak was detained by his wife; but as they were going out of the cove he appeared on the rocks, and got into the boat in spite of her threats and entreaties. No sooner was the boat put off, than she went to the canoe, which was a new one and stove it, and breaking the paddles, threw them into the water, she then went to the hut probably with an intent of committing more mischief. Banalong endeavored to pacify her, telling her that he would not be more than one day absent; but all would not do and he was put on shore—The party then proceeded to Rose-Hill, with Coalby and two other natives, none of whom ever opened their lips during the altercation: indeed they are never known to interfere in any dispute which does not concern them.

The natives slept that night at Paramata, and though some were in a sickly state, and wanted for nothing, yet the next morning they were very anxious of returning;[136] a boat was accordingly sent down with them, by the return of which it was generally expected that news would have been received of Barangaroo's being again in the hands of the surgeon for her sreaks;[137] but to the surprise of every body the next day they made their appearance, and it seemed that he had not beaten her; whether he had with-held the usual correction from what had been formerly said to him by the governor, or some other cause, could not be discovered, however a reconciliation had taken place, and they both dined with his excellency in great good humour. No sooner was the dinner ended than the lady wished to return, and Banalong said she would cry if they detained her, so that they sent a boat down in the evening with her.[138]

On the return of the governor to Sydney, not having been long absent, he learned that his game-keeper had been dangerously wounded by one of the natives with a spear. It appeared that he went out with three others, one of them was a serjeant, and in the heat of the day one of them retired to a hut they had made with boughs, and laid down to sleep. One of them awaking, heard a noise in the bushes which he supposed to be some animal; but on awaking his comrades, and coming out of the hut, four natives started up from amongst the bushes, and ran away with all their speed; the game-keeper thinking he knew one of them who had been at Sydney, followed them without a gun, notwithstanding the positive order that had been given for no one to trust himself with the natives unarmed,[139] calling on them to stop and he would give them some bread; and observing one who followed them to have a gun in his hand, desired him to lay it down, as it only frightened the natives, and they would do no harm: he had now advanced before his companions, and was not ten paces from one of the natives who stopped short, and finding they were unarmed, fixed his spear on the throwing-stick in a moment, and threw it at the man nearest him: it entered his left side, and penetrated to the lower lobe of his lungs; it was barbed and consequently could not be extracted till a supperation took place.—Immediately after throwing the spear, the native fled into the woods, and was seen no more.

They were ten miles from Sydney when this accident happened,[140] and it was with the greatest difficulty that the wounded man was brought to the settlement. Being questioned whether he had provoked the natives to this violence, he desired to have the clergyman sent for, to whom he confessed he had been a very bad man; and at the same time declared that he had never killed or wounded any native, except one, who had thrown a spear at him.[141]

Banalong and Araboo repeatedly said that it was the tribes which lived about Botany Bay who threw the spears, and killed the white man, yet as it was evident that they generally received some provocation from our people, the governor was loath to proceed to extremities whilst there was any possibility of avoiding it; especially as he had been at so much trouble in bringing them to repose some confidence in him: and a good understanding with them was essentially necessary to the happiness and prosperity of the colony.[142] Many of the natives now daily visited the settlement and were all well received; it was no unusual thing for the mothers to leave their children behind them for several days, without ever inquiring after them; and if any of them were going where the children would be an encumbrance, they made no scruple of leaving them at Sydney; Banalong, Coalby and two or three other took up their quarters there, four days a week, and all joined in the same story, and desired those natives might be killed who threw it; but governor Phillips had his suspicions that there was a great deal of art and cunning in Banalong; he had lately been seen amongst those people he now wished to be killed, he said one of them had sung a song in praise of his house, the governor, and the white men at Sydney: and he said those people would throw no more spears, as they were now all friends; this was but a few days after he was so solicitous with the governor to kill them all.

What was rather extraordinary they all knew the man that threw the spear; they said his name was Pemnlaway, of the Bejigal tribe;[143] Banalong and Coalby said they would bring him to the governor, and went off the next day, as it was supposed to Botany Bay; and his excellency, upon a report that a number of natives had been seen armed about the mouth of the harbour, went down to look out, he met Coalby there, who returned to Sydney with him, but did not seem inclined to give himself any trouble about Pemnlaway, but after dinner took his leave, saying he was going to Botany Bay to meet his wife. Banalong was absent several days; they said he was gone to assist at the ceremony of drawing a front tooth from some young men, among the Camaragals, which gave rise to the idea that the tooth is extracted as a kind of tribute.[144]

Araboo now resided with the Camaragals; when she left the clergyman's she promised to return with her sweetheart and his wife;

Plate 24 'Manhood', from *The History of New South Wales. By George Barrington* (1802).
Source: Rare Books Collection, The Library, Australian National University, Canberra.

Plate 25 'Courtship', from *The History of New South Wales. By George Barrington* (1802).
Source: Rare Books Collection, The Library, Australian National University, Canberra.

hence it appears evident that when they can procure two wives, the custom of their country does not prohibit their having them; though this custom seems very unreasonable, as the women bear no proportion to the men in point of number. It is believed that most of their wives are taken by force, or surprise, from the tribes which they are at variance; consequently their enemies retaliate, and from the disproportion of the females to the males must have been more successful in their Sabinical expeditions.[145]

Spears being frequently thrown at the settlers; it became absolutely necessary that a stop should be put to it, though his excellency wished to do it with as little severity as possible, yet he was convinced that a severe example must be made to have the desired effect. Accordingly a party was sent out, consisting of fifty privates, besides officers, they were directed to proceed to the spot where the man was wounded; and to search for the natives who dwelt thereabouts, some of whom were to be secured and brought prisoners.[146]—Spears and all other weapons which they happened to meet with were ordered to be destroyed and left on the spot, that they might see that it was intended as a punishment for them.—Particular attention was to be paid to the women and children, who were not to be molested on any account whatever; and as the governor wished to impress the idea that no deceit was ever practiced, and that they might depend on having protection whenever it was offered: he ordered that none of the party should hold up their hands, which is the signal of friendship, nor to answer such signal of friendship, if made by the natives.

Notwithstanding the most vigilant endeavours, the party was not able to get near any of them, as they made off at their approach, and eluded the pursuit. They saw Coalby near Botany Bay, where he was fishing, at whom they fired several shots. They returned to Sydney without any success; but the governor being determined if possible to make an example of some of them, again sent the party with the same orders they had before received.—They left Sydney towards the close of the evening with hopes of surprising some of the natives at their fires, but were disappointed.

It was near a fortnight before Banalong made his appearance, when he brought his wife with him; he said he had been with the Camaragals, that several young men had undergone the operation of having their front teeth drawn and Tattowing, which is making those scars which are considered as ornamental, by the natives.[147] The scars made by cutting two lines through the skin parallel to each other, with a sharp shell or flint, and stripping off the intermediate skin, the operation is repeated till the wound rises considerably above the surrounding flesh, when it is suffered to heal over. These painful embellishments are not very common among the women; Banalong shewed a throwing stick which had been cut for the purpose of knocking out the front teeth; and it was generally supposed he had been employed in that office. He was on good terms with the Camaragals, and he said they were all good people; when he was asked if he had seen the man who threw the spear at the governor, he said yes, and had slept in the same cove with him; so that his former account of having quarrelled with, and beat him, was not believed. Barangaroo, who had been with him on this occasion, was painted in a different manner from what she had been before, and there appeared to be a great deal of attention bestowed on her: her cheeks nose and upper-lip, were rubbed over with red ochre, on which, and under the eyes, were laid spots of white clay; the small of her back was likewise rubbed with red ochre, and by her deportment seemed desirous of shewing that she was finer than common. Shortly after, two of the convicts being fishing, Banalong finding they had no arms in his boat, went alongside in his canoe, and robbed them of the fish they had taken: his wife and sister being in the canoe, and having several spears, the convicts made no resistance. In consequence of this robbery, orders were given that no boat in future should go out of the cove unarmed.[148]

The next time the natives came to the settlement, they were told that if any more spears were thrown they would all be killed; but the threats did not seem to make the smallest impression on them.[149] Banalong coming soon after he was charged with taking the fish from the two white men; he denied the charge with great assurance, asserting that he was a great distance from the place at the time; but when the people were confronted with him, he endeavored to justify himself, but with so insolent an air, that he rather aggravated than excused the offence: he frequently mentioned the man who had been wounded, and threatened revenge: but on recollecting, he offered his hand to the governor, which being refused he grew violent, and seemed inclined to make use of his stick, a centinal was called in, as it was feared he might commit some extravagance that would oblige his excellency to order him to be put to death, for his behavior was savage and insolent in the extreme, and would have met with instant punishment in any other person, but they wished to bring him to reason without having recourse to violent measures; and the governor being unwilling to destroy that confidence he had been at so much pains to create in Banalong, which the slightest punishment would have done; he was, therefore, desired to come near the governor, but he refused, turning upon his heel, and went away. And as he passed the wheel-wright's shop, the workmen being at dinner, he stole a hatchet.[150]

The natives continued to visit Sydney after Banalong's bad behaviour, who conducted himself in such a manner as gave great reason to suppose he would never return; this however was not the case, for having previously visited the fishing boat, to know if Governor Philips was still angry with him, and if he would shoot him; he appeared very desirous to know if he might go to the governor's house, at the same time naming a man who had stole the hatchet, and denied having used any threats; however, not being pleased with the answers that were given him, he went away, but returned in a few days, and went to the governor's, who happening to see him come to the gate ordered him away.[151]

Governor Philips had been very desirous of learning the reason that the females had two of the joints of the little finger cut off and of seeing in what manner the operation was performed; he had now an opportunity of gratifying a part of his wish: Coalby's wife coming to the settlement with a new born female, brought her infant to the governor's house, and being told that his excellency would be present at the operation, it was accordingly performed. A ligature was applied round the second joint of the little finger, but two days after they brought the child again, the ligature was broken or taken off; this being told the mother, she took out some hairs from the head of an officer who was present, and bound them

EAST VIEW of SYDNEY.

Published by M. Jones, Paternoster Row, Feb. 3, 1803.

V. Woodthorpe fᵗ

Plate 26 'East View of Sydney', from *The History of New South Wales*. By George Barrington (1802).
Source: Rare Books Collection, The Library, Australian National University, Canberra.

very tight round the finger, after some time a gangreen[152] took place; and though the child seemed uneasy when it was touched, it did not cry, nor was any attention paid to it after the ligature was applied. This bandage was continued till the finger was ready to drop off, when its parents took it to the surgeon, who at their request, separated it with a knife.[153]

Banalong was again admitted into the favor of the governor after an absence of 3 weeks,[154] during which time he had been very active in rendering services to a boats crew, several of whom must have been lost but for his exertions, this was considered as a full atonement for his bad behaviour.—In consequence of this, the number of visitors increased and the governor's yard became their head quarters.—Their medical operations partook more of the juggling than of the Esculapian system:[155] Coalby had formerly been wounded with a fish-gig below the breast, and though it must have been done many years, as it was extremely difficult to perceive the scar; yet it was supposed as he felt some pain from the straps of a knapsack, which he carried when out on an excursion with the governor; and had travelled two or three days with it on his shoulders; and the straps pressing against his breast, he complained of pain there. He applied to an old man and his son, who had joined them in the excursion, for relief, and they prepared to perform the cure:[156] the son began the ceremony by taking a mouthful of water which he squirted on the part affected, and then applying his mouth, began to suck as long as he could without taking breath, which appeared to make him sick, and when he arose, for his patient was extended at full length on the grass, he walked about for some minutes, he then repeated the suction three times, and appeared, by drawing in his stomach to feel the same pain he pretended to extract from his patient; and having picked up a bit of stick or stone, but with so little slight of hand, that it was obvious to the whole party, he pretended to throw something away into the water. He threw something away which must have been what he picked up, but Coalby after the ceremony was over, said it was what he had sucked out of his breast, which was understood to be the barbs of a fish-gig, as he made use of the word Bullerdoul,[157] but the governor was of a different opinion, and thought he meant two pains. Before this business was finished, the doctor felt the patient's back below the shoulder, and seemed to apply his fingers as if he twiched something out; after which he sat down by the patient, and put his right arm round his back, the older man at the same time, sat down with his arm on the other side of the patient, with his face the contrary way, and clasped him round the breast with his right arm; each of them held one of the patient's hands: they continued in this situation several minutes, straining him very close, and thus the ceremony ended; when Coalby said he was well. He gave his worsted night cap, and share of his supper as a fee to his doctors, and being asked if they were both of a faculty, he said yes, and a little boy that was with them was a doctor too; from whence it was supposed that the power of healing is hereditary.[158]

As the natives frequently caught more fish than they could immediately use, great pains have been taken to induce them to barter it at Paramata for bread, vegetables, &c. Several of them carried on this traffic, and there was reason to hope that a tolerable fish-market would soon be established;[159] among those who brought their fish was a young man[160] who lived some months with the governor, but had left the settlement from time to time to go a fishing; his canoe was a good one, and being the first he was ever master of, he was a little proud of it, and accordingly valued it highly. Strict orders had been given that their canoes should not be touched, but in a very short time this amity and good understanding was intercepted by some villians, who had stove the canoe of the young man before mentioned. The moment he discovered the injury done him, he flew to the governor's in a violent rage, said the white men had broken his canoe, and that he would kill them; he had his throwing-stick and several spears in his hand, and his hair, face, arms, and breast were painted red, which is a sign of the most implacable anger.

The offenders were soon discovered, and severely flogged in the presence of Balderry, but he was far from being satisfied, till he was told that one of them had been hanged. During their examination he appeared very impatient, and said it belonged to him to punish the injury he had received. About a month after, when it was thought he had been amply compensated by various presents which the governor had given him; yet he took the first opportunity of revenging himself, which plainly shews that these people do not readily forgive an injury. A convict who had strayed from the settlement was met by two of the natives and had scarce passed them when he was wounded in the back with a spear,[161] and before he could recover himself received a second wound in the side; however he got away, and as they did not attempt to stop him to get his clothes, or take any thing from him there was no doubt but the destruction of the canoe was the cause of this attack, as especially the same evening the natives were seen round a fire, and being asked who it was that wounded the white man, they immediately answered "Baldberry". It is not a little remarkable that these people always tell the names of those who throw the spears at the colonists, or who have stole any thing from the settlement, if they are asked, though they are conscious that you mean to punish them, it might be thought to proceed from a principal of adhering to truth, did they not destroy this opinion by invariably denying any thing they may be charged with, though you see them commit the offence, and lay the blame on another who is not present.[162]

The destruction of this canoe was a most unfortunate accident, as it intimidated the natives from carrying their fish to Paramata; and no canoe visited the settlement for some time after; and besides, the governor wished to attach Balderry to himself, intending to take him to England when he returned. After absenting himself a month or five weeks Balderry began to make inquiries of the various parties he met, whether the governor was still angry, he was answered in the affirmative, and told that he would be killed for wounding a white man: yet this did not deter him from coming into the cove in a canoe, the governor upon being made acquainted with his appearance, ordered a party of marines to go and secure him. Governor Philips saw Banalong speaking to the young man in his canoe, and gave him to understand that Balderry should be killed; upon which he called out that the governor was still angry: on hearing this Balderry paddled off very briskly to the opposite side of the harbour and appeared to set them at defiance, and talked of spearing.—These people are very resolute and when provoked set very little value on their lives, so that they can be revenged; they ever contrive to be even with you, whether you praise or threaten, and whenever a blow is given they are sure to return it, though their lives should pay for it.[163] A number of natives being arrived at Sydney, amongst whom there was upwards of thirty women and children, they were treated with bread and rice as usual, they informed his excellency that Balderry was on the opposite side of the cove, with a party of his friends armed. Whether his coming after what had passed proceeded from a supposition that he should not be punished, or that he was safe whilst surrounded by so many of his countrymen, it was thought necessary to order him to be taken, as soon as the visitants should be gone, for as Balderry could not be seized without their hearing the dispute, it was probable they would suppose themselves in danger, especially as many of the guests were strangers.[164]

As soon as they had taken their leave a party of soldiers were ordered after the delinquent, but before they got sight of him, he had been advertised of his danger by Nanberre, who hearing what was going forward had left the place; a serjeant and a party were sent after him; in their way they met several of the natives, who joined them in a friendly manner, but while they were talking to the serjeant, one of them had the audacity to attempt to wrest a firelock from one of the soldiers; however, he failed in the attempt, but immediately after a spear was thrown, supposed to be by Balderry; two muskets were now fired among the natives which wounded one of them in the leg, but unfortunately neither of the offenders. A strong party were immediately ordered to some brick fields, where a pretty numerous body of them had assembled; but Nanbarre, ever faithful to his countrymen, on seeing the soldiers form on the parade, took to the woods, and stripping himself that he might not be known, joined the natives and put them on their guard: after which he returned, and saw the governor pass with some officers whilst he was hid in a bush: he afterwards met an officer's servant, and asked where the governor and soldiers were going, on being told, he laughed and said they were too late for the people were all gone.[165]

Banalong came in soon after with his wife and though he was told that the soldiers were gone to take Balderry, yet the intelligence did not prevent him eating a hearty dinner, and when he went away he left a large bundle of spears, fish-gigs,[166] and various other articles, under the care of the governor.—As the natives knew that the governor only meant to punish those who threw the spears, the late disagreement did not in the least interrupt their visits, and they called on us with the same familiarity as if nothing had happened. They were asked what became of the wounded man; they said he was gone to his tribe; that the wound was of little consequence, and would soon be healed.

Barangaroo, the wife of Banalong, was now near her time of lying-in, when the colonists had an opportunity of seeing their preparations on the occasion: she had two nets hanging from her neck, one of which being new, the governor was desirous of obtaining; and it was given him after she had taken a large piece of tea tree out of it, nicely folded up, and which was intended to lay her infant upon, and which is the only preparation previous to the ceremony of an infant's introduction to the world, that is made by lying-in women in this country. The bark of the tea tree is thick in proportion to the size of the trunk, and is composed of a great number of layers of very thin bark, not unlike in appearance to a birch tree, but so exquisitely soft that nothing this country affords can be better calculated for the purpose for which it is intended. Banalong, however, desired to have a blanket for the child, which was given him, and the next day a net being made after the English manner, which was more acceptable to his wife than the one she had given to the governor. Banalong informed the governor that his wife intended to do him the honor of lying-in at his house, this favour his excellency declined, telling him she would be much better accommodated at the hospital, so they took up their quarters there.[167]

Banalong had frequently solicited the governor to receive Balderry again into favor, but was always refused: however on being told that the poor fellow was extremely ill, the surgeon was desired to go and see him; he found him in a high fever, and the first question he asked was, whether the governor continued to be angry with him, and if he would let him go to the hospital to be cured. Banalong, who went with the surgeon, returned to the governor, who told him he was not angry now, and he might bring his companion to the settlement, he said he would, and early the next morning Balderry made his appearance. At first he was under great apprehension, but the governor taking him by the hand, and promising that when he was recovered he should live with him again—his fear subsided—he appeared very ill—and went with the surgeon and Banalong to the hospital.[168]

           ✻   ✻   ✻

I have been thus minute detailing the behaviour of the natives, and the persevering diligence and inexhaustible patience of governor Philips, in conciliating and familiarizing them in the infancy of the colony, that should they hereafter attain any degree of civilization, posterity may know to whom they are indebted for the extrication of numberless tribes from the rudest barbarism, thereby adding to society the inhabitants of a country which occupies a section of the globe to greater extent than all Europe, and capable of becoming a great and powerful Empire.[169]

With regard to religion, they sing a hymn or song of joy, from day break to sun-rise; but we have not yet been able to discover whether they have any particular object to whom they pay adoration; neither do any of the celestial bodies seem to occupy more of their attention than any of the animals which inhabit this extensive country, yet they do not appear intirely ignorant of a future state, as they say the dead are in the grave and their bodies in the clouds.[170] They burn their dead, for on opening a new made grave, a quantity of white ashes were found, which appeared to have been but lately deposited there; among the ashes were found part of a human jaw-bone, and a piece of a skull which had not been sufficiently burnt, to prevent its being perfectly ascertained. The grave was not deep, but the earth was raised as high round it as the common graves are in England.[171]

Araboo once went into fits on seeing a falling star, and said that every body would be destroyed; although some that were present insisted that she particularly alluded to the "Murray roway," the Sirins, who was lost some time after at Norfolk island.[172] From Banalong we understood that they believe in apparitions, which they call "Mane".[173] He describes them as ascending from the earth with a horrid noise, seizing any one in its way by the throat; he says apparitions singe the hat and beards of those to

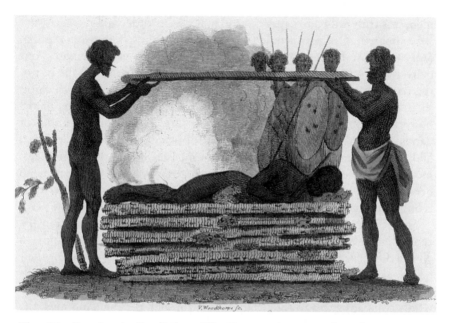

Plate 27 'Burying the Dead', from *The History of New South Wales. By George Barrington* (1802).
Source: Rare Books Collection, The Library, Australian National University, Canberra.

whom they appear, which he said was a very painful operation; rubbing the face after every application of the fire-brand.

Their principal diversion is that of dancing, for which ceremony they prepare themselves with more than ordinary attention; they are all in their birth-day suits, like so many Adams and Eves; without even a fig-tree-leaf to parry the inquisitive glance of the curious Europian. The young women employ all their art in decorating the young men, who are chiefly ornamented with streaks of white, drawn with pipe-clay, and in different forms, according to the taste of the man himself or the lady who adorns him. They are as emulous of appearing fine as the most finished petitmaitre preparing for the birth day ball of their favorite mistress.— Their paint cannot be applied without moistening, and the lady, in drawing the streaks down her face, which is the most essential part of the decoration, spits in the face of her friend whom she is adorning, from time to time, as the ochre or clay gets dry. Their dances are always at the close of the day, as they prefer the fire-light to that of the sun, on these occasions.[174]

The dance begins by a few young boys, and is increased by the men and women gradually falling in, to the number of thirty or forty;[175] but mostly men; it is truly wild and savage, yet in many parts order and regularity are very apparent. One man would frequently single himself out from the rest, and running round the whole of the performers, sing out some expressions delivered in a curious tone of voice, he would then fall in with the rest of the dancers, who alternately led forward in the centre; and they exhibit their utmost skill and dexterity in the most difficult contortions of the body, which must, in their opinion, constitute the principal beauties of dancing: one of the most striking is, that of placing their feet wide apart, and by an extraordinary exertion of the muscles of the thighs and legs, move their knees in a trembling and very astonishing manner, such as no person in the colony could any ways imitate: of course such practice is required to arrive at any degree of perfection in this single motion.

Sometimes they form a circle, with some distinguished person in the centre; at other times all the dancers have green boughs in their hands; in all the different figures, they generally finish by a certain number of their principal dancers advancing to the front, and going through the difficult part of the dance, and quivering motion of the knees, upon which the whole company faces to the front, and go through the same motions, the expertest being generally in the centre. Their music consists of two pieces of very hard wood, one of which the musician holds to his breast in the manner of a violin, and strikes it with the other, in tolerable time.—The performer sings the whole time of the dance, assisted by boys and girls who are seated at his feet, and by a manner of crossing the thighs, form a hollow between them and their belly, upon which they beat time with the flat of their hand, which makes an odd though not a disagreeable sound.[176]

They are very dextrous in striking fish, the spear of the gig with which they take them is about ten feet in length, but they can increase it by joints as we do our fishing rods in England: they have several prongs barbed with the bone of a fish or some animal. The fisher lies across the canoe, his face in the water, and his fish gig ready for darting; thus he lies motionless, and by his face being beneath the survice, he can see the fish distinctly; in this manner they strike the fish with great certainty. The women are chiefly employed with lines and hooks, the lines manufactured from the barks of trees, the hooks commonly of pearl or different shells; the talons of birds of prey they sometimes make use of, but the former are most esteemed. The women are frequently seen in a miserable canoe with two or three children, fishing the whole day in the edge of a surf, that it would terify an old seaman to trust himself near it in a good stout boat. The men are surprising divers, and remain a long time in the surfs where their canoes cannot live, whatever they bring to the surface they throw it

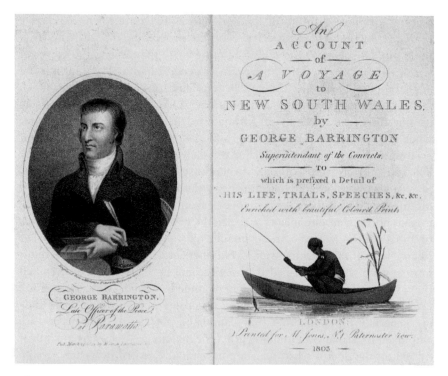

Plate 28 Frontispiece and title page of *An Account of a Voyage to New South Wales, by George Barrington, Superintendant of the Convicts* (1803).
Source: Rare Books Collection, The Library, Australian National University, Canberra.

on shore. Having a fire ready kindled for cooking, they broil or roast of their food; they have not the least conception of boiling, for one of the natives, watching an opportunity when nobody was attending the kettle, plunged his hand into the boiling water to take the fish, or course he was terribly scalded. They procure fire with great labour, by fixing the point end of a round stick into a hole made in a flat piece of wood, and whirling it round swiftly with both hands, sliding them up and down till the operator is fatigued, when he is relieved by some of his companions, each taking his turn till the fire is produced; from the labour attending this process it is no wonder they are seldom seen without a piece of lighted wood.[177] But of all their customs that of making love would be the farthest from meeting the approbation of *my* country women; the ceremony in this country is sound beating, which the lady receives as a matter of course, with all the meakness imaginable.[178]

We had now upwards of a 1000 acres of cleared land at Paramata; 350 of which were in wheat and maize; but though we had frequent showers of rain, yet, not in sufficient quantities to compensate for the excessive draught which had been experienced in the proceeding months; and from the ground being new, and requiring more work than was in the power of the settlers to bestow on it, the grain in general had a very unpromising appearance.—There are about 200 acres laid out in gardens, as much more prepared for turnips and potatoes, and the remainder closed in feeding cattle; we are badly off for manure, the colony will flourish better when it is stocked with cattle, the ground being infinitely too poor in itself even to produce crops sufficient for us solely to depend for subsistence.[179] The sudden vicissitudes of the weather must also render our harvests very precarious, as well as prove injurous to the health of the new comers; it often happens that there is no change of from 40 to 50 degrees in one day, it is no unfrequent circumstance to see the country strewed with numbers of birds fallen from the trees, unable to support themselves from the intense heat of the meridian sun.[180] Numbers of convicts fall victims, but it must not be wholly ascribed to the weather, as the weak state in which they were, for the most part when landed, would, were it a more favourable climate, be attended with a considerable mortality; and they are generally too weak that they cannot be put to any labour, but are employed in weeding and pulling grass for thatching, we have frequently 4 or 500 on the doctor's list, who are individually visited every day by the surgeon; upwards of 50 have died in a month, in the generality of whom nature appears entirely exhausted, and many of them were so fairly worn out, that they expired without a groan, and to all appearance did not experience the least degree of pain.[181]

From a most humane sugesttion of Captain Parker, of the Gorgon, the governor issued orders for a regular survey to be taken of the condition of the convicts on their landing from the different transports; and a strict investigation taking place, it appeared that some of the captains had very much abridged their unfortunate passengers of the allowance stipulated by government for their subsistance, and by this inhuman practice they had been literally starved to death. A strong and pointed representation of this circumstance was sent home to government, which will I hope put an effectual stop to such nefarious proceedings.[182]

Some of the convicts had entertained an idea that they could range along the coast until they reached some of the Chinese settlements, subsisting on oysters and other shell-fish, being told that there was a copper coloured tribe 150 miles to the northward, who were more civilized than they were at present with, who transacted with the Dutch at Timur, where they would be free. With these notions many set off from Sydney Cove and Rose Hill, but after a few days straggling, some were taken and others of their own accord, induced by the imperative command of hunger; some were supposed to be still lurking in the woods, afraid of being punished, the governor less inclined to punish than to convince them of their error, promised pardon to every person who'd return within five days, declaring that he would punish those who should be taken after. Several returned, sensible of the lenity shewn them, and some talked of repelling force by force, they were informed that no mercy would be shewn them, and any that were near those that might be so disposed would be considered as principals, and treated accordingly.[183]

The purchases I had made at the Cape, as well as the presents I had brought from England, enabled me to furnish the officers and settlers with articles that could not be had of the ships, so that in the short time I had collected the following stock:—a fowl, in pig—two fine porkers—a young she goat and two kids—an English dung-hill cock, three laying hens, and one with a brood of chickens and young ducks—these, with a kangaroo, which I had been at infinate pains in rearing myself, and a convict woman servant, and her son Timothy, a youth between twelve and thirteen, a tractable and useful lad, comprise the whole family.—Having always had a strong prediliction for agriculture, the garden employs a great deal of my time, and now is as prosperous and flourishing as any in the colony. Governor Philips when he visited Rose Hill, took great delight in it, and gave me much praise for its improvement, as well as for the appearance and spirit of industry manifested in the convicts under my superintendance.[184]

Having contracted an intimacy with a young man who had taken one of the farms on the northern boundary, about four miles from Paramata, I generally walk over once or twice a week; as I was returning from thence one afternoon with my boy Tim, (who having evinced a great partiality for me,) was now my constant companion; a large male Kangaroo crossed the path just before us; I immediately took the gun from the boy, fired at the animal, and disable one of his hind legs, which very much impended his flight, however he preserved his distance for near an hour, when getting a fair shot at him, I lodged a ball in the back part of his head, which effectually did his business.

Upon examining our prize I found it would be impossible for us to get it home without help, we, therefore, searched for a place to conceal it till the next afternoon, when I meant to return for it with a couple of men; a few paces from whence it lay we perceived a cavity on the slope of a deep ravine, to which we dragged the carcase, and covering it with stones and grass, began to think of making the best of our way to the settlement. The sun was now setting, and I began to be alarmed at being so far from home. In the eagerness of our pursuit I forgot to take my bearings by my pocket

ENTRANCE OF PARAMATTA RIVER.

Plate 29 'Entrance of Paramatta River', from *The History of New South Wales. By George Barrington* (1802).
Source: Rare Books Collection, The Library, Australian National University, Canberra.

compass, and the day closing ere we had reached any known path, increased my apprehensions in the extreme.[185] Poor Tim, though half dead with fatigue endeavoured to keep up my spirits, which he perceived were much agitated. 'He was certainly sure,' he said, that we were in the right road, and that we should get home time enough to muster the people at nine, the hour fixed for that purpose, and that if we were obliged to sleep in the woods, why, he could cut some grass for my bed, and stand centinel with the gun while I lay down, for he was not afraid to fire; and besides my dear master, you know the natives are so afraid of guns, that should they come, I only need to shew it, and they'll be off like a shot. The boy's courage and fidelity charmed me, and put me to the blush to think I had to little command of myself, as not to conceal my uneasiness from him.

After rambling for near two hours, we could not perceive that we were any nearer home than at the sun set, but rather conjectured we had taken a different route, as we did not recollect a single object that now presented itself, it being a fine star light night we could distinguish the river at some distance thro' the trees, but presented a different appearance to any we had yet seen, we quickened our pace with the hopes of speedily reaching its banks, when to my great mortification, we were stopped by a deep ravine, I now abandoned all thoughts of reaching the settlement, and as the poor boy was nearly exhausted with fatigue determined to pass the night on the spot.

We soon found a hut inhabited by the natives when hunting, as I had no apprehensions of their returning, the hunting season having just closed. I got a light from a flash of powder, and in a few minutes kindled a comfortable fire. In the corner of the hut was a bundle of grass ready dryed which we spread to lie down on, but I could not prevail on the boy to think of sleep: no, if I would trust him with the gun he would keep watch. Not being inclined to sleep myself, I took a book from my pocket, and by firelight endeavoured to amuse myself till day break, I had not perused above half a dozen pages ere poor Tim had fallen into a sound sleep, how long it was before I had followed his example, for how long I should have continued in it is difficult to determine, had I not been awoke by an acute pain in one of my hands, which I found was occasioned by the biting of some ants, whom I had accidentally molested in my sleep: I called Tim, and sallied forth, following the winding of the ravine about a mile, we arrived at its termination, and perceiving a break in the high lands before us, through which I distinctly saw Rose Hill, about six or seven miles distant, this prospect revived our spirits, which were beginning to lag, with the reflection that if we escaped every other danger, that of being starved to death was inevitable, unless we could extricate ourselves from the labyrinth in which we were involved.

Having set the spot by my compass, I found it bore W. S. W. and were proceeding slowly through the thicket, when we were alarmed by a deep groan, apparently but a few paces distant; so unlooked for a murmering sound revetted us to the spot.—Not being immediately able to perceive from whence the groan issued, I advanced with great caution about a dozen paces when I discovered a cave in the side of the rock: I was at first for retreating, but on recollecting that I might render some service to the afflicted, and that I equally stood in need of assistance, or perhaps might perish with hunger, I examined the priming of my gun, forced Tim with difficulty behind me, and approaching the entrance of the cave, a most interesting scene presented itself to my view: a young creature seated on a jet of the rock, mournfully contemplating the extended body of a man whose expiring groan had just pierced our ears: all her faculties were so absorbed with grief so that we were yet quite entirely unnoticed:[186] a sympathising sorrow pervaded all my frame; and I gave my gun to Tim, and made signs for him to retire, lest the sight should alarm her; when she

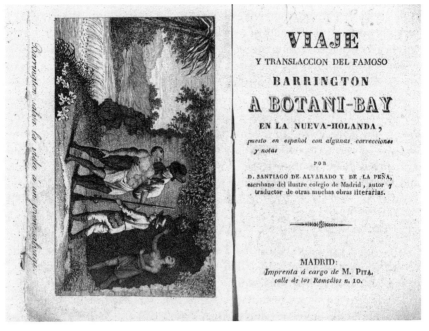

Plate 30 Frontispiece, 'Barrington salva la vida a en juven savage', from *Viaje y Translaccion del Famoso Barrington a Botani-Bay en la Nueva-Holanda* (published between 1798 and 1810)
Source: Ferguson Collection (F258a), by permission of the National Library of Australia, Canberra.

116

perceived me she gave a faint shriek and sunk motionless on the body. Observing a small pond a few paces from the cave, I sent the boy to bring some water in his hat, and gently moving her body, raised her up, supporting her in my arms; the water soon brought her too, when she raised her head, and regarded me with a look blended with grief and terror; I endeavoured by every sign I could suggest, to do away her fears and retired a few paces, leaving her at liberty to go from the cave had she chose.

Gaining confidence by my behaviour, she made me understand that the deceased was her brother, who, faint with loss of blood could not reach their habitation and night approaching they had turned from the road to shelter themselves in this cave. Examining the body I found a wound under the left pap made with a spear, part of it being barbed, remained in the wound;[187] I made her understand partly by signs, and partly by some words I had picked up, that I had unfortunately lost my way, and had been all night in the woods; she shook her head, and pointing to her brother, signifying that she could not leave him; but that their habitation was not far off, and making me observe a hill about two miles distant, she gave me to understand it was in their neighboured. I made signs to her that if she would go and acquaint her friends with her situation, I would watch by her brother till her return: her eyes glistened with joy as she gathered my meaning, and with an assenting inclination of her head, more eloquent and expressive of her feelings than in the power of the most refined language to convey, she quitted us with a celerity quickened by fraternal love, and in a few moments was out of sight.

Tim, who had been witness to several instances of the perfidy of the natives toward the settlers, strongly urged me to leave the body, and make the best of our way home. Roused by his solicitations, a momentary impulse of fear came all over me, and my mind half yielded to his importunity, but when casting my eyes upon the body, I thought I perceived it heave a feeble sigh, convinced me that life was not extinguished, the imperative call of humanity decided my operations, a death-like dew had bespread his face and limbs, which I dried with my handkerchief, and chafed his body with my hand; Tim most readily bore his part in this act of humanity, and a returning warmth encouraged us to double our efforts, in a few moments we perceived a faint pulsation, which gradually increased; at this juncture we were surprised by the return of the sister, accompanied by his father, another elderly man, and a boy about 12 years of age; seeing us busy about the body, they stopped short at the entrance of the hut, seeming at a loss for our conduct. I beckoned at my young friend who advanced with the utmost confidence, and giving her the hand of her brother, she exclaimed with great emotion,

"Diggery-goor, Digerry-goor," I thank you—and turning to her father called him to her, I immediately quitted my station and resigned him to their care; the old man examined the wound, and with great skill extracted the barb.[188] During the operation the youth lifted his eyes, and observing his father, a glance of filial affection beamed forth. Hope now tranquilized the fears of the little group; Yeariana, his sister, supporting him while the father and his friend were contriving how they should remove him to their dwelling; finding it necessary to dispatch one for their canoe, the river which passed their habitation winding within fifty paces from us, and which was the safest and only conveyance he could bear; Yeariana, proposed going for it; and it being our direct road to Paramata, I seized the opportunity of accompanying her; in less than an hour we arrived at the foot of a small mountain, when Yeariana, like an arrow from a bow, abruptly quitted us; leaving her brother, the boy before-mentioned, to be our guide, we were not long before we discovered a dozen natives with Yeariana at their head, waiting our arrival; she had sent off the canoe for her brother, and had got some dried fish, which she prepared, and led us into her hut or cave, which was a large excavated rock, on the bank of a very pleasant river. The reception we met with from these grateful people, almost bordered upon adoration! the mother of Yeariana was quite troublesome with the caresses for my services to her son; and I could perceive in the mild eye of her daughter that it anxiously sought a further acquaintance. Upon inquiry I found we were near five miles from Paramata, but that none of them ever visited the settlement; however, Botchery, her brother offered to be our conductor, provided I would take care of him, and see him part of the way back the next day; promising to see her again shortly, I took my leave, and arrived at Paramata about noon, heartily fatigued. My absence had not caused any alarm at the settlement, as they thought I had gone to Sydney Cove, which I had done twice or thrice, and staid all night.

Every object that presented itself to Botchery filled him with surprise and astonishment, and the poor lad had scarcely time to eat or drink, so much was he taken up in admiration of the wonders that surrounded him. The next morning I set him on his way home again, giving him a hatchet for himself, and a string of beads[189] for his sister, whose image had made a strong impression on my mind, being the most interesting I ever saw.[190]

The next day I made a journey to Sydney Cove, and there being a ship lying in the harbour ready for sea, I took the opportunity to remit the foregoing pages, hoping they will meet approbation and by the next conveyance will send a further account of the progress of the settlement, &c.[191]

Plate 31 'Pinchgut Island', from *The History of New South Wales*. By *George Barrington* (1802).
Source: Rare Books Collection, The Library, Australian National University, Canberra.

Editor's Notes

1. In 1788 the Territory of New South Wales extended from North Cape at the latitude of ten degrees thirty-seven minutes south, called Cape York (now identified as North Queensland), to South Cape, the land sighted at the most southerly point of Van Diemen's Land, now Tasmania, in the latitude of forty-three degrees thirty-nine minutes south, and all the country inland to the westward as far as the one hundred and thirty-fifth degree of east longitude, including all the islands adjacent in the Pacific Ocean within the latitudes of ten degrees thirty-seven minutes south and forty-three degrees thirty-nine minutes south. See *Historical Records of New South Wales*, vol. 1, pt 2, Phillip 1783–92 (Sydney: Charles Potter, Government Printer, 1892), p. 81 (henceforth *HRNSW*).

2. George Barrington (originally George Waldron), born (?1755) Maynooth, near Dublin. Died Parramatta, New South Wales, 1804 (*Australian Dictionary of Biography*, vol. 1, 1788–1850 (Melbourne: Melbourne University Press), pp. 61–2).

3. Arthur Phillip (1738–1814), first Governor of New South Wales, officially named Parramatta in November 1791, as 'that being the name given by the natives to the spot on which the town is situated': Phillip to Lord Grenville, 5 November 1791 (*HRNSW*, vol. 1, pt. 2, p. 539). The place had been initially named Rose Hill by the settlers. In the late eighteenth century London publishers frequently misspelt the name 'Parramatta' which, in the language of the Dharug people who inhabited the area, meant 'Head of the river – where the eels lie down'. The Dharug language was used over a large area with variations spoken by different clans on the coast between Botany Bay and Port Jackson, and from Parramatta to the Lane Cove River on the north side of Port Jackson. For a language map and Aboriginal clan names in the Sydney region, see D. J. Mulvaney and J. Peter White (eds), *Australians to 1788* (Sydney: Fairfax, Syme & Weldon Associates, 1985), pp. 343–65.

4. No record has been found of *An Impartial and Circumstantial Narrative of the Present State of Botany Bay in New South Wales*, henceforth *An*

Impartial and Circumstantial Narrative, in the records of Stationers' Hall (the Worshipful Company of Stationers). The inscription 'Entered at Stationers' Hall' was often used by unscrupulous publishers to imply formal registration. S. & J. Bailey of London were the only publishers to produce copies entitled *An Impartial and Circumstantial Narrative*. Other publishers in Manchester, Darlington and Preston, as well as London, published similar texts under different titles ranging from *Barrington's Voyage to New South Wales, A Voyage to Botany Bay* or *A Voyage to New South Wales,* all attributed to the pen of George Barrington. (See J. A. Ferguson, *Bibliography of Australia,* vol. 1, 1784–1830 (Canberra: National Library of Australia, 1941), pp. 80–3.)

5. D'Arcy Wentworth (1764–1827) arrived in the penal colony in June 1790 on the transport *Neptune*, a vessel of the Second Fleet. Arrested on a charge of highway robbery in 1787, Wentworth was found not guilty on two charges and was acquitted on a third. Highway robbery was then a capital offence. Tried again in 1789, he was discharged by the court, having received a guarantee of employment as Assistant-Surgeon at Botany Bay. This equated to a sentence of transportation. Like George Barrington, Wentworth was capable of impressing juries. He was intelligent, had completed his apprenticeship with a surgeon in Ireland and was well-placed, related to the Anglo-Irish Fitzwilliam family who secured his position. He went to Norfolk Island as Assistant-Surgeon after his arrival in 1790 and in December 1791 was further appointed to act as superintendent of convicts by Lieutenant Philip Gidley King (1758–1808), first commandant of Norfolk Island. Wentworth was granted land in 1806 in an area now known as Homebush Bay, on the western banks of the Parramatta River. Appointed government medical officer at Parramatta, Wentworth was also a stipendiary magistrate. Lieutenant-Colonel Lachlan Macquarie (1762–1824), Governor of New South Wales from 1810 to 1821, appointed him Superintendent of Police, establishing the first civil police force in New South Wales. There is no direct evidence to suggest that Barrington knew Wentworth personally, although this was likely as the colony's population was small and news travelled fast. By 1792 the combined population of New South Wales and Norfolk Island was estimated to be about 5000 souls; see *HRNSW*, vol. 1, pt 2, p. 575; also John Ritchie, *The Wentworths: Father and Son* (Carlton: Miegunyah Press, 1997).

6. Norfolk Island, situated approximately 1500 kilometres north-east of Sydney, was discovered by Captain Cook on his second voyage in 1774. It was named after the English Norfolk family. Naval Lieutenant Philip Gidley King was sent as its commandant in March 1788. It was a branch settlement of the penal colony of New South Wales, accommodating recalcitrant

convicts and those who committed crimes in Port Jackson. In 1808 the authorities abandoned the Island because of its difficult anchorage, upkeep costs and distance from Sydney. The bulk of the convict population was then transferred to Van Diemen's Land. Initially it was hoped that Norfolk Island would be capable of providing flax and pinewood for refurbishing vessels of the Naval Fleet. It was resettled in 1825 as a site for severe punishment and was annexed to Van Diemen's Land in 1844.

7. Barrington was sentenced by Justice Baron Eyre at the Old Bailey on Friday 17 September 1790, to transportation 'beyond the seas for the term of seven years to such a place where His Majesty, with the advice of the Privy Council, shall think fit to declare and appoint pursuant to the Statute for such cases made and provided'. Gaol Delivery Rolls, 1756–1834, series relating to George Barrington, Trials, Old Bailey (Kew: Public Record Office, Mfm 3087–3105).

8. Sir Charles Middleton (Comptroller of the Navy) advised the Under Secretary of the Home Department (Home Office), Evan Nepean, that the rule applied for victualling convicts on their passage was the same as that which applied to soldiers on board transports; this was two-thirds of the allowance for troops serving in the West Indies, spirits excepted. As convicts were confined and did not partake of strenuous exercise or labour, it was thought that this allowance was more advantageous to health than the full allowance. Middleton regarded the allowance as 'abundant when compared to bread and water which I take for granted is the prison allowance'. (See *HRNSW*, vol. 1, pt 2, pp. 91–2.) A bread allowance was one pound (500 grams) per head. The 'diet table' for the prison hulk *Justitia*, in which Barrington was imprisoned in 1777, provided barley or rice broth for breakfast, bullock's head, cheese or salt beef or pork for dinner, pease and barley soup or oatmeal for supper. Such provisions, and their quantity and quality, were the subject of a parliamentary inquiry after John Howard's reports to a House of Commons Committee inquiring into the *Prisons Acts* of 1776 and 1779. The official ration for convicts at sea was three quarts of water a day, and a weekly allowance of 7 lbs of bread or biscuits, 2 lbs salt pork, 2 lbs salt beef, 2 lbs peas, 3 lbs oatmeal, 6 lbs butter, 3/4 lbs cheese, 1/2 pint vinegar. In port, fresh vegetables might supplement, and fresh meat (up to 20 ozs) and 1 lb of rice per day. This was two-thirds of the allowance for the Naval service. See *Journal of a Voyage to New South Wales with sixty-five Plates of Non-descript Animals, Birds, Lizards, Serpents, curious Cones of Trees and other Natural Productions by John White Esq, Surgeon General to the Settlement* (London: J. Debrett, 1790), edited by Alec H. Chisholm (Sydney: The Royal Australian Historical Association and Angus & Robertson, 1962), Note 2, p. 235.

9. Three hundred and nineteen convicts were apparently mustered at Blackfriars Bridge and taken for embarkation at the end of January 1791. Two newspaper reports noted Barrington's departure. *Avis's Birmingham Gazette* for 28 February 1791 reported that Barrington was marched to Blackfriars Bridge at the head of one hundred male convicts 'with other genteel persons ... disengaged from the chain'. The *Morning Post* for 9 March 1791 reported that whilst on transport to Gravesend, Barrington was compelled to submit to the humiliating operation of having his head shaved and his clothes taken. A letter attributed to George Barrington to a 'Gentleman in the County of York', dated 1 July 1791, from the Cape of Good Hope, published in the *Western Country Magazine* for 1792, protested that 'nothing of the kind happened to me. I was permitted to retain both' (*HRNSW*, vol. 2, 1793–95, p. 785).

10. No individual benefactor has been identified. However, Barrington had previously received sympathy and attention from an unidentified benefactor who visited the prison hulk, *Justitia*, in 1776 when he was incarcerated. Barrington subsequently received an early release from his term after a supplication was sent on his behalf by an influential benefactor. Conditions on the *Justitia* were notorious, with illness caused by lack of ventilation, overcrowding and poor food. This hulk in particular was noted by the prison reformer, John Howard. See *The State of the Prisons in England and Wales: with preliminary observations and account of some foreign prisons and hospitals* (London [1777], Warrington: W. Eyres, 1784). Other evidence was given in 1778 to a Committee of the House of Commons inquiry into conditions on the 'Hulks' (*Parliamentary Reports*, vol. XXXV, 1778).

11. Barrington was usually depicted as an elegant figure, although there is one frontispiece of him looking somewhat sheepish in chains, standing in the dock of the Old Bailey. This illustrates a late edition of *The Life and Times of George Barrington* ..., published in 1820 (Canberra: Rex Nan Kivell Collection, National Library of Australia).

12. A vivid and horrifying description of the condition of convicts held in irons was sent by Captain Hill, Second Captain in the New South Wales Corps, to Samuel Wathen, a friend of William Wilberforce, from Port Jackson, on 26 July 1790. Hill was sickened by the condition of convicts held in irons on the Second Fleet transports, and likened their conditions with those of slaves taken from Guinea: 'The irons used upon these unhappy wretches were barbarous ... My feelings never have been so wounded as in this voyage, so much so, that I never shall recover my accustomed vivacity and spirits' (*HRNSW*, vol. 1, pt 2, pp. 367–8).

13. Conditions on the *Active* were extremely poor, and overcrowding and food shortages were held responsible for fatalities: 185 deaths were recorded

during the journey. Governor Phillip reported to the Rt. Hon. Henry Dundas, Principal Secretary for the Home Department: 'I am very sorry to say that most of the convicts who were received by the last ships [*Atlantic, Matilda, Active, Queen, Britannia*] still continue in the same debilitated state in which they were landed, and of whom, in less than seven months, two hundred and eighty-eight men have died' (*HRNSW*, vol. 1, pt 2, p. 596).

14. The Motherbank was a safe anchorage in the channel off Portsmouth, close to the Isle of Wight, Hampshire.

15. Watkin Tench (?1758–1833) conveyed a similar sentiment on parting, expressing his own thoughts and those of the convicts: 'By ten o'clock we had got clear of the Isle of Wight, at which time, having very little pleasure in conversing with my own thoughts, I strolled down among the convicts to observe their sentiments at this junction. A very few excepted, their countenances indicated a high degree of satisfaction, though in some the pang of being severed, perhaps forever, from their native land could not be wholly suppressed' (Tench, *A Narrative of the Expedition* (Flannery edition), p. 19).

16. The mutiny reported in Barrington's *Narrative* really did take place on the *Albemarle* on 9 April 1791. Two of the mutineers, William Siney and Owen Lyons, who wanted to take the *Albemarle* to America, were hanged from the fore-yard-arm 'to strike terror in the convicts' (*HRNSW*, vol. 1, pt 2, pp. 487–8). Those on board the *Active* and the *Admiral Barrington* must have been aware of the mutinous activity since they were anchored at Madeira at the same time. A letter describing the mutiny was most likely to have been prepared by Lieutenant Robert Parry Young, naval agent in charge of the *Albemarle*, although no manuscript survives (*HRNSW*, vol. 1, pt 2, note p. 487). An official report was made by Robert Cock to the Duke of Leeds on 13 May 1791 (*HRNSW*, vol. 2, pp. 447–8).

17. Publishers converted Barrington into a hero for apparently saving the day. The myth that Barrington had prevented a mutiny was retained and appeared without challenge in many popular accounts well into the twentieth century. Roy Bridges, for example, wrote a fictional account based on the alleged incident, *Mr Barrington: A Novel* (Sydney: The Bookstall Press, 1911). In this novel, Barrington, dressed as a gentleman in tailcoat and cravat, wresting a sword from a mutineer, figures in an illustration by the well-known Australian engraver, Lionel Lindsay.

18. While Barrington did not 'foil a mutiny', he did come to official notice. It was reported by Lieutenant-Governor King to Under-Secretary Nepean, in a private letter despatched from Table Bay dated 29 July 1791, that Barrington had become a 'religious convert' during the voyage, delivering a sermon twice on Sundays (*HRNSW*, vol. 1, pt 2, p. 505). It may have been

for this exemplary behaviour that Barrington was soon rewarded on his arrival in Port Jackson.

19. Salt junk – salt beef supplied to ships bound on long voyages. The name derives from the toughness of the preserved meat.

20. Tenerife is the main island of the Canary Island group in the North Atlantic Ocean about seventy miles west of the Moroccan coast of Africa. Santa Cruz is the capital. The Canary Islands are Spanish overseas territory and have been in Spanish possession since *c*. 1500.

21. Ortava – Puerto Orotava, the garden valley of Tenerife. This fertile area, about thirty-four miles south-west of Santa Cruz, was later described by the naturalist Alexander von Humbolt (1769–1859) as the loveliest prospect of his travels. In 1788 an orchid garden and the Botanical Gardens were established to acclimatize plants and trees brought from Asia and America for propagation in Europe.

22. Watkin Tench reported on his visit to Tenerife and the picturesque appearance of the peak. He wrote: 'The whole of the island appearing one vast mountain and a pyramidal top... The good people of Santa Cruz tell some stories of the wonderful extent of space to be seen from the summit of it that would not disgrace the memoirs of the ever-memorable Baron Munchausen' (Tench, *A Narrative of the Expedition*, p. 3). (Baron von Munchausen was a fictional figure in eighteenth-century literature, famous for his wildly exaggerated stories. He was created by the German writer Rudolf Erich Raspe in 1785.)

23. See Plate 6, 'The Peak of Teneriffe', from *An Account of a Voyage to New South Wales, by George Barrington, Superintendant of the Convicts, to which is prefixed a Detail of his Life, Trials, Speeches, &c. &c.* Enriched with beautiful Coloured Prints. London: Printed for M. Jones, No. 1 Paternoster row. 1803.

24. This episode was likely to have been plagiarized from an account by Peter Rye, *An Excursion to the Peak of Teneriffe, in 1791; being the substance of a letter to Joseph Jekyll ... from Lieutenant Rye, of the Royal Navy* (London: R. Falder, 1793). For a contemporary context, see *Maiden Voyages and Infant Colonies: Two Women's Travel Narratives of the 1790s*, edited by Deirdre Coleman (London: Leicester University Press, 1999), p. 188.

25. According to the records, the *Active*, on which Barrington was transported, did not rendezvous at Tenerife when the other vessels (*Britannia, Albemarle, Admiral Barrington*, and *Matilda*) were at anchor. On 4 May 1791 the *Active* was regarded as 'missing', but arrived safely in Sydney (*HRNSW*, vol. 1, pt 2, p. 489).

26. The 'Equinoctial line': the terrestrial equator where the hours of day and night are of equal length.

27. 'Crossing the line', or sailing across the equator, was a time for ceremonial practical joking. For sailors and travellers who had not crossed before, King Neptune summonsed them to a mock trial. Unfortunates were usually ducked by 'bears', lathered with soap and shaved. Forfeits had to be paid. Today, the ceremony is usually good-humoured although its origins may have begun as propitiatory rites to sea deities. In Barrington's time, buffoonery and rough horse-play were to be expected. Similar ceremonies were performed when a ship crossed the thirty-ninth parallel (about the latitude of Lisbon), and also when passing through the Straits of Gibraltar and rounding the Cape of Good Hope. (See *Brewer's Dictionary of Phrase and Fable* (London: Cassell, revised edition, 1981), p. 671.)

28. The correct spelling was *Albemarle*.

29. Neptune – Roman god of the sea corresponding to the Greek god Poseidon, usually represented as an elderly and stately man, carrying a trident and sometimes astride a dolphin. Amphitrite – in classical mythology the goddess of the sea, wife of Poseidon.

30. This expression meant merry, full of fun or extravagantly lively. A grig or grigg is a grasshopper or cricket (*Oxford Encyclopedic English Dictionary* (Oxford: Clarendon Press, 1994), p. 623).

31. In Barrington's *An Impartial and Circumstantial Narrative*, no mention is made of sailing to Rio de Janeiro which was the usual next port of call for vessels of the Fleet. The Third Fleet rejoined at Rio de Janeiro in late April 1791. The *Atlantic, William and Ann* and *Salamander* sailed direct from Rio de Janeiro (also called St Sebastian) to Port Jackson. In *A Voyage to Botany Bay, with a description of the Country, manners, Customs, Religion &c. of the Natives by the Celebrated George Barrington. To which is added his Life and Trial. London Printed by C. Lowndes, and sold by H. D. Symonds, No. 20, Paternoster Row* (London: H. D. Symonds, *c*. 1795), a new chapter was added (Chapter III), with a description of Port-au-Praya Bay and the island of Cobres. For comparison, see Tench's journal entry for August 1787 in *A Narrative of the Expedition*, Chapter V.

32. According to Lieutenant-Governor King to Under-Secretary Nepean, the *Active* anchored at Table Bay on 26 July 1791 (*HRNSW*, vol. 1, pt 2, p. 493).

33. No detail of the Cape of Good Hope is included in *An Impartial and Circumstantial Narrative*. In the re-worked edition, *A Voyage to Botany Bay* (*c*. 1795), new chapters IV and V presented a picture of Cape Town where Barrington is entertained by the town's affluent burghers and merchants. Readers were provided with a description of Creole slaves employed by the Dutch, as well as the 'Hottentots' (Khoikhoi) and 'Cafrees' (Kaffirs), the Xhosa, 'negroes of Madagascar and Mozambique', as well as

Malayans and Indians. Information about the Cape was added to *A Voyage to Botany Bay*, to give the edition additional currency. Ethnographic references to native habitations, social customs and physical appearance were incorporated, as well as descriptions of birds and wild animals, including an elephant and domesticated cattle. The inclusion of contemporary events characterized many of the editions of Barrington's 'histories' which followed. When the British took over the administration of the Cape Colony from the Dutch in 1795, eager publishers such as S. & J. Bailey seized the opportunity to insert material taken freely from elsewhere. For example, Captain William Paterson (1755–1810), of the New South Wales Corps, who arrived on the *Gorgon* in 1791, wrote *A Narrative of Four Journeys into the Country of the Hottentots and Caffraria* (London: J. Johnson, 1789), and works such as his were a likely target for unscrupulous publishers. (Captain Paterson succeeded Major Francis Grose as Lieutenant-Governor of New South Wales in 1800.)

34. It is unlikely that Barrington, even as a trusted convict, would have been allowed to leave the ship. There is no record of those crew members who left the *Active* to obtain supplies. The *Active* took on board official letters and 'twenty tierces and thirty barrells of salt provisions' for delivery to the commissary at Port Jackson (*HRNSW*, vol. 1, pt 2, p. 494). Supplies were obtained from Mr Petrus De Wit and were delivered to False Bay where the *Active* lay at anchor. (A tierce is a measurement of wine – one-third of a pipe, which is equivalent to 105 imperial gallons or approximately 477 litres.)

35. The colony at Port Jackson remained precariously short of flour for months at a time. Achieving self-sufficiency in grain crops was Governor Phillip's aim, but in the surrounding farmlets and at Norfolk Island, grain harvests were disappointing in 1791 and 1792. In December 1791 Phillip advised Lord Grenville that flour rations would have to be reduced (*HRNSW*, vol. 1, pt 2, pp. 556–7). By October 1792 the Governor reported that there remained in the colony only sufficient rice and flour to keep them bread-sufficient for ninety-six days, at two pounds per man for seven days (*HRNSW*, vol. 1, pt 2, p. 643). The Colony remained highly dependent upon provisions shipped from Calcutta and the Cape, while the yields from Norfolk Island continued to disappoint, and further land was put under cultivation around Parramatta and Toongabbie.

36. Convicts were never given leave to disembark during the voyage, although many tried to escape and, according to Collins and others, some were actively assisted by crew members. At Tenerife, in June 1787, a convict of the First Fleet, John Powers, lowered himself over the bow of the *Alexander*, stole a jolly boat and attempted to board a Dutch East

Indiaman, but was rejected by the crew. He was apprehended by a search party as he prepared to row to the Grand Canary Island, thirty miles away. Powers attempted another escape at the Cape of Good Hope and was chained to the deck for the remainder of the voyage. (See Donald Chapman, *1788 The People of the First Fleet* (Sydney: Cassell, 1981), p. 165.)

37. Red Point was named by Captain Cook on his voyage in 1770 and is located close to Port Kembla, due south of Botany Bay. Lieutenant William Bradley recorded the Point and a chain of remarkable sandhills resembling white cliffs in his journal for 18 January 1788. (See *A Voyage to New South Wales: The Journal of William Bradley RN of HMS Sirius 1786–1792* (Sydney: The Trustees of the Public Library of New South Wales in association with Ure Smith Pty Ltd, Sydney, 1969 (facsimile edition), p. 56.)

38. The *Active* arrived in Port Jackson on 26 September 1791. The voyage took a total of 183 days from Portsmouth. The *Active* took ninety-one days to reach Port Jackson from the Cape of Good Hope.

39. This description accords with official accounts and with Watkin Tench's observations in *A Narrative of the Expedition*. The convicts on the *Active* did not receive their full allowance of rations and although the home authorities were notified after the voyage of abuses, frauds and short rations, no official action was taken. Phillip reported that the 'greatest part' of the convicts landed from the *Active* and the *Queen* were 'so emaciated, so worn away by long confinement, or want of food, or from both these causes, that it will be long before they will recover their strength, and which many of them will never recover'. Phillip to the Rt. Hon. Henry Dundas, 19 March 1792 (*HRNSW*, vol. 1, pt 2, p. 596).

40. Information on the numbers disembarked equates with figures provided for the *Albemarle*. Lists for the *Albemarle* indicated that 282 male convicts embarked, and thirty-two died during the voyage, including the two men executed for mutiny; 250 male convicts were disembarked at Port Jackson. In addition, six women were disembarked and it is assumed that these women may have been transferred from the *Mary Ann*. See also, Charles Bateson, *The Convict Ships 1787–1868* (Sydney: A. H. & A. W. Reed, 1974), pp. 137–9.

41. Governor Phillip anticipated the need for superintendents for convicts, writing to Under-Secretary Nepean in January 1787 about the payment of people who were to superintend, noting that no one would undertake the task without some small reward, and that men from the garrison would not be spared. He also suggested that individuals be named for the purpose. Having arrived at Port Jackson, Phillip wrote to the Home Secretary, Lord Sydney, in May 1788, advising that the Marines 'declined any interference with the convicts', wishing to perform only their duties as soldiers. 'Here are

only convicts to attend to convicts, and who in general fear to exert any authority ...'. Requests for proper superintendents continued in September 1788, and by November 1791 Phillip also suggested the need for superintendents with farming expertise and experience (*HRNSW*, vol. 1, pt 2, p. 533). After a period at the government farm at Toongabbie, Barrington was appointed constable at Rose Hill in December 1791.

42. David Collins, Judge-Advocate of the Colony, reported in November 1792 that Barrington had been employed by the Governor at Toongabbie as a subordinate watchman and then as principal watchman soon after his arrival in Port Jackson, 'a situation which was likely to attract the envy and hatred of the convicts, in proportion as he might be vigilant and inflexible'. Collins noted that Barrington was 'diligent, sober and impartial; and had rendered himself so eminently servicable, that the Governor resolved to draw him from the line of convicts; and, with the instrument of his emancipation, he received a grant of thirty acres of land in an eligible situation near Parramatta'. He was later sworn in as a peace officer. Collins noted that 'Barrington found himself, through the Governor's liberality ... enjoying the immunities of a free man, a settler, and a civil officer, in whose integrity much confidence was placed'. (David Collins, *An Account of the English Colony in New South Wales with Remarks on the Dispositions, Customs, Manners, etc, of the Native Inhabitants of that Country* [London, T. Cadell & W. Davies, 1798], vol. 1, Brian H. Fletcher (ed.) (Sydney: The Royal Australian Historical Society with A. H. & A. W. Reed, 1975), p. 205, henceforth, *An Account of the English Colony*.)

43. Captain Arthur Phillip (1738–1814). Appointed Governor of New South Wales, 12 October 1786.

44. Major Robert Ross (?1740–1798). Appointed Lieutenant-Governor, 24 October 1786.

45. Captain David Collins (1756–1810). Appointed Judge-Advocate, 24 October 1786.

46. Captain John Hunter (1737–1821). Appointed second-in-command to Phillip, with a dormant commission, 28 April 1787.

47. The Governor's house, in its earliest construction built from brick and sandstone with a covered verandah, can be seen in the background of the illustration, 'East View of Sydney', Plate 26. An earlier view of the Governor's house was painted by Thomas Watling for David Collins with a date indicating *c*. 1795.

48. Farm Cove. The present Royal Botanic Gardens in Sydney are on the site of the old farm and Governor's garden. The location was marked on a map entitled 'Sketch of Sydney Cove, Port Jackson in the County of Cumberland, New South Wales, July 1788', in *The Voyage of Governor Phillip to*

Botany Bay, with an Account of the Establishment of the Colonies at Port Jackson and Norfolk Island; compiled from Authentic Papers (London: John Stockdale, 1789) (henceforth, *The Voyage of Governor Phillip to Botany Bay).*

49. Phillip reported to Lord Sydney in February 1790 on the revenge of the rats, lamenting that rodents had overrun the stores and had caused considerable damage in the gardens. He estimated that rats had destroyed 12,000 pounds weight of rice and flour (approximately 5,800 kilos), since the First Fleet's arrival (*HRNSW*, vol. 1, pt 2, p. 297).

50. Phillip's 'Additional Instructions' from the Rt. Hon. W. W. Grenville, dated 10 August 1789, provided encouragements for officers to become permanent settlers in the Colony. Every non-commissioned officer was eligible for one hundred acres of land, and every private man, fifty acres. Emancipated convicts were eligible for thirty acres. Land was free of all fees, taxes, quit rents for ten years, and thereafter an annual quit rent of one shilling was levied for every ten acres (*HRNSW*, vol. 1, pt 2, p. 257).

51. Phillip to Lord Sydney, 9 July 1788, reported that 'very good bricks' were being made. The Colony urgently required bricklayers willing to be sent out to act as superintendents of convicts who could also render valuable assistance 'to the State'. There were very few convicts with carpentry or building skills in the first wave of transportation (*HRNSW*, vol. 1, pt 2, p. 146).

52. A view of the brick hills (kilns) and high road to Parramatta are seen in the illustration 'East View of Sydney', found in Barrington's *The History of New South Wales*, 1802. See Plate 26.

53. The barracks were covered in shingles made from native timber. Illustrations of the South and East views of Sydney, found in Barrington's *The History of New South Wales*, 1802, show numerous shingled buildings. See Plates 11 and 26.

54. Contemporary spellings varied, but the cove was named in honour of the Secretary of State, first Viscount Sydney, Thomas Townsend (1733–1800). On 26 January 1788 the British flag was unfurled at the head of Sydney Cove, toasts were drunk and volleys of musketry fired. The formal proclamation of the Colony took place on 7 February 1788.

55. Phillip reported to Secretary Stephens in November 1788 that the 'natives' avoided the convicts, who frequently stole items from them, including spears, canoes and 'fizgigs'. He reported that settler 'straglers' were attacked only in revenge for thefts (*HRNSW*, vol.1, pt 2, p. 214).

56. Phillip made plans for the town of Rose Hill in July 1790. There he intended to house convicts in huts built one hundred feet from each other, each hut to contain ten convicts, with the provision of gardens to cultivate. It was

hoped that the convicts would grow vegetables which could be exchanged for 'little necessaries', so that they would feel the benefit of their industry. Phillip to Rt. Hon. W. W. Grenville, Sydney, 17 July 1790 (*HRNSW*, vol. 1, pt 2, p. 362). See Plate 26, 'East View of Sydney, from *The History of New South Wales*, 1802.

57. Barrington's appointment as a watchman was officially documented for 1791. His signature appeared on a warrant signed in 1793 when he was officially made an Officer of the Peace. He was appointed by Governor Hunter as superintendent of convicts on 17 September 1796, to replace Thomas Clark, who was returning to England. On this appointment, Barrington received an absolute pardon and a salary of fifty pounds per annum. Government and General Order for 13 September 1796 (*HRNSW*, vol. 3, 1796–99, p. 115).

58. The General Return of Male Convicts for July 1790 indicated that out of a total of 729 convicts, 316 were at work in various occupations and 413 were listed as sick. Superintendents (themselves convicts) were issued with assigned convict servants who provided labour and received rations and accommodation (*HRNSW*, vol. 1, pt 2, p. 364).

59. Once the 'tap-too' (retreat) beat was sounded, convicts were confined to their huts. If found 'stragling or lurking about' on any of the cultivated grounds, they were fired on by the watchmen on patrol. One of the duties of the watchmen was to apprehend 'all night-walkers, all disorderly and suspicious persons' and deliver them to a constable, or take them to a Justice of the Peace. Watchmen were required to 'inform themselves of all strangers who came to reside in their division' (*HRNSW*, vol. 3, 1796–99, pp. 165–6).

60. Initially, women convicts were given such tasks as laundry rather than hard labour. Later, women convicts not assigned as servants, or those who had committed crimes in the colony, were housed in the Female Factory established at Parramatta as part of the Parramatta Gaol. Weaving a coarse woollen material known as 'Parramatta cloth', along with laundry, was part of the punishment regime. In 1821 Governor Macquarie ordered the construction of a separate institution for female convicts. For recent studies on convict women, see Joy Damousi, *Depraved and Disorderly: Female Convicts, Sexuality and Gender in Australia* (Cambridge: Cambridge University Press, 1997), and Kay Daniels, *Convict Women* (Sydney: Allen & Unwin, 1998).

61. A report appeared in the *London Chronicle* for 28 August 1798 with a denial that George Barrington was about to return to England on the expiration of his sentence, with the Governor's pardon. Barrington was pardoned and free to leave, but the rumour about his return was without

foundation. Denying it, perhaps to rekindle an interest in Barrington's progress, the *London Chronicle* provided an outline of Barrington's 'colonial career', recapping his arrival in September 1791, employment at the Government Grounds at 'Toongabbee' (Toongabbie), his elevation to subordinate and then principal watchman for the protection of stores, and his receipt of a warrant of emancipation in November 1792. Within a period of thirteen months, Barrington had become a free man. He was sworn in as a Commissioner of the Peace a short time after November 1792, a result of official notice of his exemplary behaviour. He could not, however, leave the colony without the permission of the Governor and he had to provide a passage for himself. Barrington appeared to be content with his official duties and farm land and kept his promise to reform and repay society.

62. Prospect Hill was established four miles west of Toongabbie. Land grants were issued to twelve emancipated convicts by Governor Phillip in 1791. (See Collins, *An Account of the English Colony*, vol. 1, p. 144.)

63. Sydney Parkinson, the official draughtsman on board the *Endeavour*, had sketched a kangaroo in 1770 on Cook's voyage up the east coast of New Holland. Illustrations of the kangaroo, taken from a painting by George Stubbs, subsequently appeared as an engraving in John Hawkesworth's edition of Cook's *Endeavour* journal published in 1773. A further illustration of 'The Kanguroo' appeared in *The Voyage of Governor Phillip to Botany Bay* (1789). Thomas Watling produced illustrations for Surgeon-General John White, whose illustrated *Journal of a Voyage to New South Wales* appeared in London in 1790. A live kangaroo was displayed in London's Haymarket district in late 1791, and a ceramic souvenir mug decorated with a 'Kanguroo and Tigar' was in circulation *c.* 1793. Wood-thorpe's illustration of the kangaroo in Barrington's *The History of New South Wales* did not appear until 1802. This fanciful kangaroo, with enormous hind legs, had two young in the pouch and was depicted pulling acorns from a tree. See Plate 19, 'Kangaroo'.

64. Mocock – Macaco (Portuguese), from the genus *Macacus*, a monkey identified by other travellers to the Dutch East Indies (Batavia). The genus is also found in South America. The 'dark tan' colour suggested in *An Impartial and Circumstantial Narrative* describes the colour of the Red Kangaroo, but in Sydney and coastal areas it is more likely that the Eastern grey kangaroo (*Macropus giganteus*) was seen. The Aboriginal word for kangaroo was 'patagorang', noted in Tench's *Complete Account of the Settlement,* and in Collins' *An Account of the English Colony*, vol. 1, p. 614.

65. This description in *An Impartial and Circumstantial Narrative* of the physical motion of the kangaroo is a close précis of Governor Phillip's notes

made in 1788 that were presented in *An Historical Journal of the Transactions at Port Jackson and Norfolk Island, with the Discoveries which have been made in New South Wales and in the Southern Ocean, since the publication of Phillip's Voyage, compiled from the Official Papers; Including the Journals of Governors Phillip and King, and of Lieut. Ball; and the Voyages from the first Sailing of the Sirius in 1787, to the Return of that Ship's Company to England in 1792. By John Hunter, Esqr. Post Captain in His Majesty's Navy* (London: J. Stockdale, 1793), henceforth *An Historical Journal of the Transactions at Port Jackson*; see, in particular, pp. 66–7. John Hunter (1737–1821), admiral and second Governor of New South Wales from 1795 to 1800, was commander of the *Sirius*, wrecked at Norfolk Island in 1790. After this disaster he returned to England, reaching Portsmouth in 1792. Returning to the colony in 1795 as the colony's second Governor, his first task was to re-establish civil administration. Military rule had been imposed by Major Francis Grose and was continued by Captain William Paterson after Governor Phillip left the colony in 1792. While Hunter was in England, he brought together the official journals, particularly Phillip's account, and published *An Historical Journal of the Transactions at Port Jackson and Norfolk Island* (London, John Stockdale, 1793), which was subsequently published in German and Swedish editions. *An Impartial and Circumstantial Narrative* was 'scavenged' largely from information contained in *An Historical Journal of the Transactions at Port Jackson*.

66. A similar judgement on the quality of kangaroo meat is found in Phillip's notes. However, he remarked that the meat was not as 'delicate as that which we sometimes find in Leadenhall-market' (*An Historical Journal of the Transactions at Port Jackson*, p. 66).

67. In White's description, the 'New South Wales' native dog, the dingo (*Canis familiaris dingo*), is described as 'like the shepherd's dog in most countries' (*Journal of a Voyage to New South Wales*, p. 196).

68. The dingo was compared with the European greyhound. It was observed that the native dog would 'fly at young pigs, chickens, or any small animal which they might be able to conquer' (*An Historical Journal of the Transactions at Port Jackson*, p. 67).

69. In *An Historical Journal of the Transactions at Port Jackson*, Aboriginal women were described as 'generally well made', whereas in Barrington the women are described as 'rather lustier'. Women's skin colour in *An Historical Journal* is described as 'a rusty kind of black', but in Barrington the colour is described as 'brownish black, or a coffee cast'. Both accounts use the term 'mulatto'. (See *An Historical Journal of the Transactions at Port Jackson*, pp. 58–9.)

70. Barrington's account, with slight variations from *An Historical Journal of the Transactions at Port Jackson*, refers to the wearing of a piece of wood or bone, which 'dilates the nostril', while Hunter writes of wood or bone 'thrust through the septum of the nose which . . . widens the nostril'. (See *An Historical Journal of the Transactions at Port Jackson*, p. 59.)

71. Barrington's description follows wording lifted directly from *An Historical Journal of the Transactions at Port Jackson*, pp. 58–9. A later description and illustration of the tooth avulsion ceremony entitled 'Yoo-long Erah-ba-diang' appeared in Collins' *An Account of the English Colony*, vol. 1, pp. 480–1. An illustration entitled 'Manhood' appeared in Barrington's *The History of New South Wales*, 1802, showing tooth avulsion, elements of which were copied from the original plate discussed above. See Plate 24.

72. Barrington's publisher gave measurements in figures: '70 or 80 yards', whereas the original wording in *An Historical Journal of the Transactions at Port Jackson* estimated that spears could be thrown 'sixty or seventy yards'. Phillip observed that he had seen one young man throw the lance ninety yards (*An Historical Journal of the Transactions at Port Jackson*, p. 53).

73. Describing body decorations, Phillip made no observation about 'hostile expeditions' or intentions, although he observed that the decorations gave 'a most shocking appearance', making bodies look 'like so many moving skeletons' (*An Historical Journal of the Transactions at Port Jackson*, p. 57). Body decorations were applied for ceremonial purposes, clan identification, seasonal festivals and rites of passage such as initiation and mourning. Body designs designated clan totems as well as seniority. Women often had special designs of deep female significance, possibly indicating fertility. (See J. L. Kohen and Ronald Lampert, 'Hunters and Fishers in the Sydney Region', in D. J. Mulvaney and J. Peter White (eds), *Australians to 1788* (Sydney: Fairfax, Syme & Weldon Associates, 1987), pp. 342–65.)

74. Information on body decorations found in *An Impartial and Circumstantial Narrative* is taken directly from *An Historical Journal of the Transactions at Port Jackson*, pp. 60–1.

75. In *An Historical Journal of the Transactions at Port Jackson*, the original sentence states that 'each man had a green bough in his hand, as a sign of friendship', describing a leafy branch of a plant or tree. In *An Impartial and Circumstantial Narrative* the meaning becomes confused as 'Barrington' refers to a 'green bow', implying a weapon, an idea that is followed through with reference to defence. Readers were assured in *An Historical Journal of the Transactions at Port Jackson* that the Aboriginals' 'disposition was as regular as any well disciplined troops could have been' (*An Historical Journal of the Transactions at Port Jackson*, p. 57).

76. A more charitable interpretation is found in *An Historical Journal of the Transactions at Port Jackson* where Phillip referred to the 'particular care of Providence for all his creatures' and noted that 'their [the natives'] ignorance in building, is very amply compensated by the kindness of nature in the remarkable softness of the rocks' (*An Historical Journal of the Transactions at Port Jackson*, pp. 59–60).

77. In *An Impartial and Circumstantial Narrative* erasures and omissions made by the publisher lead quickly to a censorious and pejorative tone not apparent in the text of *An Historical Journal of the Transactions at Port Jackson*.

78. The squirrel, an arboreal rodent, is not found on the Australian mainland or in Tasmania. The familiar name was used to convey a description of the creature which White called the 'Hepoona Roo' in his *Journal of a Voyage to New South Wales*, and which Governor Phillip had called the 'Black Flying Opossum' in *The Voyage of Governor Phillip to Botany Bay* (London: J. Stockdale, 1789). The marsupial was the Greater Glider Possum (*Schoinobates volans*). See also, *An Historical Journal of the Transactions at Port Jackson*, p. 61.

79. The technique Aborigines used for climbing trees and hunting native animals was first briefly described in 1770 in Cook's journal of his voyage on the *Endeavour*. Phillip described the technique in a letter to Lord Sydney in May 1788 (*HRNSW*, vol. 1, pt 2, p. 135). More detailed descriptions were incorporated into accounts published in *An Historical Journal of the Transactions at Port Jackson*. Publishers of *An Impartial and Circumstantial Narrative* carefully searched and cut one section from *An Historical Journal of the Transactions at Port Jackson* (at p. 61), and joined it with a detailed description which followed (on pp. 520–1). Such judicious splicing gives modern readers an indication of the care taken by the publisher, S. & J. Bailey, to alter the text sufficiently to avoid charges of plagiarism and provide an apparently seamless narrative.

80. The figures given are 'sixty or eighty feet' in *An Historical Journal of the Transactions at Port Jackson*, p. 521.

81. Opposum is the common name given to the North American mammal. White described the Common Brush-tail possum (*Trichosurus vulpecula*), giving it the name 'Wha Tapoau Roo'; see Plate 35, *Journal of a Voyage to New South Wales*, p. 78.

82. Descriptions of fauna in *An Historical Journal of the Transactions at Port Jackson*, see pp. 68–9, also begin with 'the opposum' (possum) and end with 'the stingray' and refer to the 'vast variety of fish'. *An Impartial and Circumstantial Narrative* refers facetiously to 'the finny inhabitants of the sea'.

83. Events in *An Impartial and Circumstantial Narrative* are usually conveyed in the first person. The plural form, e.g., 'we have shot birds', is most commonly used in *An Historical Journal of the Transactions at Port Jackson*, consciously reflecting the endeavours of many.

84. This passage referring to bird life is taken from *An Historical Journal of the Transactions at Port Jackson*, pp. 68–69, but omitted from *An Impartial and Circumstantial Narrative* is a short description of eucalypts – gum trees – which display three different leaf growth stages simultaneously, a botanical feature which intrigued Phillip and Hunter. The 'Macaw, Cockatoo, Lory, Green Parrot and Paroquets' in *An Impartial and Circumstantial Narrative* provided descriptions of the variety of parrots observed in the Sydney region. The 'Macaw' was probably the Glossy Black Cockatoo, *Calyptorhynchus lathami*; the 'Cockatoo' – the Sulphur-Crested White Cockatoo, from the genera *Calyptorhyn and Cacatua*; the 'Lory' – the Crimson Rosella, *Platycercus elegans*; the 'Green Parrot' – King Parrot, *Aprosmictus scapularis*; and 'Paroquet's' – the Small Paroquet, *Psittacus pusillus*. The Crimson Rosella's name comes from an area that was known as Rose Hill. Settlers re-named the 'Lory' 'Rose-Hillers' (Rose Hill parrots), which was then contracted into the vernacular, 'Rosella'. The ingenious and able naturalist, Dr John Latham, after whom the Glossy Black Cockatoo, *Calyptorhynchus lathami*, is named, made numerous sketches of birds which appeared in Phillip's *The Voyage of Governor Phillip to Botany Bay* (1789).

85. In *An Historical Journal of the Transactions at Port Jackson*, the flesh of the ostrich [emu] is described thus: 'The flesh of this bird, although coarse, was thought by us delicious meat; it had much the appearance, when raw, of neck-beef; a party of five, myself included, dined on a side-bone of it most sumptuously' (*An Historical Journal of the Transactions at Port Jackson*, p. 70).

86. This sentence is taken from *An Historical Journal of the Transactions at Port Jackson* which refers to cooking and eating the crow: 'the pot or spit received everything which we could catch or kill, and the common crow was relished here as well as the barn-door fowl of England' (*An Historical Journal of the Transactions at Port Jackson*, p. 70).

87. The bats referred to in *An Impartial and Circumstantial Narrative* are Fruit Bats or Flying Foxes *(Pteropus poliocephalus)*, commonly found in the Sydney region. It was claimed in *An Impartial and Circumstantial Narrative* that Barrington had a domesticated bat, whereas it was reported that Governor Phillip had a female bat which lodged in his house and apparently took food from its captor, 'lapping out of the hand like a cat'. It was noted that immense numbers of bats roosted in the trees at Rose Hill (see *An*

Historical Journal of the Transactions at Port Jackson, p. 507). Fruit bats in this region continue to fly north in the early morning and south for night roosting, following established patterns of flight and timing.

88. Descriptions of 'a little wild spinach, parsley, and sorrel' appear in *An Historical Journal of the Transactions at Port Jackson*. Finding palatable native anti-scorbutic vegetables was of vital importance for the health of the early colonists. One of the most important tasks set before White and his colleagues was to find vegetables and fruits which could be eaten while domesticated European crops grew and matured. The cabbage tree palm (*Livistona australis*) provided an alternative green vegetable suitable for feeding pigs, and its shoots and buds were consumed by the colonists (see *An Historical Journal of the Transactions at Port Jackson*, p. 71). The spinach ('spinage') referred to was probably *Tetragonia tetragonoides*, commonly found in coastal districts. Native sorrell or native *oxalis* was also consumed. Plants with leaves resembling parsley may have been part of a root (carrot-type) vegetable family *Apiaceae*. See J. H. Maiden, assisted by W. S. Campbell, *The Flowering Plants and Ferns of New South Wales: with especial reference to their economic value*, Parts 1–7 (Sydney: Charles Potter, Government Printer, 1895–98). Parsley Bay, on the southern side of Sydney Harbour, was named by the settlers for its abundance of wild plants resembling parsley.

89. This description probably refers to the nut of the Burrawang palm (*Macrozamia communis*), a Cycad which is poisonous and requires intensive soaking and pounding before it can be eaten. It was used by Aborigines to produce a flour-like substance which was then baked into small flat cakes. *M. communis* is the most common Cycad in New South Wales coastal districts and is found along the banks of the Nepean River. This 'kernel' is referred to in *An Historical Journal of the Transactions at Port Jackson*, p. 479.

90. The appearance of smallpox was first noted in April and May 1789, two years prior to Barrington's arrival. Tench questioned how the disease was introduced, speculating upon the visit made by the French navigator, La Pérouse, in 1788, or that it may have arrived earlier with the navigators Cook or Dampier, or, perhaps, that the disease was already present in the indigenous population. He knew that variolous matter had been brought in bottles to inoculate, but refused any inference that the infection was introduced to the population in that way (Tench, *A Complete Account of the Settlement*, Note, pp. 103–4, see also *An Historical Journal of the Transactions at Port Jackson*, p. 134). Typical to the style of *An Impartial and Circumstantial Narrative*, additions were made to dramatize events. For example, Barrington, as narrator, speaks of the 'terrible havoc'

occasioned among the 'poor natives'. This is an understandable embellishment to text lifted from *An Historical Journal of the Transactions at Port Jackson*, which expresses only 'deep concern'. Phillip observed, 'we had never yet seen any of these people who have been to the smallest degree marked with the small-pox'. In *An Historical Journal of the Transactions at Port Jackson*, the age of the infected boy is estimated to be six or seven years and the girl about ten years. For a recent discussion of the appearance of smallpox in the colony, see Alan Frost, *Botany Bay Mirages: Illusions of Australia's Convict Beginnings* (Carlton: Melbourne University Press, 1994), chapter 10, 'The Curse of Caine?', pp. 159–210.

91. In *An Historical Journal of the Transactions at Port Jackson*, the orphaned children were named Abooroo (a thirteen-year-old girl) and Nanberry (a boy aged between seven and nine years). Abooroo, or Araboo, went to live with Revd Richard Johnson (1753–1827) and his wife, Mary Johnson, who arrived on the *Golden Grove* in the First Fleet. Johnson was the first Anglican chaplain of New South Wales and Norfolk Island, a devout evangelical and an associate of William Wilberforce. Johnson was regarded as the best farmer in the colony and lived in Sydney for its first six years. He constructed his own church and preached there from August 1793, but the building was deliberately burned down soon after. A sermon he delivered in 1792, *An Address to the Inhabitants of the Colonies Established in New South Wales and Norfolk Island* (London: Printed for the author and sold by Matthews, 1794), was the first written for distribution in the colony. Johnson returned to England on sick leave in 1800. Nanberry or Nanbaree was adopted by Surgeon John White. Lieutenant William Dawes used both children as informants (in an anthropological sense) when he collected vocabularies of Aboriginal languages. Lieutenant Dawes of the Marines (*c.* 1758[?]–1836) arrived on the *Sirius* in 1788 as second lieutenant and was appointed as engineer in 1790. He was responsible for the construction of an observatory and was appointed by the Board of Longitude at Greenwich to make astronomical observations. He left Port Jackson in 1791. His was a distinguished career; he served later three terms as Governor of Sierra Leone. Dawes Point, overlooking Sydney Harbour, was named after him.

92. The Aboriginal man was named Arabanoo (?1761–89), and was later given the name 'Manly' by Governor Phillip. In Phillip's letter to Lord Sydney dated 13 February 1790 he described the man, estimated to be about twenty-four years of age, and called him Arabanoo. Arabanoo was the first Aboriginal person to be taken hostage by the British in December 1788, at a place on the north side of Port Jackson which had been named Manly Cove by Governor Phillip in May 1788. (Phillip reported to Lord Sydney that he named the Cove thus because of his high opinion of the local Aborigines'

'confidence and manly behaviour'; *HRNSW*, vol. 1, pt 2, p. 129.) Separated from his companions on Phillip's instructions, Arabanoo was captured by Lieutenant Ball of the *Supply* and Lieutenant George Johnston of the Marines. A rope was tied around his neck and he was held in leg irons and imprisoned in a convict's hut for two weeks. Phillip wanted an intermediary to demonstrate to the local Aborigines the benefits of mixing with the new settlers. Arabanoo was placated and was gradually able to communicate with his captors, becoming close to the Governor and others in command. He wore gifts of English clothing and took to imported alcohol, English food and certain rules of etiquette, but maintained an evident sense of natural dignity. Having nursed an older Aboriginal man and his own child suffering from smallpox in 1789, Arabanoo contracted the disease himself and died in May of that year. He lived with his captors without restraint for about five months. Phillip arranged his funeral and he was buried in Phillip's private garden (*HRNSW*, vol. 1, pt 2, p. 308). (The garden was part of the first site of Government House at Sydney Cove. The Museum of Sydney is now situated on this site, where some of the foundations have been revealed by archaeologists.) Arabanoo was the first of Phillip's three Aboriginal protégés.

93. Gifts were given, especially hatchets and clothing. Captain Hunter reported that 'Ara-ba-noo' was 'a short time in conversation with some of the gentlemen, [when] one of the seamen, who had been previously directed, threw a rope around his [Arabanoo's] neck, and dragged him in a moment to the boat' (*An Historical Journal of the Transactions at Port Jackson*, p. 133).

94. *Bang-ally* was thought to be an Aboriginal word meaning decoration or ornament, although Collins noted the word *beng-al-le* to mean 'basket'. Linguists have suggested that an early lexical exchange may have taken place, so that the colonists mistook *bang-ally* for an Aboriginal term, whereas the word may have been the English word 'bangle', taken up by Aboriginals to describe an ornament or, possibly, the leg shackles worn by convicts and captured Aboriginals such as Bennelong and Colebee. For a full discussion of Australian Aboriginal contact with the English language, see Jakelin Troy, *Australian Aboriginal Contact with the English Language in New South Wales 1788 to 1845* (Canberra: Department of Linguistics, Research School of Pacific Studies, Australian National University, 1990), pp. 41–2.

95. Hunter wrote that Arabanoo learnt his name and never forgot it, and also 'expressed great desire to come on board my nowee; which is their expression for a boat or other vessel upon the water' (*An Historical Journal of the Transactions at Port Jackson*, p. 133).

96. Hunter found Arabanoo 'a very good natured talkative fellow; he was about thirty years of age, and tolerably well looked' (*An Historical Journal of the Transactions at Port Jackson*, p. 133).

97. In November 1789 Lieutenant William Bradley, with fellow officers, went on an expedition to the north part of the harbour to find and capture two Aboriginal men who could be taught enough language 'to render them useful to their countrymen' (*An Historical Journal of the Transactions at Port Jackson*, p. 166). Lieutenant William Bradley (?1758–1833) arrived on the *Sirius* in 1788. He assisted Hunter in surveying Port Jackson and Broken Bay, and surveyed Norfolk Island after the *Sirius* was wrecked in 1790. By 1812 he had risen to become Rear-Admiral of the Blue, but committed a series of inexplicable petty frauds for which he was sentenced to death. The sentence was later commuted to exile for life. He lived until his death at Tourville, near Le Havre in France. Bradley kept a detailed record of the initial journey to Port Jackson and made numerous watercolour paintings of the journey and first views of the harbour. He also recorded other Pacific islands encountered when the crew of the wrecked *Sirius* returned to England in 1792 on the Dutch vessel, the *Waakzaamheid*. Bradley's unpublished journal, *A Voyage to New South Wales: The Journal of Lieutenant William Bradley RN of HMS Sirius 1786–1792*, has been reproduced in facsimile (Sydney: Trustees of the Public Library of New South Wales & Ure Smith Pty, 1969). Bradley's Head, on the northern shore of the harbour, commemorates this officer.

98. Lieutenant William Bradley.

99. The Cadigal people were part of the Dharug language group and occupied territory on the southern side of Port Jackson, close to the area now known as Sydney Cove or Circular Quay.

100. The two men captured, Coalby and Banalong (henceforth, Colebee and Bennelong), were familiar to Hunter, Tench, Collins and Governor Phillip. In individual official accounts, the spelling of names varies, from Cole-be (in Collins), to Colbee (in Tench) and Co-al-by (in Hunter). Banalong is found as Ba-na-lang (in Hunter), Bennillong (in Collins) and Baneelon (in Tench). Today, Bennelong's name is recorded in perpetuity on Sydney Harbour at Bennelong Point, where the Sydney Opera House is now situated. Bennelong had a hut on this prominence built on the instructions of Governor Phillip in 1790.

101. Bennelong made his escape in April 1790. The escape of Bennelong and Colebee is reported in detail in *An Historical Journal of the Transactions at Port Jackson*, pp. 204–5.

102. Governor Phillip fixed a spot for 'erecting a column, or pyramid, as a mark, by which strangers might, at sea, the better know the harbour' (*An Historical Journal of the Transactions at Port Jackson*, p. 206). A Signal

Station was erected by Phillip in January 1790 at the harbour's entrance at South Head in readiness for further arrivals. The Second Fleet did not arrive until June 1790, when a flag was hoisted from the flagstaff to announce the arrival of the *Lady Juliana*.

103. This place is identified as Collins Cove which was situated to the west of Manly Cove on the north side of the Harbour. The Aborigines called the area 'Canee'.

104. The men identified were Captain David Collins, Judge-Advocate, and Captain Henry Waterhouse, surgeon. (See Note 108, below.)

105. This paraphrases Hunter's account of the meeting. Hunter describes Colebee and Bennelong as the Governor's 'old friends', reporting of the muskets that they 'found that only two of the four would strike fire, and these were loaded' (*An Historical Journal of the Transactions at Port Jackson*, p. 207).

106. One of the Aboriginal men 'called out for wine, and repeated several English words', and the Governor is said to have given them 'a few knives' (*An Historical Journal of the Transactions at Port Jackson*, p. 207).

107. According to *An Historical Journal of the Transactions at Port Jackson*, this incident took place in 1791.

108. Lieutenant Henry Waterhouse (1770–1812). Arrived as a midshipman on the *Sirius*, was promoted to third Lieutenant of the *Sirius* in December 1789, and sailed to Norfolk Island where the vessel was wrecked. He returned to England in 1791 and came back to the colony as Second Captain on HMS *Reliance* in 1794. He imported Spanish merino sheep from the Cape of Good Hope in 1796 to improve local flocks and grazed them on his land at Parramatta. He returned to England in 1801, and died in July 1812. See *Australian Dictionary of Biography*, vol. 2 (1788–1850) (Melbourne: Melbourne University Press; London; New York: Cambridge University Press, 1966).

109. Tench reported in September 1790 that Bennelong was unrecognizable until he spoke, as he was greatly emaciated and had grown a long beard. Bennelong asked after the Governor and indicated where he had been fettered on his legs. Only then was he recognized (Tench, *A Complete Account of the Settlement*, p. 119).

110. In *An Historical Journal of the Transactions at Port Jackson*, the conversation refers to 'the Governor'; see p. 460.

111. Publishers of *An Impartial and Circumstantial Narrative* took liberties by adding inflections, but also in removing important points. When Hunter described the incident, he recorded that Bennelong took Mr Waterhouse 'round the neck and kissed him'. Waterhouse personally helped Colebee put on the jacket which was given as a gift (*A Complete Account of the Settlement*, p. 208).

112. Hunter recorded that the Governor (Phillip) asked Bennelong for the spear, but that Bennelong 'either could not or would not understand him, but laid it down on the ground' (*An Historical Journal of the Transactions at Port Jackson,* p. 208).

113. The account in *An Historical Journal of the Transactions at Port Jackson* reported that Bennelong said 'Governor nanorar' – 'Governor asleep', as he imitated 'the manner in which his companion [Coleby] had ran off'. *An Impartial and Circumstantial Narrative* implies that Bennelong advised the captors that they should not sleep if they wanted to keep him and Coleby. See *An Historical Journal of the Transactions at Port Jackson,* p. 461.

114. The man in question was apparently unknown to Bennelong and Colebee, and was unfamiliar to Hunter and Governor Phillip. He was referred to as 'a stranger' in *An Historical Journal of the Transactions at Port Jackson,* p. 462. Tench identified the stranger as as Wil-ee-ma-rin. (See Note 123 below.)

115. In *An Historical Journal of the Transactions at Port Jackson,* no mention is made of 'a neighbouring tribe'. The addition of this phrase in *An Impartial and Circumstantial Narrative* hints at violent disputes, whereas the man in question may well have been punished by his own clan in customary fashion. Raids and violence between neighbouring groups did take place, but Hunter and Governor Phillip were at pains to report, at least initially, on the relatively peaceable nature of the Aborigines.

116. In *An Impartial and Circumstantial Narrative* the spear is described as 'concealed in the grass', whereas in *An Historical Journal of the Transactions at Port Jackson,* the spear was said to be 'lying on the grass'. The implication conveyed in *An Impartial and Circumstantial Narrative* is of a deliberate intention to harm, a motive not suggested in the original account. The wounding of Governor Phillip came unexpectedly. Hunter explained that fear may have provoked the attack and wrote: 'it should be remembered that the man who wounded Governor Phillip was a stranger, and might fear their [Phillip and party] taking him away, as they had carried off others ...' (*An Historical Journal of the Transactions at Port Jackson,* p. 463).

117. 'Weree, weree', or 'Wee-re', as found in Collins' list of 'New South Wales' adjectives, was an expression conveying something 'bad' (Collins, *An Account of the English Colony,* vol. 1, Appendix XII, p. 507).

118. This incident is described in *An Historical Journal of the Transactions at Port Jackson*: '[The spear] struck against Governor Phillip's collar bone, close to which it entered, and the barb came out close to the third vertebrae of the back' (*An Historical Journal of the Transactions at Port Jackson,* p. 463).

119. Captain Henry Waterhouse.

120. William Balmain (1762–1803). Arrived with the First Fleet on the *Alexander* as third assistant surgeon, and served in Port Jackson until 1791, when he was posted to Norfolk Island. He remained there until 1795, and was recalled to replace Surgeon-General John White as principal surgeon when White left the colony. An energetic man, Balmain served as a magistrate and had farming and trading interests. Balmain and White fought a pistol duel on 12 August 1788, allegedly over a matter concerning professional duty. Balmain returned to England in 1801 and died in London in November 1803. (See *Australian Dictionary of Biography*, vol. 1, 1788–1850 (Melbourne: Melbourne University Press, 1966).) The Sydney harbourside suburb of Balmain was named after him.

121. In July 1788 Phillip reported to Lord Sydney on his relationship with the local Aborigines and explained his approach: 'I have the honour of informing your Lordship that the natives have ever been treated with the greatest humanity and attention, and every precaution that was possible has been taken to prevent their receiving any insults; and when I shall have time to mix more with them every means shall be used to reconcile them to live amongst us, and to teach them the advantages they will reap from cultivating the land, which will enable them to support themselves at the season of the year, when fish are so scarce that many of them perish with hunger, at least, I have strong reason to believe this is the case' (*HRNSW*, vol. 1, pt 2, p. 177).

122. In *An Impartial and Circumstantial Narrative* also called 'Nanbarra'.

123. In *An Historical Journal of the Transactions at Port Jackson*, the man's name is given as 'Caregal', indicating the tribe. The Carigal clan inhabited the coastal region to the north of Port Jackson at Broken Bay. The Carigal were part of the Kuringgai language group. Tench referred to the man who threw the spear and wounded the Governor and identified him as 'Wil-ee-ma-rin ... belonging to a tribe residing at Broken Bay' (Tench, *A Complete Account of the Settlement*, p. 123).

124. Araboo's father is named as 'Mau-go-ran' (*An Historical Journal of the Transactions at Port Jackson*, p. 468).

125. Araboo was told that she could take all her European clothes with her, that she could come and see her friends at any time and that 'whatever she wished for should be given her'. These inducements were to persuade her to stay with Revd Johnson and his wife until her grasp of English had improved, so that she could continue to 'fully explain their intentions towards the natives as fully as could have been wished' (*An Historical Journal of the Transactions at Port Jackson*, p. 466).

126. 'Barangaroo' was Bennelong's first wife. She had been abducted from the

Cammeraigal clan who inhabited land on the north side of the Harbour. Her age was estimated to be about fifty. Bennelong had a second wife, 'Goroobarrooboollo', who came from the Kameygal clan of the Botany Bay area. She outlived Barangaroo. A detailed description of Barangaroo's cremation and burial is found in Collins, *An Account of the English Colony*, vol. 1, Appendix XI, pp. 601–8.

127. It was explained that the short spear given to the Governor was sharpened by one of the knives he had given as a gift, and that Aboriginal men preferred to use knives when they could, in preference to traditional shell sharpeners (*An Historical Journal of the Transactions at Port Jackson*, p. 467).

128. A painting of Bennelong – 'Ben-nel-long', '[As] painted when angry after Botany Bay Colebee was wounded', was made by the anonymous Port Jackson Painter some time after first contact (?1790). In this particular image, Bennelong is seen 'painted up' with traditional body decoration. As a signal of their adoption of elements of 'civilization', both Bennelong and Nanbarre were painted wearing European clothes. An engraving of Bennelong by Neagle appears in Collins, *An Account of the English Colony*, vol. 1, p. 439.

129. Momill Island. This island was called 'Mel Mel' or 'Me-mel' by the Dharug people. Hunter records it as 'Memilla' or 'Memill'. It was renamed Goat Island by the early colonists when imported goats were taken to graze upon its shrubs and rocky grounds. Goat Island is situated opposite Millers Point, in the mouth of the Parramatta River. (See *An Historical Journal of the Transactions at Port Jackson*, p. 470.)

130. This gift shield was described as fabricated from 'sole leather and covered with tin, ... likely to resist the force of their spears' (*An Historical Journal of the Transactions at Port Jackson*, p. 472).

131. The length of the Aboriginal girl's stay was stated as seventeen months (*An Historical Journal of the Transactions at Port Jackson*, p. 472).

132. Bennelong's spear 'pierced the shield and the hand of his antagonist' (*An Historical Journal of the Transactions at Port Jackson*, p. 474).

133. What Barrington's publishers excised from *An Impartial and Circumstantial Narrative* was Hunter's opinion of the honesty of the Aboriginal people. Following the episode involving Araboo's stated desire to leave and marry, Hunter wrote: 'If the natives of this country be less civilised than the inhabitants of the neighbouring islands, they are much honester; for they very seldom attempt to take any thing by stealth; and, it is certain, that when a thief is caught, they beat him to death with sticks'. This comment was related to Bennelong's absence and the possibility that he had called on the Governor for the purpose of protection rather than hospitality. Hunter

supposed that Bennelong may have been attempting to steal a neighbouring clan's spears and 'gum'. (See *An Historical Journal of the Transactions at Port Jackson*, pp. 473–4.)

134. It would appear that Araboo went to join Colebee, who subsequently 'beat her' (*An Historical Journal of the Transactions at Port Jackson*, p. 475).

135. Governor Phillip had ordered that a small hut be built for 'his own accommodation' at Rose Hill in November 1790 (*An Historical Journal of the Transactions at Port Jackson*, p. 489). By the time *An Impartial and Circumstantial Narrative* was published *c*. 1793–4, Rose Hill had been renamed Parramatta by Governor Phillip; rogue London publishers carefully amended the text and installed Barrington in the Governor's 'small house'. Barrington was granted thirty acres of land at Parramatta in November 1792 on which he built a dwelling. On his death, Barrington's effects were auctioned, including household furniture, a flock of sheep and fifty acres of cleared land on the banks of the Hawkesbury River, opposite the settlement of Cornwallis (*Sydney Gazette and New South Wales Advertiser*, Sunday 30 December 1804, p. 1).

136. The 'natives' were reportedly 'fed very plentifully' and no observation was made about illness or sickness (*An Historical Journal of the Transactions at Port Jackson*, p. 490).

137. Barangaroo received injuries to her head from her husband Bennelong, during an altercation in their canoe. According to Hunter, it was expected that 'mistress Barangaroo's head' would have been under the care of the surgeon (*An Historical Journal of the Transactions at Port Jackson*, p. 490). Barrington's version refers only to her 'sreaks' (*sic*) (shrieks), without direct reference to the beating incident.

138. Bennelong's and Barangaroo's anxiety to return to Sydney is clearly expressed in official accounts. Apparently, although living with the Governor, they disliked being at Rose Hill (Parramatta). They were, of course, out of their own clan territory and would have felt in some danger of attack even with the protection of the Governor's guards. This intimation of fearfulness is missing from *An Impartial and Circumstantial Narrative*.

139. A positive order was given by Phillip 'for no one ever to *join* the natives unarmed' (*An Historical Journal of the Transactions at Port Jackson*, p. 491 [emphasis added]).

140. The attack on the gamekeeper was said to have taken place 'eleven miles from Sydney' (*An Historical Journal of the Transactions at Port Jackson*, p. 491).

141. The attack on the gamekeeper took place in December 1790. According to Hunter, the gamekeeper was 'of the catholic persuasion' – and fearing death, asked for a clergyman to whom he could confess his past sins (*An Historical Journal of the Transactions at Port Jackson*, p. 492).

142. Consistent with the London publisher's aim to please, phrases such as this, expressing the need for the Governor to have a 'good understanding' with the natives for the 'happiness and prosperity of the colony', were inserted liberally throughout *An Impartial and Circumstantial Narrative*.

143. The Bidjigal clan, the 'Beijal', inhabited the inland region called Castle Hill by the colonists. It is situated close to Parramatta. The Bidjigal were part of the Dharug language group. Pemnlaway [Pemulwy or Pemullaway] was an acknowledged leader of the clan.

144. Tooth avulsion was practised by many Aboriginal clans on young males. Collins describes the ceremony closely in his *An Account of the English Colony* (see Appendix VI, with an accompanying engraving entitled 'Yoo-long Erah-ba-diang'). This engraving, much reduced in detail, formed the basis of the illustration entitled 'Manhood', which appeared in the 1802 edition of Barrington's *The History of New South Wales*. See Plate 24.

145. Aboriginal men frequently forcibly abducted women from neighbouring clans to take as wives. The 'Sabinical' reference made in *An Impartial and Circumstantial Narrative* is to the legend of the rape of the Sabine women. (While Sabine men attended a festival at the invitation of Romulus, Roman youths raided Sabine territory and carried off the women.)

146. Characteristically, important details are altered in *An Impartial and Circumstantial Narrative*. On 14 December 1790, two captains, two lieutenants, four non-commissioned officers and forty privates, the surgeon, a surgeon's-mate (from the *Sirius*), and three other persons, went to hunt the man who had attacked the gamekeeper. Orders were given that no women or children were to be 'injured on any account'. (*An Impartial and Circumstantial Narrative* employs the words 'molested on any account'.) The search party returned empty-handed on 17 December, and went out again on 22 December, but failed to find any suspects. (See *An Historical Journal of the Transactions at Port Jackson*, p. 496.)

147. *An Impartial and Circumstantial Narrative* refers to 'Tattowing', but the process was more likely to have been scarifying. This mutilating process, involving shell knives being drawn across the skin in regular patterns, results in permanent scarring and is fully described in *An Historical Journal of the Transactions at Port Jackson*, p. 500.

148. According to official accounts, two 'colonists' went out in the boat and were robbed of their catch by Bennelong (*An Historical Journal of the Transactions at Port Jackson*, p. 501).

149. Several Aboriginal men came to see Governor Hunter on 3 January 1791 to inform him that a 'native' who had been fired on while soldiers were trying to find the gamekeeper's assailant was near death (*An Historical Journal of the Transactions at Port Jackson*, p. 502).

150. Readers of *An Impartial and Circumstantial Narrative* were denied any knowledge of the unusually fair treatment meted out to Bennelong by Governor Phillip in the face of Bennelong's threatened violence and 'savage insolence'. It was explained elsewhere that although Bennelong's behaviour might have obliged the Governor to have him arrested and punished, or even executed, recalling that Bennelong frequently called him 'be-ah-nah', 'Governor – father', Phillip decided to forget the incident, lest he destroy the confidence that Bennelong had placed in him.

151. In versions of events relayed in official accounts, Bennelong was not 'ordered away'. Bennelong returned to see if the Governor was still displeased with him and, although Phillip was prepared to speak to him, Bennelong was denied access to the Governor's house, a privilege he had previously enjoyed. Apparently this was done as a form of shaming or punishment, to put Bennelong 'on a level with the other natives, and he [Bennelong] appeared to feel his degradation; but it did not prevent him from repeating his visits regularly' (*An Historical Journal of the Transactions at Port Jackson*, p. 509).

152. Gangrene.

153. This incident, which describes the final severing of an infant female's finger, is taken from *An Historical Journal of the Transactions at Port Jackson*, p. 510. The process of deliberate amputation was first described by Governor Phillip in a detailed letter to Lord Sydney written on 15 May 1788 (*HRNSW*, vol. 1, pt 2, p. 130).

154. Bennelong returned to the settlement after 'an absence of several days' (*Historical Journal of the Transactions at Port Jackson*, p. 511).

155. 'Esculapian' – Aesculapian – relating to medicine or physicians. This reference is to the medical or first aid assistance provided to all Aboriginal visitors at Governor Phillip's house. Treatment was always at their request.

156. Surgeon-General White and Governor Phillip were particularly careful to observe and record the use of any practices of native cures and native medicaments, and their efficacy, and they were interested in the role of the native doctors – 'the Car-ra-dy-gans' – and their methods. Other observers regarded the practices as merely superstitious or close to faith healing.

157. In Hunter's collected vocabulary, the word is shown as 'Bul-ler-doo-ul' (*An Historical Account of the Transactions at Port Jackson*, p. 522).

158. This incident is paraphrased and the subtle change in phrasing was neatly executed. In Hunter's account, the healing incident ends with the words: 'He [Colebee] gave his worsted night cap and the best part of his supper to the doctor as a fee; and being asked, if both the men were doctors, he [Colebee] said, yes, and the child was a doctor also, so that it may be

presumed the power of healing wounds descends from father to son' (*An Historical Account of the Transactions at Port Jackson*, pp. 521–2).

159. The report of exchange of fish by the Aboriginals with the colonists for bread, rice and vegetables comes from *An Historical Account of the Transactions at Port Jackson*, pp. 532ff. Phillip was anxious to encourage any system of barter which would lay the foundations for co-operation and continuing peaceful relations.

160. Balderry (also known as Boladeree, Ballederry, Ba-lo-der-ry or Boladeree) was described by Tench as a 'fine well grown lad, of nineteen or twenty years'. He accompanied Colebee and travelled with Tench and his party on their expedition in April 1791 to discover whether the Hawkesbury and Nepean were, in fact, the same river. (They were discovered to have different sources.) See 'Travelling diaries in New South Wales', Tench, *A Complete Account of the Settlement*, pp. 160–70. Balderry was banished from the settlement by Governor Phillip for spearing a convict who had stolen and destroyed his canoe. Balderry later became ill with a virulent fever and Phillip allowed him to be attended by the surgeon at the hospital. He subsequently died and was buried in Governor Phillip's garden. In Collins' *An Account of the English Settlement*, vol. 1, a detailed description of Balderry's burial ceremony appears in Appendix XI, pp. 499–504. It was said that Governor Phillip had intended to take Balderry to England.

161. Incidents of natives throwing spears at settlers and convicts are frequently recorded in early accounts. In *The History of New South Wales* (1802), attributed to George Barrington, an illustration entitled 'East View of Sydney' shows a settler being threatened by an Aboriginal man with a raised spear; see Plate 26 (at left side of view). While no explicit comments on spear attacks are included in *An Impartial and Circumstantial Narrative*, the text presented an impression of numerous unprovoked attacks. Governor Phillip recognized that many attacks were directly provoked by convicts who stole items from Aborigines, and he issued strict orders that Aboriginal property should never be touched. Severe floggings were given as punishment for any person found interfering with Aboriginal property, and those who stole from them were hanged.

162. 'Baldberry' is a corruption of the spelling found in *An Historical Account of the Transactions at Port Jackson*, pp. 533–4.

163. See Note 160, above, relating to Balderry spearing a convict who stole his canoe.

164. Hunter described the arrival of a number of natives at the settlement on 23 August 1791, and estimated that six men and twenty-eight women and children came to the Governor's house and received bread. (There is no mention of rice, although a shipment of provisions had arrived on the *Mary*

Ann transport, and two pounds of rice were added to weekly rations.) Hunter surmised that Balderry was not arrested at the time because the Governor did not want to frighten the Aboriginal visitors, 'as several of these men and women were strangers, who had now come to Sydney for the first time' (*An Historical Journal of the Transactions at Port Jackson*, p. 542).

165. Publishers of *An Impartial and Circumstantial Narrative* made a number of amendments and excisions to the text. In official accounts, Balderry is referred to by name, whereas in *An Impartial and Circumstantial Narrative* he is described as 'the delinquent'. In official accounts, it is said that the natives tried to pull 'the firelock' from a soldier, whereas *An Impartial and Circumstantial Narrative* states, 'one of them had the audacity to attempt to wrest a firelock from one of the soldiers; however, he failed in the attempt'. In cutting and pasting text, and in editing, the publishers removed the picture of a gathering. The natives were 'said to be assembled near the brick-fields; an officer was therefore ordered out with a strong party to disperse them, and to make a severe example of them, if any spears were thrown'. *An Impartial and Circumstantial Narrative* confuses the party of soldiers with the gathering of natives, and fails to inform readers that the natives were gathering on their way to 'dance at Botany-Bay' and had no violent intentions. (See *An Historical Journal of the Transactions at Port Jackson*, p. 543.)

166. A 'fish-gig' or 'fiz-gig' as it was also known, was a three- or four-pronged spear usually made from wattle tree boughs, hardened by fire, with joints fastened by gum. The spear was approximately fifteen to twenty feet in length, armed with four barbed prongs fashioned from bone or shell. Fish-gigs were usually used by men for fishing, whereas women often fished with a line and bone or shell hooks. A fine illustration of the fish-gig is found in White's *Journal of a Voyage to New South Wales*, Plate 63.

167. Barangaroo's confinement is described in *An Historical Journal of the Transactions at Port Jackson*, pp. 544–5. David Collins provided details of birth rituals, parturition and care of the new born. Collins described seeing Bennelong's wife, Barangaroo, only a few hours after she had given birth and expressed surprise at seeing her 'walking about alone, and picking up sticks to mend her fire'. For British men, married and unmarried, used only to British rituals of birth and confinement, seeing Barangaroo active and self-sufficient within hours of delivery must have occasioned wonder and consternation. (See Collins, 'Customs and Manners', *An Account of the English Colony*, vol. 1, Appendix VI, pp. 561–2.)

168. Balderry's illness appears at the end of Governor Phillip's account and forms the foundation of *An Historical Journal of the Transactions at Port*

Jackson; see p. 566. Balderry's burial ceremony is described in detail in 'Funeral Ceremonies', in Collins, *An Account of the English Colony in New South Wales*, vol. 1, Appendix XI, pp. 601–8. Immediately following Collins' description is an engraving by Neagle entitled 'Burning a Corpse'. A similar illustration appears in Barrington's *The History of New South Wales* (1802). See Plate 27, entitled 'Burying the Dead', which is a copy of a group scene produced first in Collins. Balderry died in December 1791.

169. Inconsistencies in spelling Governor Phillip's name, among others in the text, provide an indication of the rapid 'cobbling' of sources by the London publisher of *An Impartial and Circumstantial Narrative*. There was scant reverence paid to the accuracy of names as the publisher, S. & J. Bailey, undertook to produce a cheap, popular and accessible version of the more expensive subscription publication of Hunter's *An Historical Journal of the Transactions at Port Jackson*. This had been produced with seventeen plates and maps by Stockdale of Piccadilly, on fine paper, in boards. *An Impartial and Circumstantial Narrative* was priced sixpence, whereas *An Historical Journal of the Transactions at Port Jackson* was priced between £1 11s 6d and two guineas (£2 2s). (The original source of the acclamation attributed to 'Governor Philips' in Hunter's *An Impartial and Circumstantial Narrative* has not been identified.)

170. Publishers of *An Impartial and Circumstantial Narrative* spliced journal entries of events recorded at different intervals between 1790 and 1791, in an effort to make events read seamlessly. Ordering of individual paragraphs was changed and original wordings were altered to fit the style of a personal narrative. For example, references to singing are joined with questions concerning Aboriginal belief and worship, and these are run together with a description of a burial. For comparison, see *An Historical Journal of the Transactions at Port Jackson*, pp. 412–14.

171. The publisher of *An Impartial and Circumstantial Narrative* had carefully scoured *An Historical Journal of the Transactions at Port Jackson*, to pull information and observations on Aboriginal graves together. Specific details of cremations and graves came from the first descriptions written in 1788 by Governor Phillip (*An Historical Journal of the Transactions at Port Jackson*, pp. 64–5).

172. Araboo and Bennelong are cited as informants on the subject of omens and apparitions, and factual information published in *An Impartial and Circumstantial Narrative* is largely consistent with that found in *An Historical Journal of the Transactions at Port Jackson*, pp. 412–13. However, in *An Historical Journal*, the informants are referred to differently, as 'Wolare-warre' and 'the native girl'. In *An Impartial and Circumstantial Narrative*, Araboo's reference to 'Murray roway – the

Sirins', is made about the *Sirius*, the vessel which was wrecked at Norfolk Island. A combination of spelling and printing errors necessitated the publisher drastically to alter the meaning. The *Sirius* became 'The Sirins', which, to make sense, required the following insertion of 'who was lost', rather than 'the Sirius' [which] was lost ... at Norfolk Island'. 'Murray roway' was another incorrect transcription. The Aboriginal words transcribed as 'Murray nowey' referred to a description of the *Sirius*. According to Hunter's collected vocabulary of Aboriginal language, 'Murray or murrey' was an adjective meaning 'large or great', and 'nowey' referred to a 'canoe'. (See *An Historical Journal of the Transactions at Port Jackson*, p. 409.)

173. 'Mané', or 'Ma-hn' meant 'a ghost' (Collins, *An Account of the English Settlement*, Vocabulary, Appendix XII, p. 160).

174. Much of the language in this particular passage was distorted with comments added to 'popularize' the account. Hunter had observed that 'the natives ... often had a dance amongst themselves at night'. References to 'birth-day suits', or to the 'inquisitive glance of the curious Europian [sic]', do not appear in the original version from which *An Impartial and Circumstantial Narrative* was produced. The phrase that Aboriginal men 'are as emulous of appearing fine as the most finished petitmaitre preparing for the birth day ball of their favourite mistress' was undoubtedly inserted to entertain. For the original description of preparation and body decorations, see *An Historical Journal of the Transactions at Port Jackson*, pp. 210–11.

175. Following the pattern established in *An Impartial and Circumstantial Narrative*, the publisher amended the numbers involved. The number of dancers in the original account was given as between twenty and twenty-six. (See *An Historical Journal of the Transactions at Port Jackson*, p. 211.)

176. Unlike many passages in *An Impartial and Circumstantial Narrative*, this description of dancers, their movements, musical instruments and singing closely follows the original account. What was described was the corroboree, or 'cariberie' – 'good dance' – and this term was omitted from *An Impartial and Circumstantial Narrative*. (See *An Historical Journal of the Transactions at Port Jackson*, pp. 212–13.)

177. Fire-making and the carrying of a fire stick by Aboriginal people was first noted by Captain Cook. Phillip provided a description in 1791, and an illustration taken from a sketch by Second Lieutenant Phillip Gidley King (later third Governor of New South Wales (1800–1806)), subsequently engraved by Blake and entitled 'A Family of New South Wales', appears in an Appendix to *An Historical Journal of the Transactions at Port Jackson*. The sketch shows a man and woman; the man carrying a shield, a wooden

throwing stick, and a four-pronged barbed fishing spear, the woman is carrying an infant on her shoulders, with a line and fish hook and some fish in her hands, and a young boy carries fishing spears (fish gigs) and a smoldering fire stick. (See *An Historical Journal of the Transactions at Port Jackson*, pp. 413–16.)

178. Relations between Aboriginal men and women were commented upon by Tench, White, Phillip and Collins. They observed 'great cruelty' shown towards Aboriginal women by their male relations which was tolerated, apparently with little retaliation. Comments in *An Impartial and Circumstantial Narrative* regarding Aboriginal women's passivity was amended with a comment to preserve the personal narrative and 'observer's' view. In official accounts, the tone of language employed tended to be impersonal and, without necessarily condoning, took into account cultural differences: 'the women are certainly treated with great cruelty; this, however, the custom of the country seems to have perfectly reconciled them to'. (See *An Historical Journal of the Transactions at Port Jackson*, p. 501.)

179. The number of parcels of land under cultivation at Parramatta in November 1791, measured by David Burton (d. 1792), superintendent of convicts and the appointed public gardener, are listed in the official accounts (*An Historical Journal of the Transactions at Port Jackson*, p. 562).

180. The publishers of *An Impartial and Circumstantial Narrative* brought together information scattered over more than 500 pages in the original journal accounts. Temperatures, soil conditions, water supply, winds, seasons and climate changes observed over the period of the first four years of settlement provided important information for prospective settlers. Information on high temperatures and its effect upon convicts and settlers, as well as bird-life, is found in *An Historical Journal of the Transactions at Port Jackson*; see pp. 202–3 and p. 507.

181. For a description of the debilitated state of the convicts when landed, see *An Historical Journal of the Transactions at Port Jackson*, p. 561.

182. Phillip reported on the incapacitated state of convicts who had arrived on the Third Fleet transports, *Atlantic, Matilda, Active, Queen* and *Britannia*, in a detailed letter to the Rt. Hon. Henry Dundas dated 19 March 1792, commenting that high mortality rates continued well after arrival. He noted that from 1 January 1791 to 31 December 1791, 436 convicts had died – 418 males and 18 females. (See *HRNSW*, vol. 1, pt 2, Note p. 596.) George Barrington arrived on the *Active* on 26 September 1791 and his dishevelled appearance was commented upon by Tench and Collins.

183. Escaping from the penal settlement was an idea rife amongst early convicts who had little, if any, understanding of the geography and remoteness of their location. Some conceived that China was only 240 kilometres to the

north of Port Jackson. Escape attempts occurred almost within days of the First Fleet's arrival. Stowaways were discovered relatively frequently. In 1788 a group of Irish convicts evaded their marine guards and cut across country to Botany Bay where the French ships *Astrolabe* and *La Boussoule* were anchored. La Pérouse refused to take them on board and sent them packing back to Sydney Cove. This incident was reported in *An Impartial and Circumstantial Narrative*. The most famous escape of the early period was, perhaps, that of Mary (née Brand) Bryant (b. 1765), 'The Girl from Botany Bay', who, with eleven others, managed to escape from Port Jackson in 1791 in a fishing boat and reached Dutch Timor. Her story was widely celebrated in the English press; see Tench, *A Complete Account of the Settlement*, p. 108.

184. The final section of *An Impartial and Circumstantial Narrative* contains elements of fact and fiction. 'Governor Philips' – Governor Phillip – did encourage gardens and growing vegetables, and Barrington received notice for his diligence in watch-keeping, but there is no official report that refers to Barrington's gardening skills. There is no record indicating where Barrington resided in his first year after arriving in 1791, although it is known that he was sent to Toongabbie.

185. 'Barrington's' story of becoming lost in the bush follows, in its essence, the record of an expedition taken by Governor Phillip and his party who intended to reach the Hawkesbury River and cross it in order to get to an area known as Richmond Hill. This expedition took place in April 1791. During the expedition, Phillip and his party encountered the Boorooberongal people who lived in the Richmond district, and in particular an older man with a young boy. In the original account related in *An Historical Journal of the Transactions at Port Jackson,* a native shelter was found and the party rested there overnight, lighting a fire (p. 516). They continued their expedition, noting, among other features, large ant nests (p. 518). They encountered difficult terrain and small ravines in the river country. The older man's name was recorded as Yal-lah-mien-di, and the boy was called Tim-bah (p. 520). The London publisher of *An Impartial and Circumstantial Narrative* took the bones of the report of Phillip's expedition and invented a new story incorporating Barrington, his companion 'Tim', a wounded Aboriginal warrior, his family, including mother and father, and the young Aboriginal woman, 'Yeariana'.

186. See Plate 9 (p. 34). This refers to the title page of *A Voyage to Botany Bay* (*c.* 1795), an expanded version of *An Impartial and Circumstantial Narrative*. In the 1795 edition, this illustration entitled 'An interesting discovery in the woods' gives a picture of the story which concludes *An Impartial and Circumstantial Narrative*. In this, 'Tim' stands by the figure

of 'Barrington', with a young Aboriginal woman 'Yeariana' seated on a rock, looking at the prone body of her brother 'Botcherry', who has been seriously wounded with an arrow.

187. In *An Historical Journal of the Transactions at Port Jackson* it is Coleby (Colebee) who is described as having had a long-standing wound. The observer found the wound 'below the left breast with a fiz-gig, and though it must have been done many years back, or the wound must have been slight, as it was difficult to discover any scar, yet it was supposed he felt some pain'. Colebee was healed by two 'Bu-ru-be-ron-gal' – Boorooberongal men alleged to have healing powers. (See *An Historical Journal of the Transactions at Port Jackson*, p. 521.) In *An Impartial and Circumstantial Narrative*, Barrington allegedly chafed the body and restored a pulse and thus received the undying gratitude of 'Botcherry's' family.

188. The Aboriginal healer extracted what Colebee thought were two fish barbs from the old wound (*An Historical Journal of the Transactions at Port Jackson*, p. 522).

189. Governor Phillip gave the old man 'some bread, some fish-hooks, and a couple of small hatchets', in return for 'two stone hatchets, two spears, and a throwing stick', given to him by the 'old native'. Colebee gave his healers 'his worsted night cap and the best part of his supper' (*An Historical Journal of the Transactions at Port Jackson*, pp. 519–22).

190. 'Yeariana' was a composite and fictious character with a name probably devised for semi-entertaining purposes. Extensive searching across the early journals has revealed no name approximating to 'Yeariana' referring to a young woman. Watkin Tench described a young Aboriginal woman, 'Gooredeeana' (a sister of Bennelong), in glowing terms in his *A Complete Account of the Settlement* published in 1793. In Tench, Gooredeeana was said to have: 'excelled in beauty all their females I ever saw ... Her countenance ... was distinguished by a softness and sensibility unequalled in the rest of her countrywomen ...' (Tench, *A Complete Account of the Settlement* p. 207). When the expanded history attributed to Barrington appeared in 1795 as *A Voyage to Botany Bay*, the description of 'Yeariana' was similarly elaborated. From a young woman who had 'made a strong impression on my mind', 'Yeariana' became 'a form that might serve as a perfect model for the most scrupulous statuary; her face and hair unlike anything I had ever seen in this country; the first a perfect oval, or Grecian shape, with features regularly beautiful, and as fine a pair of eyes as can be imagined ... she was likewise of a much lighter colour than any of her countrywomen, and might easily have been taken for a beautiful Oriental Creole' (*A Voyage to Botany Bay* (1795), p. 117).

191. *An Impartial and Circumstantial Narrative* ends abruptly, as does *An*

Historical Journal of the Transactions at Port Jackson. Hunter closes the account with the final notes taken from the 'Journal of Governor Phillip', referring to Governor Phillip's record 'which contained the latest accounts from New South Wales; being received by the *Gorgon* that left Port Jackson in December 1791'. (See *An Historical Journal of the Transactions at Port Jackson*, p. 567.) Taking a cue from this information, Barrington's publisher probably decided to allude to the imminent departure of a ship for England without identifying the vessel, but fulfilling the promise made at the opening of *An Impartial and Circumstantial Narrative*, to relay information at the 'earliest opportunity'. The letter which opens *An Impartial and Circumstantial Narrative* from George Barrington is undated, as is the identical letter which was included in the preface of *A Voyage to Botany Bay* (1795). Many of the following histories attributed to Barrington were prefixed with Barrington's letter dated 'Paramatta, November 1793', retained because, as the publishers claimed, it had 'appeared in the First Edition of this Work'. This ploy was used, very successfully as it turned out, to authenticate the 'author's' work.

BIBLIOGRAPHY

CONTEMPORARY WORKS ATTRIBUTED TO OR ABOUT GEORGE BARRINGTON (1755–1804)

A select list of works published about or attributed to George Barrington published from 1788, to his death in Parramatta, New South Wales, in December 1804, and thereafter, up to 1820.

(Note: Spelling, capitalization, and printing errors have been retained as they appear in original titles.)

1788
The Famous Speech of George Barrington, Esq., before the Judge and Jury at the Old Bailey, London, together with the learned Recorder's Answer, 18th Sept., 1788.

1790

The Whole Proceedings on the King's Commission of the Peace, Oyer and Terminer, and Gaol Delivery for the City of London; and also The Gaol Delivery for the County of Middlesex, held at Justice Hall in the Old Bailey, on Wednesday, the 15th of September, 1790, and the following Days; Being the Seventh Session in the Mayoralty of The Right Honourable William Pickett, Lord Mayor of the City of London. Taken in Shorthand by E. Hodgson, Professor of Shorthand; And Published by Authority. Number VII. Part I. London: Printed for E. Hodgson (the Proprietor); And Sold by him, at his House, No. 14, White Lion Street, Islington. Sold also by T. Walmsley, No. 35, Chancery Lane; S. Bladon, No. 13, Paternoster Row; and J. Marsom, No. 183, High Holborn. MDCCXC.

The Life, Amours, and Wonderful Adventures of that most Notorious Pickpocket, George Barrington, from his Birth, To his conviction at the Old-Bailey, for robbing Henry Hare Townsend, Esq. Embellished with an Elegant Frontispiece, which contains a striking Likeness of Barrington. London: Printed and published by W. Mason, 21 Clerkenwell Green. Sixpence. n. d. (*c.* 1790).

A New Flash Song, made on the noted George Barrington, who was tried and found Guilty, at the last Sessions at the Old Bailey, for assaulting and Robbing Mr Henry Hare Townsend, on September the first; of his Gold Watch, three Gold Seals, and a Gold chain, on Enfield Race Course. Broadside, London, n. d. (*c. 1790*).

The Genuine Life and Trial of George Barrington, from his Birth in June 1755, to the Time of his conviction at the Old-Bailey in September 1790, for robbing Henry Hare Townsend, Esq. Of his Gold Watch, Seals, &c. London: Printed for and Sold by Mrs Mary Clements, Mr James Sadler, and Mr John Eves. Price Sixpence. n. d. (*c. 1790*).

The Genuine Life and Trial of G. Barrington, from his Birth in June 1755, to the Time of his conviction in September, 1790 at the Old Bayley, for Robbing Henry Hare Townsend Esq. of his Gold Watch, Seals, &c. Printed for J. Sadler, J. Eves, and M. Clements. Price Sixpence. n. d. (*c. 1790*).

The Genuine Life and Trial, of George Barrington, from his Birth, to the Time of his Conviction at the Old Bayley, in September 1790, for robbing Henry Hare Townsend, Esq. of his Gold Watch, Seals, &c. Printed by A. Swindells, Hanging-bridge, Manchester: and sold by J. Sadler, and T. Thomas. Price Ninepence. n. d. (*c. 1790*).

Memoirs of George Barrington, from his Birth in MDCCLV, *to his Last Conviction at the Old Bailey, on Friday, the 17th September,* MDCCXC.— London: Printed for M. Smith, opposite Fetter-lane, in Fleet-Street. MDCCXC.

A New Edition, Greatly Improved. Memoirs of George Barrington; from his Birth in MDCCLV, *to his Last Conviction at the Old Bailey, on Friday, the 17th of September,* MDCCXC. London: Printed for M. Smith, opposite Fetter-lane, in Fleet-Street. MDCCXC.

The Memoirs of George Barrington, containing every Remarkable Circumstance, from his birth to the Present Time, including the following Trials—1. *For robbing Mrs Dudman.* 2. *Elizabeth Ironmonger.* 3. *Returning from Transportation.* 4. *Robbing Sir G. Webster.* 5. *Mr Bagshaw.* 6. *Mr Le Mesurier.* 7. *For Outlawry.* 8. *For Robbing Mr Townsend. With the Whole of his Celebrated Speeches, Taken from the Records of the King's Bench, Old Bailey, &c.*— London, Printed for J. Bird, No. 22. Fetter Lane, Fleet Street; and Simmonds, No. 20, Paternoster Row. [Price One shilling.]

The only Authentic Edition. The Memoirs of George Barrington, containing every remarkable circumstance from his birth to the present time, including the following trials—With the whole of his Celebrated Speeches, Taken from the Records of the King's Bench, Old Bailey, &c. London: Printed for the Author; and sold by B. Urquhart, and all the Booksellers of the Town and Country. Price One Shilling.

The Trial at Large of George Barrington, before Lord Chief Baron Eyre, at the Sessions House in the Old Bailey, on Friday the 17th instant, for robbing Henry Townsend, Esq. at Enfield Races, for which he was found Guilty. With the Pleadings of Counsel, the Judge's Charge to the Jury, and the Prisoner's two remarkable Speeches, verbatim. By. E. Hodgson, Shorthand Writer to the Old Bailey. London: Printed for Simmonds, No. 20, Paternoster Row and R. Butters, No. 79, Fleet-Street. Price One Shilling.

1791

The Genuine Life and Trial of George Barrington, from his birth in June 1755, to the Time of his Conviction at the Old-Bailey in September 1790. For robbing Henry Hare Townsend, Esq. Of his gold Watch, Seals, &c. London: Printed for Robert Barker, in August, 1791. Price Sixpence.

1792

The Life of George Barrington, containing every Remarkable Circumstance, from his Birth to the Present Time. Including the following Trials—1. For robbing Mrs Dudman 2. Elizabeth Ironmonger 3. Returning from Transportation 4. Robbing Sir G. Webster 5. Mr Bagshaw 6. Mr Le Mesurier 7. For Outlawry 8. For robbing Mr Townsend. With the whole of his Celebrated Speeches, Taken from the Records of the King's Bench, Old Bailey, &c. To which is added A Copy of a Letter from him at the Cape of Good Hope. To a Gentleman in the County of York, dated 1st July, 1791. London: Printed for the Booksellers, 1792. Price Sixpence.

The Life of George Barrington, containing every Remarkable Circumstance, from his Birth to the present Time, including the following Trials—1. For robbing Mrs Dudman 2. Elizabeth Ironmonger 3. Returning from Transportation 4. Robbing Sir G. Webster 5. Mr Bagshaw 6. Mr Le Mesurier 7. For Outlawry 8. For robbing Mr Townsend. With the Whole of his Celebrated Speeches, Taken from the Records of King's Bench, Old Bailey, &c. The Seventh Edition. Printed and sold by Andrew Hambleton. Price Sixpence.

1793–4 [?]

AN IMPARTIAL AND CIRCUMSTANTIAL NARRATIVE OF THE PRESENT STATE OF BOTANY BAY, IN NEW SOUTH WALES: With a Description of the Country; Treatment of the Convicts on their Passage, and after their arrival. ALSO THE MANNERS, CUSTOMS, RELIGION, &c. of the NATIVES, Truly Depicted. Containing among a variety of entertaining subjects the Particulars of the Voyage; a description of the Buildings and Soil at Sydney Cove; Journey to Paramata; Convicts Houses and daily Occupations; their Emoluments from Government on the Expiration of their Term; Birds; Animals; Vegetables; manner of taking one of the Natives, who dies of the Small-Pox; entrap two others, who escape with much Ingenuity; their Retaliation upon the Governor, who very narrowly escapes Death; a reconciliation takes place; &c. &c. &c. &c. By GEORGE BARRINGTON, Now Superintendant of the Convicts at Paramata. London: Printed by S. & J. Bailey, No. 50, Bishopgate Street Within, and No. 55, Upper East-Smithfield. Price Sixpence.

1795

A Voyage to New South Wales; With a Description of the Country; The Manners, Customs, Religion, &c. of the Natives, In the Vicinity of Botany Bay. By George Barrington, now Superintendant of the Convicts at Paramatta. Price Sixpence. London. Printed for the Proprietors. 1795.

A Voyage to Botany Bay with a description of the Country, manners, Customs, religion, &c. of the Natives by the Celebrated George Barrington. Sold by H. D. Symonds, No. 20 Paternoster Row. Price One Shilling and Sixpence.

A Voyage to New South Wales; With a Description of the Country; The Manners, Customs, Religion, &c. of the Natives, In the Vicinity of Botany Bay. By George Barrington, now Superintendant of the Convicts at Paramatta. London: Printed for the Proprietor; Sold by H. D. Symonds, No. 20, Paternoster-Row. (Price Half-a-Crown.) 1795.

A Voyage to Botany Bay with a Description of the Country, manners, Customs, Religion &c. of the Natives by the Celebrated George Barrington. To which is added his Life and Trial. – London. Printed by C. Lowndes, and Sold by H. D. Symonds, No. 20, Paternoster Row.

A Voyage to New South Wales; with a Description of the Country; The Manners, Customs, Religion, &c. of The Natives, In the Vicinity of Botany Bay. By George Barrington, now Superintendant of the Convicts at Paramata, and sent to his Friend in England. Printed and Sold by J. Sadler, M. Clements, &c. Price Sixpence.

Barrington's Voyage to New South Wales; With a Description of the Country; The Manners, Customs, Religion, &c. of the Natives, in the vicinity of Botany Bay. A New Edition, by George Barrington, Now Superintendant to the Convicts at Paramata, and sent to his Friend in England. Printed for J. Sadler, J. Eves, and M. Clements. Price only Sixpence.

Barrington's Voyage to New South Wales; With a Description of the Country; The Manners, Customs, Religion, &c. of the Natives in the Vicinity of Botany Bay. A New Edition by George Barrington, now Superintendant to the Convicts at Paramata, and sent to his Friend in England. Printed by A. Swindells, Hanging-Bridge, Manchester: and sold by T. Thomas, and J. Sadler. Price only Nine-pence.

Barrington's Voyage to New South Wales; with a Description of the Country; the Manners, Customs, Religion, &c. of the Natives, in the vicinity of Botany Bay. A New Edition, by George Barrington. Now Superintendant to the Convicts at Paramata, and sent to his Friend in England. Printed by A. Swindells, Hanging-bridge. Manchester: and Sold by J. Sadler, and M. Clements. Price only sixpence.

The Life and Extraordinary Adventures of George Barrington, now transported to Botany-Bay [etc.].
Darlington. n. d. [1795].

1796

A Voyage to New South Wales; with a Description of the Country; the Manners, Customs, Religion &c. of The Natives in the Vicinity of Botany Bay. By George Barrington, now Superintendant of the Convict at Paramatta. The Third Edition. London. Printed for the Proprietor; Sold by H. D. Symonds; No. 20, Paternoster Row [Price Half-a-Crown.] 1796.

A Voyage to New South Wales; with a Description of the Country; The Manners, Customs, Religion, &c. of the Natives in the Vicinity of Botany Bay. By George Barrington, now Superintendant of the Convicts at Paramatta. The Fourth Edition. London. Printed for the Proprietor; sold by H. D. Symonds, No. 20, Paternoster-Row. [Price Half-a-Crown.] 1796.

A Voyage to New South Wales; With a Description of the Country; The Manners, Customs, Religion, &c. of the Natives, in the Vicinity of Botany Bay. By George Barrington, now Superintendant of the Convicts at Paramatta. Philadelphia: Printed by Thomas Dobson, at the Stone-House, No. 41, South Second-Street. 1796.

1798

Voyage à Botany-Bay, avec une Description du Pays, des Moeurs, des

Coutumes et de la Religion des Natifs. Par le célèbre George Barrington. Traduit de l'Anglais, sur la troisième édition. À Paris, Chez Desenne, Libraire, Palais-Égalité, Nos 1 et 2. An. VI.

A Voyage to New South Wales; With a Description of the Country; The Manners, Customs, Religion, &c. of the Natives, in the Vicinity of Botany Bay. By George Barrington, now *Superintendant of the Convicts at Parramatta, and sent to his friend in England. The Fifth Edition.* Printed and Sold by A. Hambleton. Price Six-pence.

A Voyage to New South Wales; with a Description of the Country; the Manners, Customs, Religion, &c. of the Natives, In the Vicinity of Botany Bay. By George Barrington, now *Superintendant of the Convicts at Parramatta, and sent to his Friend in England. The Sixth Edition.* Printed and Sold by A. Hambleton, Price Six-pence.

Viaje y Translaccion del Famoso Barrington a Botani-Bay en la Nueva-Holanda puesto en espagnol con algunas correccions y notas por Santiago de Alvarado y de la Pena, Madrid: M. Pita, n. d. (between 1798 and 1810).

1800

A Sequel to Barrington's Voyage to New South Wales, comprising an Interesting Narrative of the Transactions and Behaviour of the Convicts; The Progress of the Colony; An Official Register of the Crimes, Trials, Sentences and Executions that have taken place: A Topographical, Physical and Moral Account of the Country, Manners, Customs, &c. of the Natives, As likewise Authentic Anecdotes of the most Distinguished Characters, and Notorious Convicts that have been Transported to the Settlement at New South Wales. By the celebrated George Barrington, Principal Superintendant of the Convicts. London. Printed and Published by C. Lowndes, No. 66, Drury-Lane; and sold by H. D. Symonds, Paternoster Row. 1800.

1801

Barrington's Voyage to Botany Bay, in New South Wales; with a Description of the Country, & its Productions; the Manners, Customs, Religion, &c. of the Natives, in the Vicinity of the Settlement; With the manner of Treatment, and present comfortable Situation of the Convicts; State of Agriculture, &c. &c. Written by himself, Superindentant of the Convicts at Parramatta, and sent to his friend in England. Printed for J. Letbe, by M. Angus & Son, Newcastle. 1801.

Barrington's Voyage to Botany Bay in New South Wales; with a Description of the Country, & its Productions; the Manners, Customs, Religion, &c. of the Natives, in the Vicinity of the Settlement With the Manner of Treatment, and present comfortable Situation of the Convicts; State of Agriculture, &c. &c. Written by himself, Superintendent of the

Convicts at Parramatta, and sent to his friend in England. Newcastle: Printed by M. Angus & son, in the Side. 1801.

A Voyage to New South Wales, comprising an Interesting Narrative of the Transactions and Behaviour of the Convicts; The Progress of the Colony: An Official Register of the Crimes, Trials, Sentences and Executions, that have taken place: A Topographical, Physical and Moral Account of the Country, Manners, Customs &c. of the Natives. As likewise Authentic Anecdotes of the most Distinguished Characters, and Notorious Convicts that have been Transported to Botany Bay. By George Barrington, Principal Superintendant of the Convicts. To which is annexed his Life and Trial. Dublin: Printed for F. Wogan, W. Porter, H. Fitzpatrick, N. Kelly, and J. Stockdale. 1801.

A Voyage to New South Wales, comprising an Interesting Narrative of the Transactions & Behaviour of the Convicts; The Progress of the Colony; an Official Register of the Crimes, Trials, Sentences, and Executions that have taken place; A Topographical, Physical and Moral Account of the Country, Manners, Customs, &c. of the Natives. As likewise Authentic Anecdotes of the most Distinguished Characters and Notorious Convicts that have been Transported to Botany Bay. By George Barrington, Principal Superintendant of the Convicts. To which is annexed his Life and Trial. Cork: Printed by George Cherry, Circulating Library, St. Patrick's Street. 1801.

A Voyage to New South Wales, comprising an interesting Narrative of the Transactions and Behaviour of the Convicts: the Progress of the Colony; an Official Register of the Crimes, Trials, Sentences and Executions that have taken place; A Topographical, Physical, and Moral Account of the Country, Manners, Customs, &c. of the Natives. As likewise Authentic Anecdotes of the most distinguished Characters, and notorious Convicts that have been transported to Botany Bay. By George Barrington, Principal Superintendant of the Convicts. To which is annexed his Life and Trial. New-York: Printed by John Swain.

A Sequel to Barrington's Voyage to New South Wales, comprising an Interesting Narrative of the Transactions and Behaviour of the Convicts; The Progress of the Colony; An Official Register of the Crimes, Trials, Sentences, and Executions that have taken place: A Topographical, Physical and Moral Account of the Country, manners, Customs, &c. of the Natives – as likewise Authentic Anecdotes of the most Distinguished Characters, and Notorious convicts that have been Transported to the Settlement at New South Wales. By the celebrated George Barrington, Principal Superintendant of the Convicts. London. Printed and Published by C. Lowndes, No. 66, Drury-Lane; and sold by H. D. Symonds, Paternoster Row. 1801.

1802

The History of Botany Bay, in New South Wales; with a Description of the Country, Manners, Customs, Religion, &c. &c. of the Natives; including the Particulars of the Treatment of the Convicts, and a Narrative of a Voyage in a Transport Ship thereto. By George Barrington, formerly Superintendent of the Convicts. London. Printed and Published by W. Mason, 21 Clerkenwell Green. Price Sixpence.

Barrington's History of New South Wales, including Botany Bay, &c. No. 1. To be continued weekly. By George Barrington, an Officer of the Peace at Paramatta. To be completed in Twelve Numbers, elegantly Printed in Octavo, Illustrated with Elegant Engravings of Views and Customs, and Subjects of Natural History, Coloured from Nature. 'The proprietors beg leave to assure the public that nothing can impede the regular publication of the work, as the manuscript has all arrived, and the plates are in great forwardness.'

The History of New South Wales, including Botany Bay, Port Jackson, Parramatta, Sydney, and all its Dependancies from the Original Discovery of the Island: with the Customs and Manners of the Natives; and an Account of the English Colony, from its Foundation, to the Present Time. By George Barrington: superintendant of the Convicts. Enriched with beautiful Coloured Prints. London: Printed for M. Jones, No. 1 Paternoster Row. 1802.

Prologue spoken by George Barrington, on Jan. 16, 1796, at the Opening of the Theatre at Sydney, in New South Wales. [Broadside], n. d. (*c.* 1802).

1803

The Life and Trials of George Barrington, Officer of the Peace at Paramatta. Author of the Voyage to, and History of New South Wales. London: Printed by W. Flint, Old Bailey, for M. Jones, No. 1, Paternoster-Row. 1803.

Biographical Annals of Suicide, or Horrors of Self-Murder, whether impelled by Love, Penury, Depravity, Melancholy, Bigotry, Remorse, or Jealousy. Calculated to deter even the most wretched from this horrible crime, and enable them to bear with fortitude the ills of this life, by a comparative view of the miseries of some of their fellow creatures. By George Barrington. London: Printed for Tegg and Castleman, No. 23, Warwick Square: And sold by B. Crosby and Co. Stationer's Court; J. Brown, Edinburgh; M. Keene, Dublin; and Bull, Waterford. 1803.

Dedicated to His Majesty. *Barrington's Voyage to New South Wales*, No. IV. Price One Shilling to be continued weekly. (Enriched with fine coloured Prints.) To which is prefixed, the Life, Trials, &c. of the Author,

Accompanied with a fine engraved Portrait. Conditions. 1. The Voyage will be printed uniform with the History and embellished with views finely coloured after Nature. 2. That the Voyage will be completed in Twelve Numbers (all above will be given gratis) making One handsome Volume in Octavo, which, with the History, will form a complete and uniform Edition of the Works of the celebrated George Barrington, in Two elegant Volumes, neatly printed in 8vo. 3. The Work will be continued Weekly, without intermission, till completed. 4. Every Number will be embellished with a Print, finely coloured, consisting of Views, Natural History, Map of New South Wales, from the latest Discoveries. Having discharged, with Fidelity, our Engagements with the Public in the execution of the History of New South Wales, we shall not relax our Exertions in making the voyage equally deserving of their Attention and Patronage, which we so liberally experienced in the Prosecution of the History: every Arrangement being made to facilitate its Publication with Elegance and Dispatch. London: Published by M. Jones, No. 1 Paternoster-row: C. Chappell, Pall-Mall; B. Sellick, No. 3, St. James's Back, Bristol; R. Rollason, Coventry; Robinson, Nottingham; and may be had of all the Booksellers and Newsmen in Town and country. W. Flint, Old Bailey.

An Account of a Voyage to New South Wales, by George Barrington, Superintendant of the Convicts, to which is prefixed a Detail of his Life, Trials, Speeches, &c. &c. Enriched with beautiful Coloured Prints. Printed for M. Jones, No. 1 Paternoster row. 1803.

Puteschestivie v Botani-Bai: s opisaniem strany, nravov, obychaev i religii prirodnykh zhitelei, Georgiia Barringtona. Moskwa: V Universitetskoi Tipografii u Liubiia i Popova, 1803.

1804

Fairbairn's Edition of the Life, Amours, and Wonderful Adventures of that Most Notorious Pickpocket, George Barrington, giving a Full Account of his Trial, and Conviction, with Many Curious Anecdotes of this Notorious Character. Embellished with a Coloured Frontispiece. London: Printed and Published by T. Fairbairn, 110, Minories, Price Sixpence.

Barrington's New London Spy or the Frauds of London Detected being a Complete disclosure of all the dark Transactions in and about the Cities of London and Westminster to which is prefixed Belcher's Treatise on the art of Boxing ... By the celebrated George Barrington, Principal Superintendent of the Convicts at Botany Bay, and author of the Annals of Suicide. The Third Edition. London: Printed for Thomas Tegg, No. 111 Cheapside, by J. J. Hart, 23 Warwick Square. Price One Shilling and Sixpence.

Bibliography

1805

Barrington's New London Spy for 1805. Printed for Thomas Tegg, No. 111 Cheapside. Price One Shilling and Sixpence.

1807

Barrington's New London Spy or the Frauds of London Detected, 1807. London. Printed for Thomas Tegg, No. 111 Cheapside.

1808

The History of New Holland, from its First Discovery in 1616, to the Present Time. With a Particular Account of its Produce and Inhabitants: and a Description of Botany Bay. Also, A List of the Naval, Marine, Military and Civil Establishment. To which is prefixed, An Introductory Discourse on Banishment, by the Right Honourable William Eden. By Geo. Barrington. The Second Edition, illustrated with Maps. London. Printed for John Stockdale, Piccadilly. Price Six Shillings. 1808.

Barrington's New London Spy for 1808; or, The Frauds of London Detected: To which is now added, An Appendix Containing a Sketch of Night Scenes and Notorious Characters, A Ramble through the Metropolis; Being a complete Disclosure of all the dark Transactions in and about the Cities of London and Westminster. By the celebrated George Barrington, Principal Superintendant of the Convicts at Botany Bay, and Authors of the Annals of Suicide. Also, A Treatise on the Art of Boxing by Mr Belcher. Seventh Edition, considerably enlarged. Printed for Thomas Tegg, No. 111 Cheapside; Wilson and Spence, York; and Denham and Dick, Edinburgh.

1809

The London Spy: or, the Frauds of London Described: being a Complete Disclosure of all the Dark Transactions In and about that great City. By the Celebrated George Barrington, Superintendant of the Convicts at Botany Bay. Falkirk: Printed by T. Johnston, 1809.

1810

An Account of A Voyage to New South Wales, by George Barrrington, Superintendent of the Convicts, to which is prefixed a Detail of his Life, Trials, Speeches, &c. &c. Enriched with beautiful colour'd Prints. London. Printed for M. Jones, No. 5 Newgate Street and Sherwood, Neely, & Jones, Paternoster Row. 1810.

The History of New South Wales, including Botany Bay, Port Jackson, Parramatta, Sydney, and all its Dependancies, from the Original Discovery of the Island: With the Customs and Manners of the Natives, and an Account of the English Colony, from its Foundation, to the Present Time. By George Barrington: Superintendant of the Convicts.—Enriched with beautiful Coloured Prints. London: Printed for M. Jones, No. 5, Newgate Strt. & Sherwood, Neely & Jones. Paternoster Row. 1810.

1812

Barrington's New London Spy; or, the Frauds of London detected: To which is now added, an Appendix, containing a sketch of Night Scenes and Notorious Characters, in a ramble through the Metropolis: being A complete Disclosure of all the Dark Transactions in and about the Cities of London and Westminster. By the celebrated George Barrington, Principal Superintendant of the Convicts at Botany-Bay, and Author of the Annals of Suicide. Also, a Treatise on the Art of Boxing, by Mr Belcher. Ninth edition, considerably enlarged. London: Printed for Thomas Tegg, No. 111 Cheapside.

1816

Barringtons resa och deportation till Botany-Bay i Nya Holland, Stockholm: F. Cederborgh, 1816.

1820

The Life, Times, and Adventures of George Barrington, The Celebrated Thief and Pickpocket, embracing the whole of his history, and a full account of all his Extraordinary Feats, which procured him the name of 'The Prince of Thieves'; His attempted murder of O'Neill, Robbery of the Duke of Leinster, the Duke's Attack on Barrington's Wife &c.; also, Full details of the many desperate robberies committed by Barrington, in England, Ireland &c, Embellished with many beautiful engravings. London: Published by John Wilson, Oxford Street; and Sold by all Booksellers.

Second Edition. *The Life, Times, and Adventures of George Barrington, The Celebrated Thief and Pickpocket, embracing the whole of his history, and a full account of all his Extraordinary Feats, which procured him the name of 'The Prince of Thieves'; His attempted murder of O'Neill, Robbery of the Duke of Leinster, the Duke's Attack on Barrington's Wife &c.; also, Full details of the many desperate robberies committed by Barrington, in England, Ireland &c, Embellished with many beautiful engravings.* London: Published by John Wilson, Oxford Street, and sold by all Booksellers. (Price Half-a-Crown.)

Bibliography

Works Cited and Selected by the Editor

Published Records

Historical Records of Australia, vols. 1–4 (Sydney: Library Committee of the Commonwealth Parliament, Government Printer, 1914–1925).

Historical Records of New South Wales, vols. 1–2 (Sydney: Charles Potter, Government Printer, 1892–1901).

Parliamentary Reports and Official Returns

Colonial Office, C.O. 207, Entry books relating to Convicts – Records of the Superintendent of Convicts, 1788–1868 (8 vols.).

Select Committee on Hulks, House of Commons, Parliamentary Papers, vol. XXXVI, 1778.

Manuscripts

George Barrington to Mrs. Dudman, autographed letter dated 16 January 1777, Ms Ab 42/1, Mitchell Library, State Library of New South Wales, Sydney.

Bonwick Transcripts. Extracts from English and Irish newspapers, giving biographical details, accounts of various court trials and anecdotes, 1785–1804. Mitchell Library, State Library of New South Wales, Sydney.

Greater London Record Office, OB/SR, Gaol Delivery Rolls, Old Bailey, 1756–1834.

Parish Register of Births, Marriages, and Deaths for the Year 1805, St John's Anglican Church, Parramatta, New South Wales.

Riley Papers, ML A110, Mitchell Library, State Library of New South Wales, Sydney.

Facsimile Editions

A Voyage to Botany Bay, by George Barrington: together with his Life and Trial and the Sequel to his Voyage (London: Brummell Press, 1969). This limited edition combined reprints of *A Voyage to Botany Bay* (*c.* 1795) published by C. Lowndes, together with *A Sequel to Barrington's Voyage to New South Wales* (1801), also by Lowndes.

Bradley, William, *A Voyage to New South Wales: The Journal of William Bradley RN, of HMS Sirius 1786–1792* (facsimile edition) (Sydney: The Trustees of the Public Library of New South Wales in association with Ure Smith Pty Ltd, 1969).

Phillip, Arthur, *Extracts of letters from Arthur Phillip, Esq. Governor of New South Wales, to Lord Sydney* (London: J. Debrett, 1791) (facsimile edition) (Adelaide: Public Library of South Australia, 1963).

Reference Works

Australian Dictionary of Biography, vol. 1, 1788–1850 (Carlton: Melbourne University Press; London; New York: Cambridge University Press, 1966).

Australian Encyclopaedia, 5th edn. (Terrey Hills, NSW: Australian Geographic Society, 1988).

Dictionary of National Biography, vols. 1–22 (London: Oxford University Press, 1917).

Encyclopaedia of Aboriginal Australia: Aboriginal and Torres Strait Island History, Society and Culture, vol. 1, David Horton (gen. ed.), (Canberra: Aboriginal Studies Press for the Australian Institute of Aboriginal and Torres Strait Islander Studies, 1994).

Contemporary Magazines and Newspapers

(Note: Year given refers to Barrington citation only.)

Avis's Birmingham Gazette (1791)

Blackwood's Magazine (1827)

Gentleman's Magazine and Historical Chronicle (1795)

London Chronicle (1798)

London Magazine; or, Gentleman's Monthly Intelligencer (1795)

Lloyd's Evening Post (1775)

Monthly Review; or, Literary Journal (1795)

Morning Chronicle (1791)

Morning Post (1775)

Naturalist's Pocket Magazine; or, compleat cabinet of the curiosities and beauties of nature (1799)

Bibliography

The New Times (1800)

St. James Chronicle (1790)

Sydney Gazette and New South Wales Advertiser (1805)

Universal Magazine (1785, 1790)

Western County Magazine (1792)

Printed Sources

An Impartial and Circumstantial Narrative on the Present State of Botany Bay, in New South Wales: With a description of the Country; Treatment of the Convicts on their Passage, and after their arrival. Also the Manners, Customs, Religion, &c. of the Natives Truly Depicted … by George Barrington, Superintendant of the Convicts at Paramata (London: S. & J. Bailey, *c.* 1793–4).

Atkinson, Alan, *The European Settlers in Australia: A History*, vol. 1 (Melbourne: Oxford University Press, 1998).

Bateson, Charles, *The Convict Ships 1787–1868* (Sydney: A. H. & A. W. Reed, 1974).

Bentham, Jeremy, *Panopticon; or, The Inspection House: containing The Idea of a New Principle of Construction applicable to any Sort of Establishment … Written in the Year 1787 … to a Friend in England* (Dublin and London: T. Payne, 1791).

Bentham, Jeremy, *Comparative View of the System of Penal Colonization in New South Wales … to Lord Pelham*, Letters 1 & 2 (London: Wilkes and Taylor, 1802).

Bligh, William, *A Voyage to the South Sea, undertaken by command of His Majesty, for the purpose of conveying the Bread-fruit Tree to the West Indies, in His Majesty's Ship the Bounty, Commanded by Lieutenant William Bligh. Including an Account of the Mutiny on board the said Ship, and the subsequent Voyage of Part of the Crew, in the Ship's Boat, From Tofoa, one of the Friendly Islands, to Timor, A Dutch Settlement in the East Indies. The whole illustrated with charts, &c.* (London: G. Nicol, 1792).

'Botany Bay Resolutions: at a very numerous and respectable meeting of His Majesty's faithful and loyal subjects of Botany Bay, held at Port Jackson, the 20th October 1792, George Barrington, Esquire in the chair', *The Spirit of the Public Journals for 1798. Being an Impartial Selection of the Most Exquisite Essays and Jeux D'Espirits, Prose, that appear in the*

Newspapers and Publications, with explanatory notes, vol. 2 (London: James Ridgway, 1799).

Brown, Shylie and Ken, with Carol Liston and Robert Irving, *Paramatta: A Town Caught in Time* (Sydney: Hale & Iremonger, 1995).

Campbell, J. F., 'Rural Settlement about Brush Farm, 1791–1800', *Journal and Proceedings of the Royal Australian Historical Society*, vol. XIII, pt. 6, pp. 361–72.

Chapman, Donald, *1788: The People of the First Fleet* (Sydney: Cassell, 1981).

Chisholm, Alec. H., *The Romance of the Lyrebird* (Sydney: Angus & Robertson, 1960).

Clarke, C. M. H. (ed.), *Select Documents in Australian History 1788–1850* (London and Sydney: Angus & Robertson, 1977) (reprint).

Coleman, Deirdre (ed.), *Maiden Voyages and Infant Colonies: Two Women's Travel Narratives of the 1790s* (London: Leicester University Press, 1999).

Collins, David, *An Account of the English Colony in New South Wales: with remarks on the Disposition, Customs, Manners &c. of the Native Inhabitants of that Country. To which are added, some particulars of New Zealand; compiled, by permission, from the Mss. of Lieutenant-Governor King. By David Collins, Esquire, late Judge Advocate and Secretary of the Colony* (London: T. Caddell, Jun. and W. Davies, 1798).

Crowley, F. K. (ed.), *A New History of Australia* (Melbourne: Heinemann, 1974).

Dalrymple, Alexander, *A Serious Admonition to the Publick, on the Intended Thief-Colony at Botany Bay* (London: J. Sewell, 1786).

Damousi, Joy, *Depraved and Disorderly: Female Convicts, Sexuality and Gender in Australia* (Cambridge: Cambridge University Press, 1997).

Daniels, Kay, *Convict Women* (Sydney: Allen & Unwin, 1998).

Emmett, Peter, *Fleeting Encounters: Pictures and Chronicles of the First Fleet* (Sydney: Historic Houses Trust of New South Wales, 1995).

Ferguson, J. A., 'A Bibliography of Literature, ascribed to, or relating to, George Barrington', *Journal and Proceedings of the Royal Australian Historical Society*, vol. XVI, pp. 51–80.

Ferguson, John Alexander, *Bibliography of Australia, vol. 1, 1784–1830* (facsimile edition) (Canberra: National Library of Australia, 1975).

Fitzhardinge, L. F. (ed.), *Sydney's First Four Years being a reprint of A Narrative of the Expedition to Botany Bay and A Complete Account of the Settlement at Port Jackson* (Sydney: Library of Australian History in association with the Royal Australian Historical Society, 1979).

Flannery, Tim (ed.), *1788 Comprising A Narrative of the Expedition to Botany Bay and A Complete Account of the Settlement at Port Jackson: Watkin Tench* (Melbourne: The Text Publishing Company, 1996).

Fletcher, Brian (ed.), *An Account of the English Colony in New South Wales with Remarks on the Dispositions, Customs, Manners, etc, of the Native Inhabitants of that Country* [London, T. Cadell & W. Davies, 1798] (Sydney: The Royal Australian Historical Society with A. H. & A. W. Reed, 1975).

Frost, Alan, *Botany Bay Mirages: Illusions of Australia's Convict Beginnings* (Carlton: Melbourne University Press, 1994).

Hirst, John, *Convict Society and Its Enemies: A History of Early New South Wales* (Sydney: George Allen & Unwin, 1983).

Howard, John, *The State of the Prisons in England and Wales: with preliminary observations and account of some foreign prisons and hospitals* (London [1777], Warrington: W. Eyres, 1784).

Hunter, John, *An Historical Journal of the Transactions at Port Jackson and Norfolk Island, with the Discoveries which have been made in New South Wales and in the Southern Ocean, since the publication of Phillip's Voyage, compiled from the Official Papers; Including the Journals of Governors Phillip and King, and of Lieut. Ball; and the Voyages from the first Sailing of the Sirius in 1787, to the Return of that Ship's Company to England in 1792. By John Hunter, Esqr. Post Captain in His Majesty's Navy* (London: John Stockdale, 1793).

Jose, A., 'The Barrington Prologue', *Journal and Proceedings of the Royal Australian Historical Society*, vol. XIII, pp. 292–4.

Lackington, James, *Memoirs of the forty-five first years of The Life of James Lackington*, 7th edn (London: Lackington, 1794).

Lambert, R. S., *George Barrington: The Prince of Pickpockets, A Study of George Barrington Who Left His Country for His Country's Good* (London: Faber & Faber, 1930).

Maiden, J. H., assisted by W. S. Campbell, *The Flowering Plants and Ferns of New South Wales: with especial reference to their economic value*, Parts 1–7 (Sydney: Charles Potter, Government Printer, 1895–98).

Mann, D. D., *The Present State of New South Wales; illustrated with four large coloured views, from drawings taken on the spot, of Sydney, the seat of government: with a plan of the colony ... by D. D. Mann* (London: J. Booth, 1811).

McCormick, Tim, Robert Irving, Elizabeth Imashev, Judy Nelson and Gordon Bull, *First Views of Australia 1788–1825: A History of Early Sydney* (Chippendale, NSW: David Ell Press, Longueville Publications, 1987).

McPhee, J., *Australian Decorative Arts in the Australian National Gallery* (Canberra: Australian National Gallery Publications, 1982).

Milius, Pierre Bernard, *Recit du Voyage aux Terres Australes par Pierre Bernard Milius, second sur le 'Naturaliste' dans l'expedition Baudin, (1800–1804)*, transcription du texte original par Jacqueline Bonnemaine et Pascale Haugel (Le Havre: Societe havraise d'etudes diverse, Museum d'histoire naturelle du Havre, 1987).

Mulvaney, D. J., and White, J. Peter (eds), *Australians to 1788* (Sydney: Fairfax, Syme & Weldon Associates, 1987).

Neville, Richard, *A Rage for Curiosity: Visualising Australia 1788–1830* (Sydney: State Library of New South Wales, 1997).

Paine, Thomas, *Rights of Man: being an answer to Mr. Burke's attack on the French Revolution* (Dublin: G. Burnet, 1791).

Paterson, Captain William, *A Narrative of Four Journeys into the Country of the Hottentots and Caffraria* (London: J. Johnson, 1789).

Phillip, Arthur, *The Voyage of Governor Phillip to Botany Bay; with an Account of the Establishment of the Colonies of Port Jackson & Norfolk Island; compiled from Authentic Papers, which have been obtained from the several Departments. To which are added, the Journals of Lieuts Shortland, Watts, Ball, & Capt. Marshall, with an Account of their New Discoveries embellished with fifty-five Copper Plates, the Maps and Charts taken from Actual Surveys, & the Plans & Views drawn on the Spot, by Capt. Hunter, Lieuts Shortland, Watts, Dawes, Bradley, Capt. Marshall, &c.* (London: J. Stockdale, 1789).

Rickard, Suzanne, 'Barrington, George (1755–1804)', in *An Oxford Companion to the Romantic Age: British Culture 1776–1832*, Iain McCalman (gen. ed.) (Oxford: Oxford University Press, 1999), p. 417.

Ritchie, John, *The Wentworths: Father and Son* (Carlton: Miegunyah Press, 1997).

Robson, L. L., *The Convict Settlers of Australia* (Carlton: Melbourne University Press, 1976).

Ryan, R. J., *The Third Fleet Convicts: An Alphabetical Listing of the Names, Giving Place and Date of Conviction, Length of Sentence & Ship of Transportation* (Sydney: Castle Books, 1981).

Rye, Lt. Peter, *An Excursion to the Peak of Teneriffe, in 1791; being the substance of a letter to Joseph Jekyll ... from Lieutenant Rye, of the Royal Navy* (London: R. Falder, 1793).

Shaw, A. G. L., *Convicts and the Colonies: A Study of Penal Transportation from Great Britain & Ireland to Australia and Other Parts of the British Empire* (Carlton: Melbourne University Press, 1966).

Smith, Bernard, *European Visions and the South Pacific*, 2nd edn (Melbourne: Oxford University Press, 1989).

Stephenson, P. R., *The History and Description of Sydney Harbour* (Adelaide: Rigby, 1966).

Steven, Margaret, *First Impressions: The British Discovery of Australia* (London: British Museum (Natural History), 1988).

Tench, Watkin, *A Narrative of the Expedition to Botany Bay; with an account of New South Wales, its productions, inhabitants, &c. to which is subjoined, A List of the Civil and Millitary Establishments at Port Jackson. By Captain Watkin Tench, of the Marines* (London: J. Debrett, 1789).

Tench, Watkin, *A Complete Account of the Settlement at Port Jackson, in New South Wales, including an accurate description of the Situation of the Colony; of the Natives; and of its natural productions: Taken on the spot, By Captain Watkin Tench, of the Marines* (London: G. Nicol, 1793).

Troy, Jakelin, *Australian Aboriginal Contact with the English Language in New South Wales 1788 to 1845* (Canberra: Department of Linguistics, Research School of Pacific Studies, Australian National University, 1990).

White, John, *Journal of a Voyage to New South Wales with Sixty-five Plates of Nondescript Animals, Birds, Lizards, Serpents, curious Cones of Trees and other Natural Productions By John White Esqr. Surgeon General to the Settlement* (London: J. Debrett, 1790).

Wraxall, Nathaniel William (Sir), *A Short Review of the Political State of Great Britain at the commencement of the year 1787*, 8th edn (London: J. Debrett, 1787).

INDEX